Sunday's Coming!

G. Edward Reid

Omega Productions
P.O. Box 600
Fulton, MD 20759

Distributed by
Review and Herald®
Publishing Association
55 West Oak Ridge Drive
Hagerstown, MD 21740

This book was
Edited by Lincoln E. Steed
Designed by Freshcut Design
Cover designed by Bill Kirstein
Cover photo: Getty Images/R&H files
Typeset: Times 11.5/13.5

PRINTED IN U.S.A.

09 08 07 06 05   5 4 3 2 1

ISBN 0-9711134-3-2

Introduction

Prophecy continues to be fulfilled at an ever-increasing pace. In the nearly 10 years since *Sunday's Coming!* was first printed, much has happened to confirm the validity of its premise. This new edition has nine entirely new chapters, and the remaining six have been fully revised and updated. The appendix containing the basic prophetic interpretations remains unchanged.

"I will come again" is a red print standout in the Bible. Jesus said it, and it's a promise we can count on. With strong confidence in Jesus' ministry and His stated plan to return, the apostle Peter stated, "We did not follow cunningly devised fables when we made known to you the power and coming of our Lord Jesus Christ, but were eyewitnesses of His majesty. . . .We have the prophetic word confirmed, which you do well to heed as a light that shines in a dark place, until the day dawns and the morning star rises in your heart" (2 Peter 1:16,19).

God's Word outlines very clearly the course of earth's history from the time of the prophet Daniel right to the end of the world and the second coming of Christ. Jesus has revealed to us what will happen just before He comes to earth the second time. And I believe we are seeing these events taking place right now.

Close attention to the details of prophecy indicate that there would be a falling away from orthodox Christianity before the coming of the Lord. In addition, elements of the church would think to change times and laws. The purpose of this book is to explain in laymen's language how this happened and what may be expected to transpire in the near future. These pages reveal in a well-documented manner an overview of church and political history that reveals not only a falling away from orthodoxy, but also a mingling of church and state—religion and politics. It is clear that the stage is being set for the final merger of government and religion that will cause all both small and great to receive either the seal of God or the mark of the beast.

The final test for the inhabitants of this earth will be over the issue of the worship of God and the relationship of the professed followers of God to His never-changing and eternal law that He wrote with His own hand on tablets of stone. The countdown has begun. It is time to renew our covenant with God. Time to get a vision of our God—high and lifted up above this ever more sinful world.

This book will strengthen your confidence in the prophetic record, make an understanding of prophecy real and permanent with you, and aid in the realization that current events in the United States and the world reveal that *Sunday's Coming!*

Because compromise and change take place over a period of time, it is rarely visible to those in the midst of change how serious will be the consequences of such change. But by standing back and taking a look at a bigger picture these changes are quite apparent and portend of things to come.

The Bible frequently uses the analogy of the Christian life as a journey that involves many choices. For example, "There is a way that seems right to a man, but its end is the way of death" (Proverbs 14:12). And again in the counsel of Jesus, "Enter by the narrow gate; for wide is the gate and broad is the way that leads to destruction, and there are many who go in by it. Because narrow is the gate and difficult is the way which leads to life, and there are few who find it" (Matthew 7:13, 14). The question we should all ask ourselves from time to time is, "Will the road I am now traveling take me to where I really want to go?" For many in the world, it is time for a midcourse correction. What about you?

Contents

CHAPTER 1

From Loss to Restoration

T he entire "plan of salvation," the story of salvation history, covers God's dealing with man from the Garden of Eden all the way to the New Earth. It is the grand theme of Scripture. It describes a battle between the forces of good and evil. The struggle is referred to as "the great controversy." John Bunyan, in his book *Pilgrim's Progress,* described the salvation process as a road that each of us must travel. Nearing our heavenly home, we look ahead and see the last waymarks—the "signs" telling us that it is very close. This is exciting to those who have traveled a great distance, a long time, or through difficult times. However, we know that the last mile of this grand quest may be the most difficult. Our adversary, the devil, has come down with great wrath because he knows that he has only a short time (Revelation 12:12).

Like "Christian" in *Pilgrim's Progress,* we have a weapon to counteract the devil's wiles. "And take the helmet of salvation, and the sword of the Spirit, which is the word of God" (Ephesians 6:17). God's Word also provides light and guidance. "Your word is a lamp to my feet and a light to my path" (Psalm 119:105). A brief description of what is soon to happen on the earth and how the Bible reveals this is described as follows: "Angels are now restraining the winds of strife, that they may not blow until the world shall be warned of its coming doom; but a storm is gathering, ready to burst upon the earth; and when God shall bid His angels loose the winds, there will be such a scene of strife as no pen can picture.

"The Bible, and the Bible only, gives a correct view of these things. Here are revealed the great final scenes in the history of our world, events that already are casting their shadows before, the sound of their approach causing the earth to tremble and men's hearts to fail them for fear" (*Education,* pp. 179, 180).

The Bible warns, "There is a way that seems right to a man, but its end is the way of death" (Proverbs 14:12). If the way that seems right—isn't—what does one do? Again the Bible has the answer. "Trust in the Lord with all your heart, and lean not on your own understanding; in all your ways acknowledge Him, and He shall direct your paths" (Proverbs 3:5, 6).

One of the truly awesome things about the Incarnation, the life of Christ, is that He came to this earth to show us the way. He said, "I am the way, the truth, and the life. No one comes to the Father except through Me" (John 14:6). The Sermon on the Mount makes it plain that each of us has a decision to make—a gate to pass through—and a destination at the end of the road. "Enter by the narrow gate; for wide is the gate and broad is the way that leads to destruction, and there are many who go in by it. Because narrow is the gate and difficult is the way which leads to life, and there are few who find it" (Matthew 7:13, 14).

When Adam and Eve sinned, God responded with love. He let them know of His love by providing clothes for them and outlining the plan of salvation. There was a way out of the mess, but it would take a long time. And yes, there was an immediate price to pay. They had to leave their garden home. They could no longer eat of the tree of life and thereby perpetuate their life of evil. As it was, in the course of his 930 years Adam lived to see the almost total degradation of the race. Late in his life he was for a time contemporary with Enoch and Methuselah. Possibly he learned from them of God's plan to destroy the earth with a flood.

To Noah, faithful Noah, God revealed His plan to save the righteous in an ark. For 120 years Noah's life was one of excitement—anticipating the Flood and building the ark—and also frustration by the constant barrage of criticism, scorn, and ridicule. He saved himself and his family. But after the Flood wickedness increased, and God again acted in righteousness, scattering the rebels at the Tower of Babel. But He gathered the righteous into one family through the promise to Abraham.

The call of Abraham, the birth of Isaac, and the experiences of Jacob began the long history of "the people of God." All three of these men made serious mistakes in their lives, but God has identified Himself since then as the God of Abraham, Isaac, and Jacob.

Later God called Moses to deliver Israel from bondage in Egypt. Moses, who had been adopted into the family of the pharaoh, had to decide between the wealth and pleasures of Egypt or joining with the people of God. He chose the latter, and with God's power delivered Israel and led them to the borders of Canaan.

Inspired by God, Moses wrote the first five books of the Bible. He outlined salvation history from the Creation to the Exodus. He chronicled the giving of God's laws in written form. The Law combines poetry, salvation history, legislation, and exhortation. The three major divisions of the Law, as outlined in Deuteronomy 4:44, 45, are the testimonies (moral duties), the statutes (ceremonial duties), and the judgments or ordinances (civil and social duties). The moral portion of the Law is summarized in the Ten Commandments.

The reign of King David, about 1,000 years before Christ, was a high point in the experience of ancient Israel, a golden age, the "Camelot" kingdom of a man after God's own heart. But David compromised God's will for Israel, sowing in his own family the seeds of discord that would later divide the kingdom. Later kings led the people into apostasy. Because of increasing worldliness and disobedience, God allowed the Babylonian captivity. But it was during this period that God used faithful young men to represent Him in that foreign land. Daniel, the statesman/prophet, was used by God to outline the course of history from his day to the end of time. The time prophecies of Daniel and those of the apostle John in his Revelation of Jesus Christ give us a picture of where we are in this world's history and what can be expected in the time remaining. When we compare the predictions of these men of God with the events transpiring in the world today, it is clear that the stage is set for the final, closing scenes of earth's history. In order to get a "big picture" view of current events I have included a review of some Early Church history, some Reformation history, some Early American history, and a great deal of history in the making—current events of prophetic significance. It will be very clear to you after reading this book that the last acts in the great controversy are about to be played.

Questioned privately by His disciples, Jesus revealed much about end-time events. He gave a number of "signs of the end" and described events in the world and the church that would indicate His coming was near—at the very doors.

Of course it was Christ Himself who laid out all of history and prophecy. "The history which the great I AM has marked out in His word, uniting link after link in the prophetic chain, from eternity in the past to eternity in the future, tells us where we are today in the procession of the ages, and what may be expected in the time to come. <u>All that prophecy has foretold as coming to pass, until the present time, has been traced on the pages of history, and we may be assured that all which is yet to come will be fulfilled in its order.</u> The final overthrow of all earthly dominions is plainly foretold in the word of truth. . . . That time is at hand. Today the signs of the times declare that we are standing on the threshold of great and solemn events" (*Education,* pp. 178, 179).

We have briefly traced the lives of some of the major players in God's salvation history. They are part of history. Their part is written in the Scriptures and the history books. <u>Now the last chapter is being written and we are the characters!</u>

"The word came to Noah, 'Come thou and all thy house into the ark; for thee have I seen righteous before Me.' Noah obeyed and was saved. The message came to Lot, 'Up, get you out of this place; for the Lord will destroy this city' (Gen. 7:1; 19:14). Lot placed himself under the guardianship of the heavenly messengers, and was saved. So Christ's disciples were given warning of the destruction of Jerusalem. Those who watched for the sign of the coming ruin, and fled from the city, escaped the destruction. <u>So now we are given warning of Christ's second coming and of the destruction to fall upon the world.</u> **Those who heed the warning will be saved**" (*The Desire of Ages,* p. 634).

The purpose of this book, from the author's perspective, is to give assurance and warning. Several of the new chapters are really just investigative reports. They will be of great significance to you if you understand God's great prophetic outline. Things are happening in detail just like we have been told that they would. Truly we live in a grand and awful time. It is a time for confidence and trust in God and His many wonderful promises. My hope is that this book will serve as a call to Christians everywhere to awake and be vigilant.

It is my personal judgment based on my study of prophecy and an observation of current events that the stage is set for the final events. I believe that the activities of the Religious Right as expressed through the Evangelical Protestants and Roman Catholics with organizations such as the Moral Majority Coalition, Focus on the Family Action, the Catholic Alliance, and events such as the *Reclaiming America for Christ* weekend rallies conducted by D. James Kennedy and others, though the participants are apparently sincere and God-fearing, will lead to consequences that will fulfill the 13th chapter of Revelation.

A statement from Ellen White seems to be especially timely right now: "Through the two great errors, the immortality of the soul and Sunday sacredness, Satan will bring the people under his deceptions. While the former lays the foundation of spiritualism, the latter creates a bond of sympathy with Rome. The Protestants of the United States will be foremost in stretching their hands across the gulf to grasp the hand of spiritualism; they will reach over the abyss to clasp hands with the Roman power; and under the influence of this threefold union, this country will follow in the steps of Rome in trampling on the rights of conscience" (*The Great Controversy,* p. 588).

Spiritualism is making major inroads into the Catholic Church with Marian apparitions, and a great emphasis on contact with the dead. In addition, there is a growing emphasis on urging Sunday as a mandated day of rest.

We are at the point where we can say, "We are living in the time of the end. The fast-fulfilling signs of the times declare that the coming of Christ is near at hand. The days in which we live are solemn and important. The Spirit of God is gradually but surely being withdrawn from the earth. Plagues and judgments are already falling upon the despisers of the grace of God. The calamities by land and sea, the unsettled state of society, the alarms of war, are portentous. They forecast approaching events of the greatest magnitude.

"The agencies of evil are combining their forces and consolidating. They are strengthening for the last great crisis. Great changes are soon to take place in our world, and the final movements will be rapid ones" (*Testimonies,* vol. 9, p. 11).

Readers with an understanding of Bible prophecy study will realize that the last two major players in earthly history are the papacy, or the Roman Catholic Church, and the United States of America, now the world's only remaining superpower. Other readers may find it necessary to review the major prophecies of the Bible and trace God's outline of prophecy down through time. If you desire to review the prophecies or to see them explained in a simple manner as a foundation for the material that will follow, I have included six extra chapters as an appendix at the back of the book. The appendix includes a review of the world empires as given in Scripture and history, the rise and fall of the little horn power, the predicted role of the United States in world affairs, an unmasking of the antichrist, and an explanation of the seal of God and the mark of the beast.

This material brings the student of prophecy down to our day, when the great powers of the United States and the Roman Catholic Church cooperate to bring about the last events on earth. These last two powers do not simply emerge out of thin air. God has plainly and simply outlined the course of history that brings us to our present-day scenario—the last act in the drama of the ages.

Before going on to the next chapter, you may wish to mark your place here and go to the appendix and read the six prophetic chapters there to establish a better foundation upon which to gain an understanding of the material to follow.

CHAPTER 2

Sunday's Coming!

T he Bible predicts a time of religious intolerance at the very end of time—in the near future for us. Seventh-day Adventists have understood that this intolerance, and eventual persecution, will involve the object and manner of worship. In short, we believe that crucial to the chain of events just before Jesus comes will be a law requiring all to worship on Sunday.

This in itself will not be a great problem for us, because we can use the day for Bible study, Christian fellowship, and witnessing. The real problem will come, we believe, when the law is broadened to prohibit worship on Sabbath.

You might ask, "Do we see any evidence that such a law is desired by the antichrist power today and is it supported by a religio/political power in America?" **The answer to both questions is Yes!**

Some critics suggest that in studying eschatology—end-time events—we see a Sunday law behind every rock and every bush. There is a tendency, they say, to "create evidence" where no such evidence exists. I will let you be the judge of that as we examine what I see as unmistakable evidence that the climate in the United States today is ripe for just such a law.

Some of the more conservative believe that there is a national Sunday law already drafted and those supporting it are just waiting for the right time to spring it on the American people. More "liberal" thinkers, on the other hand, think and talk as though a Sunday law in America is a long way off, if it ever materializes at all. They point to the fact that our laws protect the civil and religious rights of citizens and in fact we are a watch dog country for civil and religious liberties around the world. The true situation is probably somewhere between those two positions. I believe we are so close to the end of time that we should be seeing the beginning stages or the foundation upon which a Sunday law will rest. We already see the players who will push for it, and we are already beginning to see the power and intolerance of those who will support it.

There have been serious Sunday laws in the United States before. Sunday blue laws, as they were called, existed in America from Colonial days. But it was not until the late 1880s and early 1890s that Sunday laws became a widespread issue in the United States. During that period 17 of the 48 states with Sunday laws were actually using them to prosecute Sabbathkeepers. Arkansas and Tennessee were the worst. In fact, in the two years of 1895 and 1896 "no less than 76 Seventh-day Adventists were prosecuted in the United States and Canada under existing Sunday laws. Of these, 28 served terms of various lengths in jails, chain gangs, etc., aggregating 1,144 days" (*American State Papers,* p. 562; see also, Warren L. Johns, *Dateline Sunday,* U.S.A., pp. 43-57).

From the beginning the devil has actively tried to subvert the kingdom of God and His Sabbath sign of commitment. In Old Testament times there was the ever-present sun worship to distract mankind from the worship of God Himself.

In post New Testament times, with the "conversion of Constantine," many pagan rituals came into the Christian church—including the first historically recorded Sunday law that I am aware of. Enacted by the Roman Emperor Constantine in 321 A.D., it reads as follows:

"Let all judges and all city people and all tradesmen rest upon the venerable day of the sun. But let those dwelling in the country freely and with full liberty attend to the culture of their fields; since it frequently happens that no other day is so fit for the sowing of grain or the planting of vines; hence the favorable time should not be allowed to pass, lest the provisions of heaven be lost.

"Given the seventh of March, Crispus and Constantine being consuls, each for the second time (321)" (*"Codex Justin,"* lib. iii, tit. xii, 1, 3).

It is interesting to note that this first Sunday law was obligatory only on the city people.

America's First Sunday Laws

Many of the early settlers in America arrived from European countries seeking religious liberty. But even they had to learn the hard lesson of what religious liberty is all about. "In short, religious liberty as we understand the concept today existed nowhere in colonial America outside of William's Rhode Island. Citizens were usually taxed to support religion. Strict Sunday laws were strictly enforced. Blasphemy was a capital offense. Some colonies were flat-out theocracies; others came very close to it" (Robert Boston, *Why the Religious Right Is Wrong*, pp. 53, 54).

The old *Present Truth* magazine printed an article about Sunday laws in its February 1, 1930, issue. The article listed several of the Sunday laws from the Colonial period. While many later Sunday laws had a somewhat secular flavor, it is easy to see in these early Sunday laws an overt religious connotation.

VIRGINIA
America's First Sunday Law
1610

Every man and woman shall repair in the morning to the divine service and sermons preached upon the Sabbath day, and in the afternoon to divine service, and catechizing, <u>upon pain for the first fault to lose their provision and the allowance for the whole week following; for the second, to lose the said allowance</u>

<u>and also be whipt; **and for the third to suffer death.**</u>

This interesting law primarily required church attendance upon pain of financial loss, public whipping, and on the third offense—death. Remember, all of these laws were written and enforced in the Colonies before the U.S. Constitution and the Bill of Rights were established.

MASSACHUSETTS
1650

Further bee it enacted that whosoever shall prophane the Lord's day by doing any servill work or any such like abuses, <u>shall forfeite for every such default tenn shillings or be whipt.</u>

CONNECTICUT
1656

Whosoever shall profane the Lord's day, or any part of it, either by sinful servile work, or by unlawful sport, recreation, or otherwise, whether wilfully or in a careless neglect, <u>shall be duly punished by fine, imprisonment, or corporally,</u> according to the nature, and the measure of the sin, and offense. But if the court upon examination, by clear, and <u>satisfying evidence find that the sin was proudly, presumptuously,</u> and with a high hand committed against the known command and authority of the blessed God, such a person therein despising and reproaching the Lord, **shall be put to death,** <u>that all others may fear and shun such provoking rebellious courses.</u>

MARYLAND
1692-1715

Forasmuch as the sanctification and keeping holy the Lord's Day commonly called Sunday, hath been and is esteemed by the present and all the primitive Christians and people, to be principal part of the worship of Almighty God, and the honor due to His holy name; Be it enacted, . . . That from and after publishing of this law, no person or persons whatsoever within this Province, shall work or do any bodily labor or occupation upon the Lord's Day, commonly called Sunday, . . . (the works of absolute necessity and mercy always excepted) . . . nor shall abuse or profane the Lord's Day by drunkenness, swearing, . . . And if any person or persons . . . shall offend in any or all of these premises, <u>he . . . shall forfeit and pay for every such offense the sum of one hundred pounds of tobacco.</u>

This is just a sampling of the many such laws enacted in the Colonies, there being no central government at that time. The later persecution resulting from Sunday laws in 1895 and 1896 was again tied to the violation of state Sunday laws.

One of the most interesting and significant Sunday agitations in American history to date was the introduction in 1888 by Senator H. W. Blair of New Hampshire of a proposed national Sunday law. It was quite significant to Adventists for two reasons. First, because 1888 was a very pivotal year in Adventist history, and second, because the proposed law would have national force and not just be a matter of state law. The proposed law was quite comprehensive and attracted the attention and opposition of Adventists. A. T. Jones wrote an account of his presentation before the Senate Committee on Education and Labor on December 3, 1888. Jones states that his presentation was interrupted repeatedly by questions from Senator Blair, so the 192-page book he wrote is written as though each question received a proper answer. He noted that "I was interrupted by the Chairman alone, *one hundred and sixty nine times in ninety minutes,* as may be seen by the official report of the hearing." Jones includes a copy of the Blair Bill in the book. It reads as follows:

THE BLAIR BILL

"50th CONGRESS-}

} S. 2983.

1st SESSION}

"In the Senate of the United States, May 21, 1888, Mr. Blair introduced the following bill, which was read twice, and referred to the Committee on Education and Labor:

"A bill to secure to the people the enjoyment of the first day of the week, commonly known as the Lord's day, as a day of rest, and to promote its observance as a day of religious worship.

"Be it enacted by the Senate and House of Representatives of the United States of America in Congress Assembled, That no person, or corporation, or the agent, servant, or employee of any person or corporation, shall perform or authorize to be performed any secular work, labor, or business to the disturbance of others, works of necessity, mercy, and humanity excepted; nor shall any person engage in any play, game, or amusement, or recreation, to the disturbance of others, on the first day of the week, commonly known as the Lord's day, or during any part thereof, in any territory, district, vessel, or place subject to the exclusive jurisdiction of the United States; nor shall it be lawful for any person or corporation to receive pay for labor or service performed or rendered in violation of this section.

"SEC. 2. That no mails or mail matter shall hereafter be transported in time of peace over any land postal route, nor shall any mail matter be collected, assorted, handled, or delivered during any part of the first day of the week: Provided, That whenever any letter shall relate to a work of necessity or mercy, or shall concern the health, life, or decease of any person, and the fact shall be plainly stated upon the face of the envelope containing the same, the postmaster-general shall provide for the transportation of such letter.

"SEC. 3. That the prosecution of commerce between the States and with the Indian tribes, the same not being work of necessity, mercy, or humanity, by the transportation of persons or property by land or water in such way as to interfere with or disturb the people in the enjoyment of the first day of the week, or any portion thereof, as a day of rest from labor, the same not being labor of necessity, mercy, or humanity, or its observance as a day of religious worship, is hereby prohibited; and any person or corporation, who shall willfully violate this section, shall be punished by a fine of not less than ten or more than one thousand dollars, and no service performed in the prosecution of such prohibited commerce shall be lawful, nor shall any compensation be recoverable or be paid for the same.

"SEC. 4. That all military and naval drills, musters, and parades, not in time of active service or immediate preparation therefore, of soldiers, sailors, marines, or cadets of the United States, on the first day of the week, except assemblies for the due and orderly observance of religious worship, are hereby prohibited, nor shall any unnecessary labor be performed or permitted in the military or naval service of the United States on the Lord's day.

"SEC. 5. That it shall be unlawful to pay or to receive payment or wages in any manner for service rendered, or for labor performed, or for the transportation of persons or of property in violation of the provisions of this act, nor shall any action lie for the recovery thereof, and when so paid, whether in advance or otherwise, the same may be recovered back by whoever shall first sue for the same.

"SEC. 6. That labor or service performed and rendered on the first day of the week in consequence of accident, disaster, or unavoidable delays in making the regular connections upon postal routes and routes of travel and transportation, the preservation of perishable and exposed property, and the regular and necessary transportation and delivery of articles of food in condition for healthy use, and such transportation for short distances from one State, district, or Territory, into another State, district, or Territory as by local laws shall be declared to be necessary for the public good, shall not be deemed violations of this act, but the same shall be construed, so far as possible, to secure to the whole people rest from toil during the first day of the week, their mental and moral culture, and the religious observance of the Sabbath day."

The bill, vigorously opposed by Jews, Seventh Day Baptists, Seventh-day Adventists, and other groups, was defeated in 1888 and also the amended 1889 version was likewise defeated. Of particular interest to those concerned with Sunday laws today is the counsel of Ellen White during this proposed legislation and also during the persecutions of 1895 and 1896. She continued to warn against such laws and even into the next century counseled to be vigilant in this area. She firmly believed that a national Sunday law would highlight the final events in the great controversy. It is my belief that the counsel she gave then will apply as well to the time when the final Sunday agitation arises.

It is axiomatic that in the end-time/Sunday law scenario Protestants in the United States will join with Roman Catholics to bring about a Sunday law in America. Remember Ellen White's prediction: "Through the two great errors, the immortality of the soul and Sunday sacredness, Satan will bring the people under his deceptions. While the former lays the foundation of spiritualism, the latter creates a bond of sympathy with Rome. <u>The Protestants of the United States will be foremost in stretching their hands across the gulf to grasp the hand of spiritualism; they will reach over the abyss to clasp hands with the Roman power;</u> and under the influence of this threefold union, this country will follow in the steps of Rome in trampling on the rights of conscience" (*The Great Controversy,* p. 588).

"Protestants of the United States," she stated. Who hasn't heard of Chuck Colson, coauthor of *Evangelicals and Catholics Together?* And what about Pat Robertson's letter to the pope and visit with him in New York? And who hasn't heard of Ralph Reed, formerly with the Christian Coalition and its auxiliary organization, the Catholic Alliance? To me, these men and their activities are <u>a direct fulfillment of the predictions of *The Great Controversy!*</u> Their current counterparts are discussed in later chapters in this book.

Note "the threefold union" mentioned above. Anglican Charismatic leader Michael Harper in 1986 sent a message to Pope John Paul II, saying, "We're with you for a united evangelization of Europe." He has been very active in ecumenism. He has spoken of his own ecumenical pilgrimage in terms of "'the three major spiritual influences in the contemporary church.' In his book, *This Is the Day,* Canon Harper speaks of <u>three sisters whose names are Evangeline, Charisma, and Roma, representing the Evangelical and Charismatic movements and the Roman Catholic Church,</u> 'which was once anathema to him, but in which he has found a deepening of profound, loving commitment to Christ and God'" (Michael Semlyen, *All Roads Lead to Rome,* p. 30).

The establishment of diplomatic relations between the United States and the Holy See, the escalating progress of the ecumenical movement, the pope's visits to the U.S., and the Catholic Campaign for America show clearly that <u>the predictions of Ellen White and the traditional Adventist interpretation of Revelation 13 and 17 are proving to be very correct.</u> But what is it all leading to? We turn again to *The Great Controversy* for the answer: "In the movements now in progress in the United States to secure for the institutions and usages of the church the support of the state, Protestants are following in the steps of papists, Nay, more, they are opening the door for the papacy to regain in Protestant America the supremacy which she has lost in the Old World. <u>And that which gives greater significance to this movement is the fact that the principal object contemplated is the enforcement of Sunday observance</u>—a custom which originated with Rome, and which she claims as the sign of her authority" (*The Great Controversy,* p. 573).

We are going to examine evidence that the foundation for Sunday enforcement is being established now. But why aren't we seeing it mentioned prominently? Here is an answer.

"While men are sleeping, Satan is actively arranging matters so that the Lord's people may not have mercy or justice. <u>The Sunday movement is now making its way in darkness.</u> The leaders are concealing the true issue, and many who unite with the movement do not themselves see whither the under-current is tending. Its professions are mild, and apparently Christian; but when it shall speak, it will reveal the spirit of the dragon" (Ellen G. White, *The Watchman,* paragraph 11, Dec. 25, 1906).

Another similar statement points out the hidden nature of the Sunday movement. "Prophecy [Rev. 13] represents Protestantism as having lamb-like horns, but speaking like a dragon. Already we are beginning to hear the voice of the dragon. <u>There is a satanic force propelling the Sunday movement, but it is concealed.</u> Even the men who are engaged in the work, are themselves blinded to the results which will follow their movement." With this in mind, Ellen White goes on to counsel, "Let not the commandment-keeping people of God be silent at this time, as though we gracefully accepted the situation. There is the prospect before us, of waging a continuous war, at the risk of imprisonment, of losing property and even life itself, to defend the law of God, which is being made void by the laws of men. This Bible text will be quoted to us, 'Let every soul be subject unto the higher powers. . . . The powers that be are ordained of God'" (*Advent Review and Sabbath Herald,* Jan. 1, 1889).

So, apparently, initially we are not going to see a lot of overt action on the Sunday law, though behind-the-scenes steps are clearly being taken. In 1991 Pat Robertson, founder and past president of the Christian Coalition, authored a book titled *The New World Order.* (My paperback edition states on the cover that it was on the New York *Times* best-seller list.) Robertson's main thrust is that the "secular humanists" are trying to take over the world and provide a "new world order." As citizens of "God's world order" Christians have several obligations. One is: " 'Remember the Sabbath day, to keep it holy,' is a command for the personal benefit to each citizen. Our minds, spirits, and bodies demand a regular time of rest. Perhaps God's greatest gift to mankind's earthly existence is the ability to be free from work one day a week. Only when people are permitted to rest from their labors, to meditate on God, to consider His way, to dream of a better world can there be progress and genuine human betterment.

"Galley slaves and coolies forced to work seven days a week became no better than beasts of burden. Higher civilizations rise when people can rest, think, and draw inspiration from God. Laws in America [blue laws] that mandated a day of rest from incessant commerce have been nullified as a violation of church and state. . . . What idiocy our society has indulged in by refusing to acknowledge the wisdom of God."

Robertson concludes his "Sabbath" admonition by quoting Scripture and making a commitment. "I never gave the issue of a day of rest much thought until I read God's Word spoken through the Prophet Isaiah on the subject:

If you turn away your foot from the Sabbath,
From doing your pleasure on My holy day,

And call the Sabbath a delight,
The holy day of the Lord honorable, . . .
(Not) finding your own pleasure,
Nor speaking your own words,
Then you shall delight yourself in the Lord;
And I will cause you to ride on the high hills of the earth,
And feed you with the heritage of Jacob your father.

Isaiah 58:13, 14

"Since exaltation and promised rewards came from one day of rest and worship, I determined to remake my Sundays according to the biblical model" (Pat Robertson, *The New World Order,* pp. 236, 237).

The Christian Coalition's "Religious Liberty" department was initially headed up by Catholic attorney Keith Fournier. His book, *A House United,* with a foreword by Pat Robertson, applauds the work of Protestants and Catholics in uniting together. Both Robertson and Fournier were signers of the *Evangelicals and Catholics Together* document. In his book Fournier subtly states that Jesus kept Sunday: "The Son did not become man simply to be religious on Sundays or to do religious things" (*A House United,* p. 107). He also states, without any biblical support, of course, that the apostles kept Sunday. I quote, "All Christians also shared the same core beliefs, which came to them from the apostles and was first memorialized in creeds, The earliest creedal statements show up in the New Testament. These creeds predate the writing of the New Testament books in which they are cited. . . . All of these early creeds, probably formulated between AD 30 and 50, focus on the Person and work of Jesus of Nazareth. They show what even the pre-New Testament apostolic church was taught and believed about the central Figure of the faith. These core beliefs included twelve historical facts. [I will quote only his points 9 and 10] . . . As a result of this preaching, (9) the church was born and grew, (10) with **Sunday** as the primary day of worship" (*ibid.,* p. 165). This statement is of course absolutely false. There simply is no historical or biblical support for believing that the apostolic church kept Sunday, yet thousands who read Fournier's book will blindly believe they are reading truth!

Believe it or not, there is more to this book than his praising the *Evangelicals and Catholics Together* document and strongly supporting the ecumenical movement. Fournier apparently believes that

Christians can get back together faster if they get back to the "core be-liefs of the New Testament church." Accordingly, he tries to lead his readers to conclude that Jesus and the disciples kept Sunday as their day of rest. He goes on to discuss the church at the time of the early church fathers. This period is after the apostles had passed away but before the Council of Nicea in 325 A.D. Fournier states, "When one looks at the early church, one cannot divorce practice from values. For the most part, Christians conducted their lives according to their moral convictions and religious beliefs, even if it meant losing their posses-sions and their lives. One of the most revealing observations of this fact is conveyed by an early Roman governor, Pliny the Younger.

"Pliny's description of some of the practices and values of the early Christians corresponds to those taught by Jesus, the apostles, and other New Testament writers. Pliny's list also finds parallels in the writings of the church Fathers. What all of these show is that Christians met on the same day for worship—Sunday" (*ibid.,* pp. 170, 171). Fournier's point here is that if we want to get together today and be unified as the early church was, then we would also have the same common day of worship—Sunday.

Another indication of the way Christians are thinking about Sunday laws is recorded in the papers written for the Massachusetts Council of Churches that was printed in Boston, January 1993. The ar-ticles were written under the title **SUNDAY CLOSING LAWS RE-VISITED, A Biblical, Ethical, and Sociological Study of a Common Day of Rest.**

Bradley Googins, Ph.D., of Boston University writes, "Clearly the need for family time is more dire than ever. Yet the battle over Blue laws is a fierce one. At its most basic level, the attempt to repeal the laws is a manifestation of the dominance of the economic order and the perception that we have no choice but to follow the drumbeat of commercialism if we are to survive economically as a state and as a country." He then makes a "Call for Action." "Where then is all of this leading? In 'Chicago's' lyrics, 'Does anybody know what time it is?' is followed by 'Does anybody really care?' From what I have seen, there is an increas-ing concern that the fabric of life is unraveling around us. What can we do about our deteriorating families and communities? How can we pro-tect our children? These questions are being raised with growing frequency and urgency as we confront increasing violence, stress, addiction and other signs of community and family breakdown.

"Up until now, groups in favor of repealing Blue Laws have been very successful in getting their agenda before the public and gaining a fair degree of acceptance. For the other side, however, there has been no strong voice or organized movement arguing for a time out to reflect on the problems afflicting our lives. Unless a broad constituency is formed to fight for this alternative, the L. L. Bean model [open 24 hours a day 365 days a year in Freeport, Maine] will soon be here, resulting in an even more materialistic society and frenetic Sundays.

"It seems to me that it is up to the clergy and others among us concerned with the quality of life to speak out strongly for a value system which is supportive of our families and communities. We must articulate a vision of life which values family time, reflective time and communities built on caring and mutual support. Only by framing the Sunday closing laws in this manner do we have a chance for insuring a basic quality of life for our families and communities."

Dr. Barbara Darling-Smith wrote the article "The Meaning of Sabbath Rest in the World of Commerce" for the series. She wrote that "The benefits of Sabbath for humans and our environment are too precious to be left to the vagaries of the marketplace, to the luck of where one finds employment, or to the good intentions of one's employer. Like the question of family leave, a basic human need of this sort needs **legislative** support; otherwise workers will be exploited."

But what about those who do not worship on Sunday such as Muslims, Jews, and Seventh-day Adventists? David M. Barney, of the Trinity Episcopal Church in Concord, MA, gives his answer to that question in his article "A View From a Parish." He asks, "In the face of these two considerations, the rights of minorities and the commandment to keep the Sabbath, what grounds have we for supporting Sunday closing laws?" His answer, "In America, Sunday remains our common day of rest for want of any practical alternative. Naturally it suits the Christian majority, but other religious and non-religious communities have adapted to it more or less happily. I cannot foresee having two or more days in which closing laws would be enforced. Since we have to choose one day in order for the whole community to enjoy it together, I see no alternative to Sunday.

"My impression is that the owners of businesses and employers generally oppose Sunday closing laws while the workers generally support closing laws. I always sleep better at night when I take the side of the workers against owners.

"The benefits of the workers' and community's time of rest also outweighs the benefits of increased profits. As a matter of justice, let our Commonwealth set some limit to the demands made on working people."

In concluding a Council of Churches session Dr. Ruy Costa stated, "Only with a renewed vision, with a statewide grassroots effort, and, with the will to be political in defense of the Sunday laws, will common day of rest advocates in this Commonwealth be able to persevere against the tremendous odds faced in defense of the current Sunday Closing laws."

THE CATHOLIC PERSPECTIVE ON SUNDAY LAWS

Pope Leo XIII, in an encyclical letter, *Rerum Norarum,* released on May 15, 1891, gave a reflection on the meaning of the Sabbath that views it as "intrinsic and fundamental to our common human dignity." He stated in part:

"Here follows necessary cessation from toil and work on Sundays and Holy Days of obligation. Let no one, however, understand this in the sense of greater indulgence of idle leisure, and much less in that kind of cessation from work, such as many desire, that encourages vice and promotes wasteful spending of money, but solely in the sense of a repose from labor made sacred by religion. Rest combined with religion calls man away from toil and the business of daily life to admonish him to pay his just and due homage to the Eternal Deity. This is especially the nature, and this is the cause of the rest to be taken on Sundays and Holy Days of Obligation, and God has sanctioned the same in the Old Testament by a special law: 'Remember thou keep holy the Sabbath Day,' and He Himself taught it by His own action: namely the mystical rest taken immediately after He had created man: 'He rested on the seventh day from all His work which He had done.'"

Here the pope is using Sabbath texts to promote Sunday rest. This is of necessity, of course, because there is no biblical indication that Sunday is holy, or set apart, as anything but a common working day.

Exactly 100 years after Pope Leo's encyclical, Pope John Paul II issued an encyclical titled "ON THE HUNDREDTH ANNIVERSARY OF RERUM NOVARUM." Then he gives his letter the subtitle of "Centesimus Annus." Pope John Paul in reviewing Leo's letter affirms the right of the working man to have time for rest and to receive a just wage. Then referring directly to the former encyclical he says, "He [Leo] affirms the need for Sunday rest so that people may turn their thoughts to heavenly things and to the worship which they owe to Almighty God. No one can take away this human right, which is based on a commandment; . . . and consequently, the State must guarantee to the worker the exercise of this freedom. . . . In this regard, one may ask whether existing laws and the practice of industrialized societies effectively ensure in our own day the exercise of this basic right to Sunday rest."

Apparently, he believed that the state should have laws that provide the "basic right to Sunday rest."

In an *Adventist Review* article (October 12, 1995) pastor Wellesley Muir reported a shocking discovery. "While preparing for a Revelation Seminar not long ago, I came across a new Catholic catechism and turned to the section dealing with the Sabbath. I was shocked by what I found. Under the heading 'Cooperation by the Civil Authorities Regarding This Commandment,' I read as follows: 'The civil authorities should be urged to cooperate with the church in maintaining and strengthening this public worship of God, and to support with their own authority the regulations set down by the church's pastors.' The next paragraph added, 'For it is only in this way that the faithful will understand why it is Sunday and not the Sabbath day that we now keep holy.'

"*The Roman Catechism* (1985), from which the above statement was taken, is no fly-by-night document, either! John Paul II called it 'a work of the first rank as a summary of Christian teaching.' And Silvio Cardinal Oddi, prefect of the Sacred Congregation of the Clergy, wrote concerning it as follows: 'The United States of America holds a special place in our heart, and we believe that *The Roman Catechism* will contribute to give the faithful in this great country a true *summa* of the main truths of the Catholic faith.' "

I had a similar shock when I read the 1994 edition of the *Catechism of the Catholic Church*. This edition was the first fully revised and updated edition of the official catechism of the Catholic Church since 1566—Reformation era. In addition, the church says that it is the first unabridged edition of the Catechism ever translated and printed in

English. This Catechism is 800 pages in length and has the "imprimatur" of the Vatican. In the first six months of circulation the Catechism sold 2.3 million copies in the United States and 10 million copies worldwide.

On the upper-left corner of the first page of the 1994 Catechism I read, "Imprimi Potest—Joseph Cardinal Ratzinger." Ratzinger? Somehow that name rang a bell. Then I remembered the *Time* magazine article I read (and saved) from the December 6, 1993, issue. He is now the new pope Benedict XVI!

REOPENING THE OFFICE OF THE INQUISITION

The article titled "Keeper of the Straight and Narrow" had a subtitle, "The Pope's chief enforcer of doctrine and morals, **Joseph Cardinal Ratzinger,** is the most powerful prince of the Church and one of the most despised." The *Time* article was three full pages. I will share just part of the first paragraph to let you know how significant it is that Ratzinger's name appears with the imprimatur.

"The world's most powerful cardinal lives a stone's throw from St. Peter's Square, above the terminus of the No. 64 bus, a line infamous for pickpockets. Each morning he sets off on foot at a brisk pace, crossing over cobblestones to arrive at 9:00 a.m. at the palazzo that once bore the title of the Roman and Universal Inquisition. Soft spoken and courteous, Joseph Cardinal Ratzinger, 66, looks too benign to be an inquisitor. But his Congregation for the Doctrine of the Faith is the Roman Inquisition's latest incarnation, and as the Catholic Church's chief enforcer of dogma, the Cardinal stands in direct succession to the persecutors of Galileo and the compilers of the index of banned books. The weight of history is borne in the attention that Ratzinger receives." Pope John Paul II named his friend Ratzinger to this position in 1981, just three years after he began his pontificate.

I was interested to see what the new catechism would say about the fourth commandment—the Sabbath commandment. By using the index I found the section that dealt with the Ten Commandments. I turned to the fourth commandment and read, "Honor your father and your mother . . ." Nothing has changed, I mused. Since the second commandment is dropped from the ten by Catholicism the fourth becomes the third, etc. Then in order to make ten, the "tenth" commandment is divided to make nine and ten.

So back I went to the third commandment. It started out great—"Remember the sabbath day, to keep it holy, Six days you shall labor, and do all your work; but the seventh day is a sabbath to the Lord your God; in it you shall not do any work." Then follows a page and a half of high praise for the biblical Sabbath including, "God entrusted the sabbath to Israel to keep as a *sign of the irrevocable covenant*" (italics in the Catechism). Then somewhat mysteriously paragraph (they are all numbered) number 2175 states—**"Sunday—fulfillment of the sabbath.** Sunday is expressly distinguished from the sabbath which it follows chronologically every week; for Christians its ceremonial observance replaces that of the sabbath." The section summary states in number 2190: "The sabbath, which represented the completion of the first creation, has been replaced by Sunday which recalls the new creation inaugurated by the Resurrection of Christ."

The most significant paragraphs with regard to the scope of this book are numbers 2187 and 2188 on page 528. Number 2187 states in part, "Sanctifying Sundays and holy days requires a common effort. . . . In spite of economic constraints, public authorities should ensure citizens a time intended for rest and divine worship. Employers have a similar obligation toward their employees." Several points in this statement jump out at me. First, how does one "sanctify Sunday"? Only God can sanctify or make holy—something that He did not do with respect to Sunday. Second, who are "public authorities" that "should ensure citizens a time intended for rest and divine worship"? Public authorities are not church leaders—they are civil leaders, law makers, law enforcers. Here the Catechism states that civil authorities should ensure citizens a time for rest and worship. How could they do that? Only by passing a law!

Paragraph 2188 is the most revealing of the papal strategy. "In respecting religious liberty and the common good of all, Christians should seek recognition of Sundays and the Church's holy days as legal holidays. Note the key words here. "Religious Liberty"—to the Catholic mind this means the right to believe as a Catholic. "The common good of all"—this wording is similar to the preamble to the U.S. Constitution. In addition it sounds much like the words of the Catholic Campaign for America: "It is time that we demonstrate our Catholic vitality and engage in the public policy debate. We have the power and the people to embark on this movement—a movement that will benefit all Americans.

"Christians should seek recognition of Sundays . . . as legal holidays." Who makes things legal? For example, who made Martin Luther King day a "legal holiday"? The Congress of the United States, that's who. In common language this statement says Christians should encourage or pressure the civil authorities to make Sunday a legal holiday by passing a Sunday law! This will give you a clue as to how the Sunday law will be enacted—by pressure from the people. This is exactly how Ellen White said it would happen. In this way Catholicism defeated Communism in Eastern Europe. By orders of the Vatican and local bishops literally thousands upon thousands of people took to the streets in 1989 to demand a change in government—and as we all know it worked.*

The Catholic plan for urging a Sunday law from the grass roots, outlined in the new Catechism, has literally gone out to millions and millions of homes in the United States and around the world. The Catechism is even being advertized to Protestant clergy in the pages of *Christianity Today*—so that they can be informed regarding *"the richness and beauty of the Catholic faith."*

Ponder this short insight from Ellen White on how the Sunday law will come about and compare this with what you have just learned from the new Catechism. "To secure popularity and patronage, legislators will yield to the demand [from Christian citizens] for a Sunday law. **On this battlefield comes the last great conflict** of the controversy between truth and error" (*Testimonies for the Church,* vol. 5, p. 451).

Here's an illustration from current life that demonstrates the power of the people over leaders. **"Chicago's public schools can close on Good Friday,** a federal judge said. U.S. District Judge Ann Williams ruled last summer that the schools could not do so because it was a religious holiday. But last month the school system said a survey showed that 90 percent of its teachers would not work on Good Friday. [Judge] Williams provided a loophole: officials have the power to close schools for non-religious reasons on any day, she said. The officials reclassified Good Friday as an emergency closing day that will not have to be made up at the end of the year" (*National & International Religion Report,* Vol. 9, No. 8, p. 5, April 3, 1995).

There are many ongoing "under the radar" unofficial and subtle encouragements for Sunday rest. Here are a few more current articles.

Christianity Today, November 2003, featured a two-page article, "Take Back Your Sabbath." The author stated, "Our churches and families need to return to a Sabbath consciousness that can provide a platform for counterculture witness. Without being legalistic about it, Christians have a duty to protest the oppressive tyranny of time and productivity and an economic order that tries to squeeze inordinate productivity out of people's energies.

"Such a witness will take varied shapes, but along with church worship it should be characterized by a cessation from paid employment, a respite from commercial activity, an investment in relationships, a receptivity to divine wisdom, a celebration of creation, and intentional acts of kindness.

"Churches and small groups should experiment with mutual covenants to take back their Sabbath time. And in the course of experimentation and mutual feedback, they will find a blessing." This article was written to protest so many stores being opened on Sunday—including "Christian" bookstores. It noted that these Sunday store openings are "another sign of the culture turning Sunday into one more day in the rat race."

In the same month (One must wonder if there is some kind of collusion here), November 1, 2003, *Christian Century* featured a five-page article, "Reclaiming the Sabbath—Take the Day Off." The article starts off by indicating that most people are in such a hurry with their lives today that they really don't enjoy any time for themselves or their families, much less time with God. Then a large portion of the article details how the Jewish community welcomes and enjoys the Sabbath each week and what we are missing by not doing the same on Sunday. Then the author notes, "But there is something in the Jewish Sabbath that is absent from most Christian Sundays: a true cessation from the rhythms of work and world, a time wholly set apart, and, perhaps above all, a sense that the point of Shabbat, the orientation of Shabbat, is toward God." The article concludes with a resolution by the author: "As for me, I am starting small. I have joined a Bible study that meets Sundays at five, a bookend to my day that helps me live into Shabbat. There's not enough time between church and Bible study to pull out my laptop and start working, so instead I try to have a leisurely lunch with friends from church." She adds, "I have forsworn Sunday shopping (a bigger sacrifice than you may realize), and I sometimes join my friend Ginger on her afternoon visits to church shut-ins." This article, written from a woman's perspective, encourages the readers to stop and smell the roses, to enjoy life, and get closer to God.

Guideposts calls itself "a monthly inspirational, interfaith, non-profit magazine written by people from all walks of life. Its articles help readers achieve their maximum personal and spiritual potential." Their August 2004 edition featured a three-page article lamenting the fact that we no longer seem to have time for the Sabbath. Mary Ann O'Roark, the roving editor, reminisced, *"The Sabbath.* Guiltily I thought of the commandment I'd committed to memory growing up in small-town West Virginia. 'Remember the Sabbath day to keep it holy.' My parents made sure we did. Sundays were special. First came church, where we would sit in a front pew with our dad and listen to Reverend Boak, and to Mother singing in the choir. Then came dinner with pork roast and brown-and-serve rolls. Afterward we'd go for a drive in the countryside. Stores were closed, and we weren't to do work. Mother explained this was because the Sabbath was a day of rest, a day set aside for God. A day when we stopped thinking about the things we had to do and thought about what God wanted.

"Has the Sabbath changed so much that it no longer feels different from any other day? Do we even have time for rest anymore, what with our incessantly chirping cell phones and overloaded schedules? Back in my apartment I pulled out some books I'd been given about the Sabbath. I got comfortable on my sofa and started reading. . . . My mind drifted back again to Sundays in West Virginia. I could hear Reverend Boak, his voice reaching the rafters of our church and into my heart, 'Come unto me, ye who are weary and heavy laden and I will give you rest. . . . I yearned for the peace and serenity of those long-ago Sabbaths." It is really interesting how God is moving on the hearts of many to restore the Sabbath. Unfortunately, for many this means Sunday, the first day of the week. But we can thank God for those who are searching.

Another August 2004 article on the Sabbath—like the one above in *Guideposts*—appeared in *Time* (August 2, 2004). One could still wonder why these "Sabbath" articles seem to come out at the same time in different publications. The *Time* was an essay by Nancy Gibbs titled "And on the Seventh Day We Rested? Maybe Those Old Blue Laws

Weren't So Crazy After All." I'll note just two sentences from her arti-cle: "The idea that rest is a right has deep roots in our history. Blue laws were a gift as much as a duty, a command to relax and reflect."

And finally, from Zenit news agency in Rome (February 27, 2005) comes this item: **"KEEPING SUNDAY HOLY.** Trying to ensure Christians celebrate Sunday as a special day is one of the aims of the Year of the Eucharist the Church is now observing. In his apostolic let-ter on the year, 'Mane Nobiscum Domine,' John Paul II wrote, 'In a particular way I ask that every effort be made this year to experience Sunday as the day of the Lord and the day of the church."

So from many sources the public is being reminded of what they are missing by not keeping Sunday as a day of rest. Are you beginning to get the picture? Everything is in place for the Sunday law. Religio-political leaders writing in favor of a Sunday law; Evangelicals and Catholics, who together make up over 50 percent of the U.S. population, are organizing at the grass roots—precinct level for voting in the national elections; and U.S. leadership positions at all levels, Executive, Legislative, Judicial, oc-cupied by activist Roman Catholics.

If the millions of readers of the new Catechism follow its counsel and urge a Sunday law in America, what could be the result? Many years ago we were told that "When our nation, in its legislative coun-cils, shall enact laws to bind the consciences of men in regard to their religious privileges, enforcing Sunday observance, and bringing op-pressive power to bear against those who keep the seventh-day Sabbath, the law of God will, to all intents and purposes, be made void in our land; and national apostasy will be followed by national ruin" (*Maranatha*, p. 193).

---

*For more information about how Catholicism in a "holy alliance" with the U.S. defeated Communism, see chapter five and the appendix to chapter five in my book *Even at the Door.*

CHAPTER 3

Luther and the Reformation

It was a time of desolation and disease. When Martin Luther was born in Germany in 1483 the plague was wiping out entire towns in a matter of days. One fourth of the children died before the age of 5.

In this seemly hopeless world there was one consolation—the church, and its promise of heaven. This promise had made the church the most powerful institution on earth. It was rich beyond counting, mightier than kings, but also corrupt and tyrannical. Yet this was an empire that would be overturned by one man—Martin Luther.

Luther was swept from devotion to rebellion with a quest that would set all of Europe afire, spread revolution across nations, and unleash a voice of freedom that still resounds throughout the modern world. In fact, a reluctant revolutionary, Luther became the most famous man in Europe.

It is impossible to write a modern history of western culture without talking about Luther. The idea that we should stand up for what we believe in; the idea that every person is precious in the sight of God, are taken for granted today. But these were things that Luther had to fight for. Luther has to be ranked with the great emancipators of human history. He put emphasis on the individual, the courage of the individual, and the willingness of the individual to face death for his beliefs.

Luther took on the immense and enduring institution of the Catholic Church, and said, "You are wrong! Let us now come to the right." There are very few cases in history where you find a single individual standing literally before the arrayed might of the world and saying, "No, I won't back down."

Later in his life, Luther wrote, "There has been no one in a thousand years that has been hated as much as me. May our Lord come soon and quickly take me away." He had challenged the supremacy of the Catholic Church and the pope.

Luther grew up in a tiny village of Eisleben, a hardworking community in northern Germany where the church reigned supreme. The most important thing to remember about late medieval religion is that Roman Catholic Christianity was the only game in town. It was the only major story that was allowed to be told. It was told systematically and embedded in institutions everywhere you would turn.

The church stood at the center of Luther's childhood world. Its churches, monasteries, and convents lay scattered across an empire that stretched from the far west of Ireland to the southern tip of Sicily. The church's power lay in the one great comfort it promised. If you followed its rules, performed its rituals, you would escape the horrors of this world, and find eternal happiness in heaven.

But the church claimed as much control over life on earth as it did in heaven. Its rules and laws permeated every aspect of life. The church declared whose birth was legitimate. It declared whose marriages were lawful. It declared whose wills were valid. And in that way it actually inserted itself and its legal system into the lives of ordinary people—not just its own members, but all of the community.

As many around him, young Luther embraced the church. He served as an altar boy and sang in the choir. His father, a copper smelter, wanted a better life for his son and determined that he would get a proper education and become a lawyer. So, at age 18, Luther left his small home community and moved to Erfurt, where he enrolled in the university. Erfurt was a great center of the church with 25 parish churches. All were Roman Catholic. Luther did well in school and made many close friends. He finished his basic university courses and had to take only his course in law to become a lawyer, when in 1505 traumatic events changed the course of his life. The plague struck Erfurt, and three of Luther's close friends died. Luther began to feel his own mortality and feared the wrath of God. The Black Death had killed nearly half of Europe's population in the previous hundred years, and now Luther had been affected personally.

That same year as Luther was returning to Erfurt after a visit with his family, he encountered a tremendous thunder and lightning storm that caused him to fear for his life. Without the protection of an automobile or train, he feared for his life. Falling to his knees, he struck a bargain with God. He vowed that if God would spare his life, he would become a monk.

Monastic life required religious services seven times a day. That meant choir singing, and saying parts of the liturgical services. Luther believed that if he were to be saved at last he would have to completely renounce the world; so he immersed himself in a community that completely cut him off from it. Two weeks after the lightning experience, Luther joined one of the most severe monastic orders in Germany—the Arimite Augustinians of Strict Observance. His hair was cut and he was clothed in the white robes of the novice monk. He prostrated himself before the Abbott, and was welcomed into the very heart of the Catholic Church.

Luther's order was not the type of order that you would choose if you wanted a comfortable or easy life. His new home was as much a business as a spiritual retreat. The Abbott was running a thriving trade in dyeing cloth. In addition, the monks had a brewery where they distilled a popular beer. The monastery also owned land in the community and had a significant income from rent and tithe.

THE TURNING POINT

In spite of the fact that Luther entered wholeheartedly into monastic life, he still despaired of ever achieving salvation. He worked for five years in the monastery without relief. Then he and a fellow monk were asked to take a pilgrimage to Rome—the capital of the Roman Catholic Church. The two monks walked the entire way. In October of 1510 they finally arrived at the eternal city. It had taken them two months!

In Rome the monks discovered a very earthly institution—for the church was as much about money as religion. The papacy was sucking in money from all over Europe.

They found a great display of wealth that they realized was being supported by taxes and tithes from monasteries like their own and fees that were charged for everything from a marriage license to a Cardinalship.

In the 16th century the papacy had all the trappings of a state government with a bureaucracy, palaces, and magnificent buildings. Rome was a spiritual place filled with a lot of unspiritual people. In Rome Luther discovered a cynicism that shocked him to the core. He also discovered that the church was happy to profit from its pilgrims. For example, for a fee he was able to view the church's holy shrines that earned him an indulgence that would help to pay his way out of purgatory—a place where your sins would be burned out of you for a period of thousands of years before you could be allowed to enter heaven. Buying time off your stay in purgatory was an extremely attractive offer to the faithful and very profitable to the church.

After trekking to all of the holy sites in Rome, Luther was confronted with a haunting question: "Could all of this really bring me closer to God?" He came to the realization that Rome did not reflect true Christianity. His trip to Rome, rather than being the great spiritual high that he had anticipated, brought instead only dissolution and doubt. Life back in the monastery now offered even less consolation than before. He spent his time in endless confession and penance.

In 1511 Luther was sent to a new smaller monastery in Wittenberg. It was a small community with only a couple of churches and a newly founded university. The leader of the new order asked Luther to teach a few classes at the university. While preparing for his lectures Luther discovered the biblical teaching that salvation is a free gift. It was not long after this life-changing discovery that Luther was again shocked to the core.

Seven years after Luther's trip to Rome, Pope Julius II died. He was succeeded by Leo X. A member of the Medici family of Florence, Leo was a man devoted to the pleasures of the flesh. At his dinner parties he would regularly serve a great cake out of which would jump little naked boys. Within two years, sumptuous festivals and wild boar hunts had emptied the papal treasuries. Leo was forced to halt work on the church's greatest extravagance yet—the glorious Basilica of St. Peter's. This structure was one of the greatest architectural feats in all of Europe. The greatest artists, sculptors, and architects of the time were all working on it.

But Leo was unconcerned. To meet this challenge and fill the church's treasury he turned to one of the most proven fund-raising methods—the selling of indulgences—charging the faithful for entry into heaven. An indulgence was simply a piece of paper that was sold for a sum of money, which promised the bearer, on demand, forgiveness of sins. Leo's indulgences had a number of unique benefits. You could buy one not just for yourself, but also for your dead relatives. And it promised forgiveness for an array of sins. It was claimed that it would even forgive adultery with the virgin Mary had that been possible. Here was salvation in exchange for a sum of money.

POPE LEO'S INDULGENCES

This 1517 indulgence raised massive amounts of money for Rome. In modern terms it would be many millions of dollars. In preparation for the sale of these indulgences, Leo brought in a Dominican friar named Johann Tetzel to handle the sales and public relations. And as part of his sales gimmick, Tetzel prepared a jingle that said, "When the coin in the coffer rings, then the soul to heaven wings." Tetzel's main market for selling the new indulgence was Germany.

The people of Wittenberg quickly learned of the great bargain offered by the church. Luther found that many of his congregation were being sucked into this deceptive practice and were rushing to spend their hard-earned money on Tetzel's offer. He had learned through his study that salvation was a gift from God—a gift received through faith. And that meant that the church had no right to sell redemption.

Luther was very upset by the sale of the indulgences because he knew that people's lives were at stake over this. The monk who had once been the church's most devoted servant now turned on the institution to which he had vowed his life. On the evening of October 31, 1517, Luther sat down and wrote out 95 bullet points against the pope and the sale of indulgences and then, as was the custom in initiating public protest on issues, he nailed them to the door of the Wittenberg castle church. It was a blistering attack on the greatest power of the day.

A DOCUMENT THAT CHANGED THE WORLD

Luther may not have intended for his 95 Theses, as they later came to be known, to be published. After all, he had written them in Latin, the language of the church. But others did this for him. He was about to become one of the top-selling authors in history. Fewer than 70 years before, another German, Guttenburg, had perfected the printing press. And so Luther's 95 Theses were translated into German, printed, and spread like wildfire across Germany, setting Luther and all of Europe on a path no one could have anticipated. The 95 Theses undermined the authority of the pope, who was ultimately responsible for the production and sale of the indulgences.

In Rome, the capital of the Catholic Church, the 95 Theses caused outrage and horror. Luther's books were burned as heresy, and Luther, upon his failure to retract the Theses, was excommunicated as a heretic. In those days heretics were killed in a rather hypocritical way

—without the shedding of blood—which usually meant that they were either burned at the stake or drowned. One hundred years earlier, Reformer John Huss, asked to appear before the church to answer for his faith, had been granted a "safe conduct," which meant that he would not be jailed or tortured. But when he arrived at the tribunal he was immediately arrested, tried, condemned, and roasted alive at the stake.

But Luther squared off with the church with a style it had never encountered before. He was utterly dismissive of its threats. Pope Leo had used his ultimate weapon on Luther—excommunication. This meant that he was damned to an eternity in hell in the next life and to be an outcast in the present life.

For Martin Luther these threats from the Catholic Church did not inspire doubt and fear but rather an extraordinary faith and confidence in God, which would grow only stronger with every attack he faced. Luther felt that if the Christian life was being lived authentically, then you must expect to suffer.

In the course of time a new emperor, Charles V, ascended the throne of The Holy Roman Empire, and representatives from Rome hastened to present their congratulations and induce the monarch to employ his power against the Reformation. On the other hand, the elector of Saxony, to whom Charles was in a great degree indebted for his crown, urged him to take no step against Luther until he was granted a hearing. Charles was put in a position of perplexity and embarrassment. The papists wanted him to sentence Luther to death, but the leaders of the German states insisted on giving Luther a public hearing.

THE DIET OF WORMS

It was finally decided that since the assembly of the German states would soon be convened at Worms (in 1521) to consider important political questions and interests of the national council, Luther should be summoned to this "Diet" to answer for himself. And so it was that Luther, following a rather lengthy illness, made the two-week trip to Worms. Ellen White records the meeting as follows: "At length Luther stood before the council. The emperor occupied the throne. He was surrounded by the most illustrious personages in the empire. Never had any man appeared in the presence of a more imposing assembly than that before which Martin Luther was to answer for his faith. 'This appearance was of itself a signal victory over the papacy. The pope had condemned the man, and he was now standing before a tribunal which, by this very act, set itself above the pope. The pope had laid him under an interdict, and cut him off from all human society; and yet he was summoned in respectful language, and received before the most august assembly in the world. The pope had condemned him to perpetual silence, and he was now about to speak before thousands of attentive hearers drawn together from the farthest parts of Christendom. An immense revolution had thus been effected by Luther's instrumentality. Rome was already descending from her throne, and it was the voice of a monk that caused this humiliation.' D'Aubigne, b. 7, ch. 8" (*The Great Controversy,* p. 155).

Luther had spent the night before his defense in earnest prayer that the Word of God would be vindicated and God would be glorified in his presentation. Then as he stood before the vast crowd of dignitaries he spoke with confidence and joy of newfound faith in God. "Luther had spoken in German; he was now requested to repeat the same words in Latin. Though exhausted by the previous effort, he complied, and again delivered his speech, with the same clearness and energy as at the first. God's providence directed in this matter. The minds of many of the princes were so blinded by error and superstition that at the first delivery they did not see the force of Luther's reasoning; but the repetition enabled them to perceive clearly the points presented.

"Those who stubbornly closed their eyes to the light, and determined not to be convinced of the truth, were enraged at the power of Luther's words. As he ceased speaking, the spokesman of the Diet said angrily: 'You have not answered the question put to you. . . . You are required to give a clear and precise answer. . . . Will you, or will you not, retract?'

"The Reformer answered: 'Since your most serene majesty and your high mightinesses require from me a clear, simple, and precise answer, I will give you one, and it is this: I cannot submit my faith either to the pope or to the councils, because it is clear as the day that they have frequently erred and contradicted each other. Unless therefore I am convinced by the testimony of Scripture or by the clearest reasoning, unless I am persuaded by means of the passages I have quoted, and unless they thus render my conscience bound by the word of God, *I cannot and I will not retract,* for it is unsafe for a Christian to speak against his conscience. Here I stand, I can do no other; may God help me. Amen.'—D'Aubigne, b. 7, ch. 8.

"Thus stood this righteous man upon the sure foundation of the word of God. The light of heaven illuminated his countenance. His greatness and purity of character, his peace and joy of heart, were manifest to all as he testified against the power of error and witnessed to the superiority of that faith that overcomes the world.

"The whole assembly were for a time speechless with amazement. At his first answer [the day before] Luther had spoken in a low tone, with a respectful, almost submissive bearing. The Romanists had interpreted this as evidence that his courage was beginning to fail. They regarded the request for delay as merely the prelude to his recantation. Charles himself, noting, half contemptuously, the monk's worn frame, his plain attire, and the simplicity of his address, had declared: 'This monk will never make a heretic of me.' The courage and firmness which he now displayed, as well as the power and clearness of his reasoning, filled all parties with surprise. The emperor, moved to admiration, exclaimed: 'This monk speaks with an intrepid heart and unshaken courage.' Many of the German princes looked with pride and joy upon this representative of their nation.

"The partisans of Rome had been worsted; their cause appeared in a most unfavorable light. They sought to maintain their power, not by appealing to the Scriptures, but by a resort to threats, Rome's unfailing argument. Said the spokesman of the Diet: 'If you do not retract, the emperor and the states of the empire will consult what course to adopt against an incorrigible heretic.'

"Luther's friends, who had with great joy listened to his noble defense, trembled at these words; but the doctor himself said calmly: 'May God be my helper, for I can retract nothing.'—*Ibid.*, b. 7, ch. 8" (*The Great Controversy,* pp. 159-161).

ROME'S DOUBLE CHALLENGE

Rome faced two great challenges: What to do with Luther and what to do to stem the Reformation. In Luther's speech before the Diet, the papacy had sustained a defeat which would be felt among all nations and in all ages. Feeling tremendous pressure from the papacy to eliminate Luther, Charles V decided to pronounce Luther a heretic. The leaders of the church urged him to execute Luther right then and there, but Charles said he would honor the safe conduct and allow Luther to return home before arresting him. Charles did not want to be remembered as was the embarrassed Sigismund, who a hundred years earlier had violated a safe conduct and burned Huss at the stake.

Many of Luther's supporters urged him to reach a compromise with the papacy in order to spare his life. But Luther stood firm in his convictions. Those familiar with the tactics of Rome believed he would never make it home alive. Shortly after Luther started for home the supporters of the papacy prevailed upon the emperor to issue an edict against him. The edict stated that as soon as the safe-conduct expired, severe measures would be put in place to stop Luther's work, sealing the fate of the Reformation. His writings were to be destroyed, and anyone who helped him in any way would suffer the same condemnation.

It appears to many that God stepped in to protect Luther. Frederick, the elector of Saxony, arranged for Luther to be kidnapped during his journey home, and taken into hiding. Frederick chose not to know where they took him so that he would not have to divulge his whereabouts. Luther was taken to a mountain fortress called the castle of Wartburg. He spent nearly a year in this secluded location, during which time he wrote many tracts that were circulated throughout Germany. He also translated the entire New Testament into German for the benefit of his fellow countrymen.

During the year that Luther spent at Wartburg, the Reformation literally swept across Germany. Luther and the Reformation were supported so strongly by the Germans that Rome was afraid to touch him. Though it seemed on many an occasion that Luther would die a martyr's death, he died of natural causes in 1546.

THE AUGSBURG CONFESSION

In 1530 the German princes were summoned to Augsburg, Germany, to appear before the emperor, Charles V, to give a confession of their faith. And so it was that on June 25, 1530, they appeared before him and submitted what is now known as the "Augsburg Confession." There are two parts to the confession. Part one is the "Chief Articles of Faith," consisting of 21 articles, and part two is titled "Abuses Corrected," consisting of articles 22 through 28. Article 28 addresses "Ecclesiastical Power." In this article the princes addressed the abuse of power by the Roman bishops. Article 28 begins:

"1] There has been great controversy concerning the Power of Bishops, in which some have awkwardly confounded the power of the Church 2] and the power of the sword [civil power]. And from this confusion very great wars and tumults have resulted, while the Pontiffs, emboldened by the power of the Keys, not only have instituted new services and burdened consciences with reservation of cases and ruthless excommunications, but have also undertaken to transfer the kingdoms of this world, 3] and to take the Empire from the Emperor. These wrongs have long since been rebuked in the Church 4] by learned and godly men. . . . 33] They [the bishops] refer to the Sabbath-day as having been changed into the Lord's Day, contrary to the Decalogue, as it seems. Neither is there any example whereof they make more than concerning the changing of the Sabbath-day. Great, they say, is the power of the Church, since it has dispensed with one of the Ten Commandments!

"34] But concerning this question it is taught on our part (as has been shown above) that bishops have no power to decree anything against the Gospel." [1]

This great confession by the German princes and reformers at Augsburg was considered to be "the greatest day of the Reformation, and one of the most glorious in the history of Christianity and of mankind"—D'Aubigne, b. 14, ch. 7.[2]

Here the Protestant leaders, both secular and religious, in what is surely the Magna Carta of the Reformation, acknowledged that the change of the Sabbath was the work of the church and not a mandate from Christ or the Bible writers.

THE COUNCIL OF TRENT

"In 25 separate sessions, from 1545 [the year before Luther died] to 1563, the Council Fathers met in Ecumenical Council at a small town in the Austrian Tyrol, named Tridentum—in English, Trent. That meeting—the Council of Trent—produced a large number of canons and decrees, condemned the errors of the Protestant Reformation, and shone as a beacon to all the world. Of the twenty-one Ecumenical Councils of the Catholic Church, the Council of Trent is universally regarded as the greatest."[3] This is the Catholic evaluation of the significance of the Council of Trent.

This great council is generally considered to be the church's most significant action in the Counter-Reformation. In the "Bull of the Convocation" calling for the council, Pope Paul III stated in part, "Whilst we deemed it necessary for the integrity of the Christian religion and for the confirmation within us of the hope of heavenly things, that there be *one fold and one shepherd* (John 10:16) for the Lord's flock, the unity of the Christian name was well-nigh rent and torn asunder by schisms, dissensions and heresies."[4] In the same document he stated that the council was being called "to succor the tottering state of Christendom," and to "aid the Christian commonwealth, already reduced to the greatest immediate danger."[5]

As can be easily understood from these reasons given by the pope for calling the council, the Reformation was bringing the Roman Church to its knees. Something had to be done to stop it. The church intended the Council of Trent to do just that.

Protestants claimed the Bible and the Bible only as their rule of faith and practice. *Sola Scriptura*—only the Bible—was their watchword. The Roman Catholic leaders, on the other hand, stated that "Scripture and tradition" were the dual sources of authority for Christians. Apparently, the "Bible alone" position was quite appealing for a significant group of Catholic leaders. In fact historians record that the pope's supporters sent him a letter stating that there was "a strong tendency to set aside tradition altogether and to make Scripture the sole standard of appeal." But, of course, if the church took this position it would have the affect of supporting the Protestant position. The 16th session of the Council of Trent was suspended in 1552 partly because the church leaders could not come to an agreement on the issue of scriptural authority.

A decisive moment came when, 10 years later, the 17th session was reconvened under a new pope—Pius IV. At the opening session of the newly opened council, after a long and intensive debate, the question was finally decided following a speech made by the Archbishop of Reggio—Gaspar de Fosso. He stated, "Such is the condition of the heretics of this age that on nothing do they rely more than that, under the pretense of the word of God, they overthrow the authority of the church; as though the church, His body, could be opposed to the word of Christ, or the head to the body. On the contrary, the authority of the church, then, is illustrated most clearly by the Scriptures; for while on the one hand she recommends them, declares them to be divine, offers them to us to be read, in doubtful matters explains them faithfully, and condemns whatever is contrary to them; on the other hand, the legal precepts in the Scriptures taught by the Lord have ceased by virtue of the same authority. <u>The Sabbath, the most glorious day in the law, has been changed into the Lord's Day.</u> Circumcision, enjoined upon Abraham and his seed under such threatening that he who had not been circumcised would be destroyed from among his people, has been so abrogated that the apostle asserts: 'If ye be circumcised, ye have fallen from grace, and Christ shall profit you nothing.' <u>These and other similar matters have not ceased by virtue of Christ's teaching (for He says He has come to fulfill the law, not to destroy it), but they have been changed by the authority of the church.</u>" [6]

Another credible historian gives essentially the same report. Holtzmann states, "Finally, at the last opening session on the eighteenth of January, 1562, all hesitation was set aside: the Archbishop of Reggio, made a speech in which he openly declared that tradition stood above Scripture. The authority of the church could therefore not be bound to the authority of the Scriptures, because the church had changed circumcision into baptism, Sabbath into Sunday, not by the command of Christ, but by its own authority. With this, to be sure, the last illusion was destroyed, and it was declared that tradition does not signify antiquity, but continual inspiration." [7]

A third historical source adds additional confirmation to the fact that the Council of Trent was influenced in its decision to elevate tradition over Scripture by the speech of the Archbishop of Reggio. It is *The History of the Council of Trent,* by Peter Polano. The author was born in Venice in 1552 and was therefore 10 years old when Reggio's speech was given at the Council of Trent. At age 22 he was consecrated as a Catholic priest and spent the major portion of his life as a researcher and scholar. On the first page of his history he stated his reason and method for the study. "My purpose is to write a History of the Council of Trent. For though many famous Historians of our Age have made mention in their Writings of some particular accidents [incidents] that happened therein, and John Sleidam, a most diligent Author, hath related, with exquisite industry, the causes that went before, notwithstanding all these things put together would not suffice for an entire narration.

"For my self, so soon as I had understanding of the affairs of the World, I became exceeding curious to know the whole proceedings thereof: and after I had diligently read whatever I found written, and the publick instructions, whether Printed or divulged by pen, I betook my self, without sparing either pains or care, to search in the remainder of the writings of the Prelates, and others who were present in the Council, the Records which they left behind them, and the Suffrages or opinions delivered in publick, preserved by the Authors themselves, or by others, and the Letters of advice written from the City whereby I have the favour to see even a whole register of Notes and Letters of those persons, who had a great part in those negotiations. Having therefore collected so many things as may minister unto me sufficient matter for a narration of the progress [process], I am resolved to set it down in order." [8]

Here is Polano's description of the opening of the Seventeenth Session:

"Therefore in conformity of the resolution, when the eighteenth day [of January, 1562] was come, a Procession was made of the whole Clergy of the City, of the Divines and Prelates, who, besides the Cardinals, were one hundred and twelve, that did wear Miter, accompanied by their families, and by many Country people armed going from Saint Peters Church, to the Cathedral; where the Cardinal of Mantua sang the Mass of the Holy Ghost, and *Gasparo del Fosso,* Archbishop of Rheggio, made the Sermon. His subject was the authority of the Church, Primacy of the Pope, and the power of Councils. He said that the Church had as much authority as the Word of God; that the Church hath changed the Sabbath, ordained by God, into *Sunday,* and taken away Circumcision, formerly commanded by his Divine Majesty, and that these Precepts are changed, not by the preaching of Christ, but by the authority of the Church. Turning himself to the Fathers, he exhorted them to labour constantly against the Protestants, being assured that, as the Holy Ghost cannot erre, so they cannot be deceived." [9]

So there you have it, on the testimony of three historians, that the Council of Trent, in response to the Reformation elevated the authority of the church above Scripture in matters of faith and practice. The fact that the church changed the day of rest and worship from Saturday, the seventh day, to Sunday, the first day of the week, is also uniformly stated in modern catechisms. Note the following examples:

CATHOLIC CATECHISMS ADDRESS THE SABBATH

Peter Geiermann's catechism states:

"Q. *Which is the Sabbath day?*

"A. Saturday is the Sabbath day.

"Q. Why do we observe Sunday instead of Saturday?

"A. We observe Sunday instead of Saturday because the Catholic Church transferred the solemnity from Saturday to Sunday."[10]

Stephen Keenan's catechism states:

"Q. *Have you any other way of proving that the Church has power to institute festivals of precept?*

"A. Had she not such power, she could not have done that in which all modern religionists agree with her; she could not have substituted the observance of Sunday the first day of the week for the observance of Saturday the seventh day, a change for which there is no scriptural authority."[11]

Catechism of the Council of Trent for Parish Priests:

"But the Church of God has thought it well to transfer the celebration of the Sabbath to Sunday."[12]

It is very significant to note that the Council of Trent—the greatest of the church councils, and the Augsburg Confession—the greatest statement of the Reformation, both explicitly state that the Sabbath was changed from the seventh day to Sunday, the first day of the week, not by Christ or the apostles, but by the authority of the church!

The material in this chapter has been given in order to document that there was no question in the minds of anyone during the days of the Reformation that the church had placed its authority above Scripture in the change of the Sabbath and in the condemnation of the Reformation. While the church, and specifically Pope John Paul II, later claimed that in some convoluted way the Sabbath has morphed into Sunday "the eighth day," the fact remains that both the church and the Reformers recognized during the Reformation that the church had changed the Sabbath to Sunday and dispensed with one of the Ten Commandments! Just how this change came about will be the subject of the next chapter.

[1] The Augsburg Confession, *The Confession of Faith which was submitted to His Imperial Majesty Charles V at the Diet of Augsburg in the year 1530 by certain princes and cities.* (Translated by the Evangelical Lutheran Synod), part 2, article 7 [Article 28 overall]. Note: This translation and citation is taken from the public posting of the Augsburg Confession on the Web site of the Evangelical Lutheran Synod.

[2] As cited in *The Great Controversy,* p. 207.

[3] *Canons and Decrees of the Council of Trent,* English Translation, by Rev. H. J. Schroeder, O.P. Tan Books and Publishers, Inc., Rockford, Illinois 61105, 1978, Back Cover.

[4] *Ibid.,* p. 1.

[5] *Ibid.,* pp. 3, 4.

[6] Gaspare [Ricciulli] de Fosso (Archbishop of Reggio), Address in the 17th session of the Council of Trent, Jan. 18, 1562, in Mansi SC, vol. 33, cols, 529, 530. Latin.

[7] Heinrich Julius Holtzmann, "Canon and Tradition," *Kanon und Tradition* (Ludwigsburg: Druck und Verlag von Ferd. Riehm, 1859), p. 263. German. [FRS No. 72.]

[8] *The History of the Council of Trent,* Containing Eight Volumes [in one book] in Which, Besides the Ordinary Acts of the Council are declared many notable Occurrences, which happened in Christendom, during the space of forty years and more. And Particularly the Practices of the Court of Rome, To hinder the Reformation of their Errours, and to maintain their Greatness. Written in Italian by Pietro Soave Polano, and faithfully translated into English by Sir Nathaniel Brent, Knight, Printed by F. Macock, London, 1676, Vol. I, p. 1.
Note: Through the generosity of a kind friend, I have on loan at the time of this writing a first edition of this book (the 1676 English translation) open on the desk before me. It is likely the oldest book I have ever opened and read. The author was born Peter Sarpi and as a priest took as his religious name Father Paul, hence Pietro Polano.

[9] *Ibid.,* Vol. VI, p. 439.

[10] Peter Geiermann, *The Convert's Catechism of Catholic Doctrine* (1957 ed.), p. 50. Copyright 1930 by B. Herder Book Co., St. Louis. Note: This work received the "apostolic blessing" of Pope Pius X, Jan. 25, 1910.

[11] Stephen Keenan, *A Doctrinal Catechism* (3d American ed., rev.; New York: T. W. Strong, late Edward Dunigan & Bro. 1876), p. 174.

[12] *Catechism of the Council of Trent for Parish Priests,* trans. by John A. McHugh and Charles J. Callan (1958), p. 402. Copyright 1934 by Joseph F. Wagner, Inc., New York.

CHAPTER 4

The Change of the Sabbath

Both the Council of Trent and the Augsburg Confession, the greatest of the church councils and the greatest statement of the Reformation, respectively, proclaim that the Roman Catholic Church changed the day of worship from Sabbath to Sunday by her authority. But how did this change come about? While a great many books have been written to document that process, I have elected to use the work of the late church history professor Kenneth A. Strand to explain the change.

Many years ago Strand was asked by *These Times,* a magazine that later merged with *Signs of the Times,* to explain the change in the day of worship. In harmony with this request, Dr. Strand summarized his full-quarter seminary class into one succinct magazine article.

Most compromises with error happen over a period of time. Take, for example, failure to be faithful in tithes and offerings. It has been my observation over the years that rarely does an individual just decide out of the clear blue to stop returning his tithe and offerings to the Lord. What usually happens is that over time a person may become upset with something that happened either in church or with an individual in church that begins to erode his love for and support for the church. Other factors may enter in, such as a financial crisis where the funds are "needed" for personal use. It may be that one's interests are drawn away from church activities to more secular interests over time. Eventually the person experiencing such life-changing circumstances finds himself no longer wishing to spend "his money" to support something that he no longer cares that much about. At first his conscience may bother him a lot or a little, but eventually, after a period of non-tithing, his conscience no longer bothers him, and, in fact, he has developed a rationalization that God has given him the responsibility of using his money however he feels it will do the most good.

In like manner, many who become involved in an "affair" or an adulterous relationship gradually lower their standards, thinking that they can stop at any time. But over time their conscience bothers them less and less. At length they have even developed a rationalization that comforts them by saying that God wants them to be happy and doesn't intend for them to be in an unhappy relationship with his or her rightful spouse.

From a historical perspective, this is what happened with the change of the Sabbath. Gradually over time, and not at a precise moment, the compromise with paganism occurred. In fact, Sunday worship never became a universal practice. Credible historical records indicate that seventh-day Sabbathkeeping had support from isolated groups down through time.

The departure from the Sabbath commandment was not a teaching of Christ or the apostles. It appeared about the middle of the second century A.D., beginning with the early Church Fathers. The most ardent proponents of first-day festivities were "converts" from Grecian philosophy and paganism. The Sun's-day had been a leading weekly pagan festival for many centuries, and therefore it naturally formed a common ground on which paganism and apostatizing Christianity could meet.

The gradual elevation of Sunday in place of the biblical Sabbath was further supported by opposition to Judaism. The church Councils of Nicaea in A.D. 325 and the regional Council in Laodicea in A.D. 364 mention the desire to avoid association with Judiasm. As Kenneth Strand points out in the following article, the church should have been a guardian of the faith that was delivered to the saints; instead it aided in gradually transferring the day of rest from the biblical seventh day to the pagan first day of the week. Sundaykeeping in the church is indeed a "child of the papacy." Kenneth Strand's summation of the historical change of the Sabbath is reproduced below without any comments or editorializing by me in order to protect the integrity of his original work.

HOW SUNDAY BECAME THE POPULAR DAY OF WORSHIP
by Kenneth A. Strand

Contrary to what many Christians believe, Sunday was not observed by New Testament Christians as a day of worship. They kept Saturday, the seventh day of the week.

The question of how Sunday, the first day of the week, replaced Saturday, the seventh day of the week, as the main day of Christian worship has received increasing attention in recent years. One widely acclaimed study, for example, suggests that the weekly Christian Sunday arose from Sunday-evening Communion services in the immediate postresurrection period, with Sunday itself being a workday until after the time of Constantine the Great in the early fourth century.[1] Eventually, however, Sunday ceased to be a workday and became a Christian Sabbath. Some simpler and more popular views are that either (1) Sunday was substituted immediately after Christ's resurrection for the seventh-day Sabbath, or (2) Sundaykeeping was introduced directly from paganism during the second century or later. But is either of these views correct? What do the actual source materials tell us?

BOTH DAYS OBSERVED

One thing is clear: The weekly Christian Sunday—whenever it did arise—did not at first generally become a substitute for the Bible seventh-day Sabbath, Saturday; for both Saturday and Sunday were widely kept side by side for several centuries in early Christian history. Socrates Scholasticus, a church historian of the fifth century A.D., wrote, "For although almost all churches throughout the world celebrate the sacred mysteries [the Lord's Supper] on the sabbath of every week, yet the Christians of Alexandria and at Rome, on account of some ancient tradition, have ceased to do this."[2] And Sozomen, a contemporary of Socrates, wrote, "The people of Constantinople, and almost everywhere, assemble together on the Sabbath, as well as on the first day of the week, which custom is never observed at Rome or at Alexandria."[3] Thus, "almost everywhere" throughout Christendom, except in Rome and Alexandria, there were Christian worship services on both Saturday and Sunday as late as the fifth century. A number of other sources from the third to the fifth centuries also depict Christian observance of both Saturday and Sunday. For example, the Apostolic Constitutions, compiled in the fourth century, furnished instruction to "keep the Sabbath [Saturday], and the Lord's day [Sunday] festival; because the former is the memorial of the creation, and the latter of the resurrection." "Let the slaves work five days; but on the Sabbath-day [Saturday] and the Lord's day [Sunday] let them have leisure to go to church for instruction in piety."[4] Gregory of Nyssa in the late fourth century referred to the Sabbath and Sunday as "sisters."[5] And about A.D. 400 Asterius of Amasea declared that it was beautiful for

Christians that the "team of these two days comes together"—"the Sabbath and the Lord's day,"[6] which each week gathers together the people with priests as their instructors. And in the fifth century, John Cassian refers to attendance in church on both Saturday and Sunday, stating that he had even seen a certain monk who sometimes fasted five days a week but would go to church on Saturday or on Sunday and bring home guests for a meal on those two days.[7] It is clear that none of these early writers confused Sunday with the Bible Sabbath. Sunday, the first day of the week, always followed the Sabbath, the seventh day. Furthermore, the historical records are clear in showing that the weekly cycle has remained unchanged from Christ's time till now, so that the Saturday and Sunday of those early centuries are still the Saturday and Sunday of today. Later in this article we will return to data from early church history of the second and subsequent centuries to trace the manner in which Sunday eventually eclipsed the Sabbath, but first it is important here to take a look at the New Testament evidence, inasmuch as the New Testament is normative for Christian practice.

HOW DID CHRIST AND THE APOSTLES REGARD THE SABBATH AND SUNDAY?

According to Luke 4:16, it was Christ's "custom" to go to the synagogue on the Sabbath day. Moreover, at the time of Christ's death and burial, the women who had followed Him from Galilee "rested the sabbath day according to the commandment" (Luke 23:56), indicating that there had been no instruction from Him to the contrary. They were still observing the seventh day of the week! We may, in addition, take note of the fact that the implication of this text is that when Luke wrote the account several decades after Christ's crucifixion, he took for granted that no change in Sabbath observance had occurred. He reports this Sabbath observance "according to the commandment" in a totally matter-of-fact way, with no hint that there had been any new day of worship added in the interim. On the other hand we must also recognize, of course, that Christ was accused of Sabbathbreaking by the scribes and Pharisees. We may take, for example, the incident where Christ's disciples plucked grain as they walked through a grain field, rubbed it in their hands, and ate it (Matthew 12:1-8). And we could also notice several instances of Christ's healing work that ran counter to the

Sabbathkeeping views of the Jewish leaders—perhaps most strikingly the incident regarding the man with a withered hand (verses 10-13). What do these experiences mean? In order to understand the situation, one must recognize that Jewish Sabbath observance in Christ's day did not mean simply following Scripture laws but also adherence to strict regulations in Jewish oral tradition. The Mishnah, wherein multitudinous regulations of this so-called oral law were written down about A.D. 200, gives an idea of what Sabbath observance was like among the scribes and Pharisees.

THERE WERE BOTH MAJOR LAWS AND MINOR LAWS

The thirty-nine major laws listed in the tractate (or section) of the Mishnah entitled "Shabbath" are given as follows: "The main classes of work are forty save one: sowing, ploughing, reaping, binding sheaves, threshing, winnowing, cleansing crops, grinding, sifting, kneading, baking, shearing wool, washing or beating or dyeing it, spinning, weaving, making two loops, weaving two threads, separating two threads, tying [a knot], loosening [a knot], sewing two stitches, tearing in order to sew two stitches, hunting a gazelle, slaughtering or flaying or salting it or curing its skin, scraping it or cutting it up, writing two letters, erasing in order to write two letters, building, pulling down, putting out a fire, lighting a fire, striking with a hammer, and taking out aught from one domain into another. These are the main classes of work: forty save one." [8] These thirty-nine laws had many variations and ramifications. It would make a difference, for instance, whether two letters of the alphabet were written in such a way that they could both be seen at the same time. If water were to be drawn from a well in a gourd, a stone used as a weight in the gourd would be considered as part of the vessel if it did not fall out. However, if it should happen to fall out, it would be considered as an object being lifted, and therefore the individual with such an experience would be guilty of Sabbathbreaking. [9] Objects could be tossed on the Sabbath, but there were regulations pertaining to allowable distance and as to whether the object went from a private domain to a public domain, for example. [10] The foregoing are but a very few of the specifics mentioned in the tractate "Shabbath." And in addition to the laws mentioned in that tractate, the Mishnah contains other Sabbath regulations, the largest number of which deal with the Sabbath day's journey. (These are treated in the tractate "Erubin.")

In the context of this sort of casuistry regarding Sabbathkeeping, it is obvious why Christ's disciples were being accused of Sabbathbreaking by their picking and rubbing kernels of grain. One of the thirty-nine major Sabbath laws was "reaping"; another was "threshing." Thus Christ's disciples were both reaping and threshing—breaking two of the major laws of the Sabbath. If they blew the chaff away, they could also possibly have been considered as engaged in "sifting"—in which case they would have broken three different major Sabbath laws. Such "Sabbathbreaking," it must be emphasized, was not against God's commandments as given in Scripture but was purely and solely against the Jewish restrictions. In considering the various miracles that Christ performed on the Sabbath for the purpose of alleviating suffering, it is interesting that Christ Himself never accepted the Pharisees' criticism that He was breaking the Sabbath. Indeed, in connection with the case of the man with the withered hand, He raised a question, "What man shall there be among you, that shall have one sheep, and if it fall into a pit on the sabbath day, will he not lay hold on it, and lift it out? How much then is a man better than a sheep? Wherefore it is lawful to do well on the sabbath days" (Matthew 12:11, 12). After this, He proceeded to heal the man. Thus He emphasized the lawfulness of this kind of deed on the Sabbath.

HOW ABOUT THE APOSTLES?

But now, what can we say about apostolic practice after Christ's resurrection? The book of Acts reveals that the only day on which the apostles repeatedly were engaged in worship services on a weekly basis was Saturday, the seventh day of the week. The apostle Paul and his company, when visiting Antioch in Pisidia, "went into the synagogue on the sabbath day, and sat down" (Acts 13:14). After the Scripture reading, they were called upon to speak. They stayed in Antioch a further week, and that "next sabbath day came almost the whole city together to hear the word of God" (verse 44). In Philippi Paul and his company went out of the city by a riverside on the Sabbath day, to the place where prayer was customarily made (Acts 16:13). In Thessalonica, "as his manner was," Paul went to the synagogue and "three sabbath days reasoned with them [the Jews] out of the scriptures" (Acts 17:2). And in Corinth, where Paul resided for a year and a half, "he reasoned in the synagogue every sabbath, and persuaded the Jews and the Greeks" (Acts 18:4; compare verse 11). Thus the evidence in the book of Acts is multiplied regarding apostolic attendance at worship services on Saturday.

THE LORD'S DAY

Some believe that "the Lord's day" mentioned in Revelation 1:10 refers to Sunday. However, when we read the passage, we find no hint of it being either a Sunday or a worship day. John here simply states that he "was in the Spirit on the Lord's day." Although it is true that eventually the term "Lord's day" came to be used for Sunday, no evidence indicates this was the case until about a century after the book of Revelation was written![11]

Most pointedly of all, there is neither prior nor contemporary evidence that Sunday had achieved in New Testament times a status that would have caused it to be called "Lord's day." Another day—the seventh-day Sabbath—had, of course, been the Lord's holy day from antiquity (see Isaiah 58:13) and was the day on which Christ Himself and His followers, including the apostle Paul, had attended religious services, as we have seen.

In fact, there is not one piece of concrete evidence anywhere in the New Testament that Sunday was considered as a weekly day of worship for Christians. Rather, Christ Himself, His followers at the time of His death, and apostles after His resurrection regularly attended worship services on Saturday, the seventh day of the week. Moreover, when widespread Christian Sunday observance finally did become evident during the third to fifth centuries, this was side by side with the seventh-day Sabbath, as we have seen. The question now arises as to when and how Christian Sunday observance arose.

The first clear evidence for weekly Sunday observance by Christians comes in the second century from two places—Alexandria and Rome. About A.D. 130 Barnabas of Alexandria, in a highly allegorical discourse, refers to the seventh-day Sabbath as representing the seventh millennium of earth's history. He goes on to say that the present sabbaths were unacceptable to God, who would make "a beginning of the eighth day [Sunday], that is, a beginning of another world. Wherefore, also, we keep the eighth day with joyfulness, the day also on which Jesus rose again from the dead." [12] About A.D. 150, Justin Martyr in Rome provides a more clear and direct reference to Sunday observance, actually describing briefly in his Apology the worship service held on Sunday: "And on the day called Sunday, all who live in cities or in the country gather together to one place, and the memoirs of the apostles or the writings of the prophets are read, as long as time permits; then, when the reader has ceased, the president verbally instructs, and exhorts to the imitation of these good things." Next follow prayer, communion, and an offering for the poor.[13] The same writer in his Dialogue With Trypho the Jew manifests an anti-Sabbath bent in a number of statements, including the following: "Do you see that the elements are not idle, and keep no Sabbaths? Remain as you were born." [14]

Thus both Barnabas of Alexandria and Justin Martyr in Rome not only refer to the practice of Sunday observance, but they both also manifest a negative attitude toward the Sabbath. Interestingly, it is precisely these same two cities—Alexandria and Rome—that are mentioned by two fifth-century historians, Socrates Scholasticus and Sozomen, as being exceptions to the general rule that worship services were still held on Saturday throughout the Christian world as late as the fifth century. What particular circumstances could have led Rome and Alexandria to their early adoption of Sunday observance? Moreover, why was Sunday observance soon (at least by the third century) so readily accepted throughout the rest of Christendom, even when the Sabbath was not abandoned? Obviously, the evidence thus far presented shatters the theory that Sunday was substituted for the seventh-day Sabbath immediately after Christ's resurrection. But likewise incorrect is the opposing view that the Christian Sunday was borrowed directly from paganism early in post-New Testament times. Not only does this theory lack proof, but the sheer improbability that virtually all Christendom suddenly shifted to a purely pagan practice should alert us to the need for a more plausible explanation. Especially is this so when we remember that numerous early Christians accepted martyrdom rather than compromise their faith. Justin himself was such a Christian, suffering martyrdom in Rome about A.D. 165.

NOT A SUBSTITUTE FOR THE SABBATH

At such a time as this, would a purely pagan worship day have suddenly captured the entire Christian world, apparently without any serious protest? Furthermore, if this were the case, how would we account for the fact that the Christian Sunday, when it did arise, was regularly looked upon by the Christians as a day honoring Christ's resurrection, not as a Sabbath? This latter point deserves special attention. In the New Testament, Christ's resurrection is symbolically related to the firstfruits of the harvest just as His death is related to the slaying of the Paschal lamb (see 1 Corinthians 15:20 and 5:7). The offering of the wave sheaf (grain sample) of the firstfruits of the barley harvest was an annual event among the Jews. But in New Testament times there were two different methods of reckoning the day for this celebration. According to Leviticus 23:11, the wave sheaf was to be offered in the season of unleavened bread on "the morrow after the sabbath." The Pharisees interpreted this as the day after the Passover sabbath. They killed the Paschal lamb on Nisan 14, celebrated the Passover sabbath on Nisan 15, and offered the firstfruits wave sheaf on Nisan 16, regardless of the days of the week on which these dates might fall. Their celebration thus would parallel our method for reckoning Christmas, which falls on different days of the week in different years.

THE RESURRECTION FESTIVAL

On the other hand, the Essenes and Sadducean Boethusians interpreted "the morrow after the sabbath" as the day after a weekly Sabbath—always a Sunday. Their day of Pentecost also always fell on a Sunday—"the morrow after the seventh sabbath" from the day of the offering of the firstfruits (see Leviticus 23:15, 16).[15] It would be natural for Christians to continue the firstfruits celebration. They would keep it, not as a Jewish festival, but in honor of Christ's resurrection. After all, was not Christ the true firstfruits (see 1 Corinthians 15:20), and was not His resurrection of the utmost importance (see verses 14, 17-19)? But when would Christians keep such a resurrection festival? Would they do it every week? No. Rather, they would do it annually, as had been their custom in the Jewish celebration of the firstfruits. But which of the two types of reckoning would they choose—the Pharisaic or the Essene-Boethusian? Probably both. And this is precisely the situation we find in the Easter controversy that broke out toward the end of the second century.[16] At that time Asian Christians (in the Roman province of Asia Minor) celebrated the Easter events on the Nisan 14-15-16 basis, irrespective of the days of the week. But Christians throughout most of the rest of the world—including Gaul, Corinth, Pontus (in northern Asia Minor), Alexandria, Mesopotamia, and Palestine (even Jerusalem itself)—held to a Sunday-Easter. Early sources indicate that both practices stemmed from apostolic tradition.[17] This is a view more plausible than that the Sunday-Easter was a late Roman innovation. After all, at a time when Christian influences were still moving from east to west, how could a Roman innovation so suddenly and so thoroughly have uprooted an entrenched apostolic practice throughout virtually the whole Christian world, East as well as West?[18] A reconstruction of church history that sees the earliest Christian Sunday as an annual Easter one rather than as a weekly observance makes historical sense. The habit of keeping the annual Jewish firstfruits festival day could be easily transferred into an annual resurrection celebration in honor of Christ, the FirstFruits. But there was no such habit or psychological background for keeping a weekly resurrection celebration. It is probable that the weekly Christian Sunday developed later as an extension of the annual one.

Various factors could have had a part in such a development. In the first place, not only did almost all early Christians observe both Easter and Pentecost on Sunday, but the whole seven-week season between the two holidays had special significance.[19] As J. van Goudoever has suggested, perhaps the Sundays between the two annual festivals had special importance too.[20] If so, elements already present could have aided in extending Sunday observance to a weekly basis, spreading first to the Sundays during the Easter-to-Pentecost season itself and then eventually throughout the entire year.[21] Thus the annual Sunday celebration could have furnished a source from which the early Christians in Alexandria and Rome inaugurated a weekly Sunday as a substitute for the Sabbath. But there is no reason why this kind of weekly resurrection festival had to supplant the Sabbath. And indeed, elsewhere throughout Christianity we find it simply emerging as a special day observed side by side with the Sabbath.

SUNDAY REPLACES SABBATH IN ROME

But what factor or factors prompted the displacement of the Sabbath by a weekly Sunday in Rome and Alexandria? Undoubtedly the most significant was a growing anti-Jewish sentiment in the early second century. Several Jewish revolts, culminating in that of Bar Cocheba in A.D. 132-135, aroused Roman antagonism against the Jews to a high level—so high, in fact, that Emperor Hadrian expelled the Jews from Palestine. His predecessor, Trajan, had been vexed too with Jewish outbreaks; and

Hadrian himself, prior to the Bar Cocheba revolt, had outlawed such Jewish practices as circumcision and Sabbathkeeping.[22]

Especially in Alexandria, where there was a strong contingent of Jews, and in the Roman capital itself would Christians be prone to feel in danger of identification with the Jews. Thus, especially in these two places would they be likely to seek a substitute for the weekly Sabbath to avoid being associated with the Sabbathkeeping Jews. Moreover, with respect to Rome (and some other places in the West), the practice of fasting on the Sabbath every week also tended to enhance the development of Sunday observance by making the Sabbath a gloomy day. This obviously had negative effects on the Sabbath and could have served as an inducement in Rome and in some neighboring areas to replace such a sad and hungry Sabbath with a joyous weekly resurrection festival on Sunday. As the weekly Sunday arose side by side with the Sabbath throughout Christendom, elsewhere than at Rome and Alexandria, perhaps it was inevitable that eventually the two days would clash quite generally, as they had done as early as the second century in Rome and Alexandria. This did in fact happen, and later in this article we will survey the process by which Sunday finally displaced the Sabbath as the main day for Christian worship throughout Christendom.

A brief summary of the facts ascertained thus far will now be in order:

1. The New Testament silence about the weekly observance of Sunday, in contrast to the recurring statements about the Sabbath, provides convincing evidence that there was no such Sunday observance in New Testament Christianity. (Moreover, the second-century silence regarding the Sabbath and Sunday, except for Rome and Alexandria, is in large part a result of the fact that basically no controversy had developed over the two weekly days except in those two places.)

2. The mushrooming literary evidence from the third through fifth centuries reveals that at last a weekly Sunday had become quite generally observed. Furthermore, throughout most of Christendom it was observed side by side with the Sabbath.

3. The background from Judaism for an annual "firstfruits" celebration on Sunday provided the basis for an annual resurrection celebration among Christians. This was undoubtedly the first step toward a weekly Sunday resurrection festival.

INCREASED REFERENCE TO BOTH SABBATH
AND SUNDAY

It is a curious fact that the references dealing with both Sabbath and Sunday increased sharply in the fourth century A.D. and that many of these had overtones of controversy. In some instances, there was an emphasis to keep both days (as, for example, in the Apostolic Constitutions).

On the other side, however, stood the anti-Sabbath church leaders. For example, John Chrysostom, a contemporary of Gregory and Asterius, went so far as to declare, "There are many among us now, who fast on the same day as the Jews, and keep the sabbaths in the same manner; and we endure it nobly or rather ignobly and basely"![23] Earlier we noted that the Sabbath fast—which made the Sabbath a sad and hungry day—helped bring about the rise of Sunday observance in Rome and in some other places in the West. Indeed, as early as the first quarter of the third century Tertullian of Carthage in North Africa argued against the practice.[24] About the same time Hippolytus in Rome took issue with those who observed the Sabbath fast.[25] However, in the fourth and fifth centuries evidence of controversy on this matter heightened. Augustine (died A.D. 430) dealt with the issue in several of his letters, including one in which he gave rebuttal to a zealous Roman advocate of Sabbath fasting—an individual who caustically denounced those who refused to fast on the Sabbath.[26] As another evidence of the controversy, Canon 64 of the Apostolic Constitutions specifies that "if any one of the clergy be found to fast on the Lord's day, or on the Sabbath-day, excepting one only, let him be deprived; but if he be one of the laity, let him be suspended." [27] The interpolater of Ignatius, who probably wrote at about the same time, even declared that "if any one fasts on the Lord's Day or on the Sabbath, except on the paschal Sabbath only, he is a murderer of Christ." [28] (On the Paschal Sabbath, the anniversary of the Sabbath during which Christ was in the tomb, Christians considered it appropriate to fast.) The last two sources noted may indicate that the controversy had extended beyond Western Christianity; but as far as the actual official practice was concerned, only Rome and certain other Western churches adopted it. John Cassian (died about A.D. 440) speaks of "some people in some countries of the West, and especially in the city [Rome]" who fasted on the Sabbath.[29] And Augustine refers to "the Roman Church and some other churches . . . near to it or remote from it" where the Sabbath fast was observed. But Milan, an important church in northern Italy, was among the Western churches that did not observe the Sabbath fast, as Augustine also makes clear.[30] Nor did the Eastern churches ever adopt it. The question remained a point of disagreement between East and West as late as the eleventh century.[31]

The increase in references about the Sabbath—both for and against— indicate that some sort of struggle was beginning to manifest itself on a rather widespread basis. No longer did the controversy center in only Rome and Alexandria. What could have triggered this struggle on such a wide scale in the fourth and fifth centuries?

Undoubtedly, one of the most important factors is to be found in the activities of Emperor Constantine the Great in the early fourth century, followed by later "Christian emperors." Not only did Constantine give Christianity a new status within the Roman Empire (from being persecuted to being honored), but he also gave Sunday a "new look." By his civil legislation, he made Sunday a rest day. His famous Sunday law of March 7, 321, reads: "On the venerable Day of the Sun let the magistrates and people residing in cities rest, and let all workshops be closed. In the country, however, persons engaged in agriculture may freely and lawfully continue their pursuits; because it often happens that another day is not so suitable for grain-sowing or for vine-planting; lest by neglecting the proper moment for such operations the bounty of heaven should be lost." [32] This was the first in a series of steps taken by Constantine and by later "Christian emperors" in regulating Sunday observance. It is obvious that this first Sunday law was not particularly Christian in orientation (note the pagan designation "venerable Day of the Sun"); but very likely Constantine, on political and social grounds, endeavored to merge together heathen and Christian elements of his constituency by focusing on a common practice. In A.D. 386, Theodosius I and Gratian Valentinian extended Sunday restrictions so that litigation should entirely cease on that day and there would be no public or private payment of debt.[33] Laws forbidding circus, theater, and horse racing also followed and were reiterated as felt necessary.

REACTION TO EARLY SUNDAY LAWS

How did the Christian church react to Constantine's Sunday edict of March, 321, and to subsequent civil legislation that made Sunday a rest day? As desirable as such legislation may have seemed to Christians from one standpoint, it also placed them in a dilemma. Heretofore, Sunday had been a workday, except for special worship services. What would happen, for example, to nuns such as those described by Jerome in Bethlehem, who, after following their mother superior to church and then back to their communions, the rest of their time on Sunday devoted "themselves to their allotted tasks, and made garments either for themselves or else for others"?[34] There is no evidence that Constantine's Sunday laws were ever specifically made the basis for Christian regulations of the day, but it is obvious that Christian leaders had to do something to keep the day from becoming one of idleness and vain amusement. Added emphasis on worship and reference to the Sabbath commandment in the Old Testament seem to have been the twin routes now taken. Perhaps a first inkling of the new trend comes as early as the time of Constantine himself—through the church historian Eusebius, who was also Constantine's biographer and keen admirer. In his commentary on Psalm 92, "the Sabbath psalm," Eusebius writes that Christians would fulfill on the Lord's day all that in this psalm was prescribed for the Sabbath—including worship of God early in the morning. He then adds that through the new covenant the Sabbath celebration was transferred to "the first day of light [Sunday]."[35] Later in the fourth century Ephraem Syrus suggested that honor was due "to the Lord's day, the firstborn of all days," which had "taken away the right of the firstborn from the Sabbath." Then he goes on to point out that the law prescribes that rest should be given to servants and animals.[36] The reflection of the Old Testament Sabbath commandment is obvious.

With this sort of Sabbath emphasis now being placed on Sunday, it was inevitable that the Sabbath day itself (Saturday) would take on lesser and lesser importance. And the controversy that is evident in literature of the fourth and fifth centuries between those who would honor it reflects the struggle. Moreover, it was a struggle that did not terminate quickly, for as we have seen, the fifth-century church historians Socrates Scholasticus and Sozomen provide a picture of Sabbath worship services alongside Sunday worship services as being the pattern throughout Christendom in their day, except in Rome and Alexandria. It appears that the "Christian Sabbath" as a replacement for the earlier biblical Sabbath was a development of the sixth century and later. The earliest church council to deal with the matter was a regional eastern one meeting in Laodicea about A.D. 364. Although this council still manifested respect for the Sabbath as well as Sunday in the special lections (Scripture readings) designated for those two days, it nonetheless stipulated the following in its Canon 29: "Christians shall not Judaize and be idle on Saturday, but shall work on that day; but the Lord's day they shall especially honour, and, as being Christians, shall, if possible, do no work on that day. If, however, they are found Judaizing, they shall be shut out from Christ." [37] The regulation with regard to working on Sunday was rather moderate in that Christians should not work on that day if possible! However, more significant was the fact that this council reversed the original command of God and the practice of the earliest Christians with regard to the seventh-day Sabbath. God had said, "Remember the sabbath day, to keep it holy. Six days you shall labor, and do all your work; but the seventh day is a sabbath to the Lord your God; in it you shall not do any work" (Exodus 20:8-10, RSV). This council said, instead, "Christians shall not Judaize and be idle on Saturday, but shall work on that day."

WORK FORBIDDEN ON SUNDAY

The Third Synod of Orleans in 538, though deploring Jewish Sabbatarianism, forbade "field labours" so that "people may be able to come to church and worship." [38] Half a century later, the Second Synod of Macon in 585 and the Council of Narbonne in 589 stipulated strict Sunday observance.[39] The ordinances of the former "were published by King Guntram in a decree of November 10, 585, in which he enforced careful observance of the Sunday." [40] Finally, during the Carolingian Age a great emphasis was placed on Lord's day observance according to the Sabbath commandment. Walter W. Hyde, in his *Paganism to Christianity in the Roman Empire,* has well summed up several centuries of the history of Sabbath and Sunday up to Charlemagne: "The emperors after Constantine made Sunday observance more stringent but in no case was their legislation based on the Old Testament. . . . At the Third Synod of Aureliani (Orleans) in 538 rural work was forbidden but the restriction against preparing meals and similar work on Sunday was regarded as a superstition.

"After Justinian's death in 565 various epistolae decretales were passed by the popes about Sunday. One of Gregory I (590-604) forbade men 'to yoke oxen or to perform any other work, except for approved reasons,' while another of Gregory II (715-731) said: 'We decree that all Sundays be observed from vespers to vespers and that all unlawful work be abstained from.' . . . "Charlemagne at Aquisgranum (Aachen) in 788 decreed that all ordinary labor on the Lord's Day be forbidden, since it was against the Fourth Commandment, especially labor in the field or vineyard which Constantine had exempted."[41] And thus Sunday came to be the Christian rest day substitute for the Sabbath. But the seventh-day Sabbath was never entirely forgotten, of course. This was true in Europe itself. But particularly in Ethiopia, for example, groups kept both Saturday and Sunday as "Sabbaths," not only in the early Christian centuries but down into modern times.

Nevertheless, for a good share of Christendom, the history of the Sabbath and Sunday had by the sixth through eighth centuries taken a complete circle. For most Christians, God's rest day of both Old Testament and New Testament times had through a gradual process become a workday and had been supplanted by a substitute rest day. God's command that on the seventh day "you shall not do any work" had been replaced by the command of man: Work on the seventh day; rest on the first. However, all Christians who consider the New Testament as the normative guide for their lives, rather than the decisions of men hundreds of years later, will ask whether the worship day of Christ and the apostles—Saturday, the seventh day of the week—should not still be observed today. We believe it should.

---

[1] Willy Rordorf, *Sunday: The History of the Day of Rest and Worship in the Earliest Centuries of the Christian Church,* trans. by A.A.K. Graham from the German ed. of 1962 (Philadelphia, 1968).

[2] Socrates Scholasticus, *Ecclesiastical History,* book 5, chap. 22, in The Nicene and Post-Nicene Fathers (NPNF) Second Series, Vol. II, p. 132.

[3] Sozomen, *Ecclesiastical History,* book 7, chap. 19, in NPNF, Second Series, Vol. II, p. 390.

[4] *Apostolic Constitutions,* book 7, sec. 2, chap. 23, and book 8, sec. 4, chap. 33 in The Ante-Nicene Fathers (ANF), Vol. VII, pp. 469, 495.

[5] Gregory of Nyssa, De Castigatione ("On Reproof"), in J. P. Migne, *Patrologia Graeca,* vol. 46, col. 309 (Greek) and col. 310 (Latin).

[6] Asterius, Homily 5, on Matthew 19:3, in Migne, *Patrologia Graeca,* vol. 40, col. 225 (Greek) and col. 226 (Latin).

[7] Cassian, *Institutes of the Coenobia,* book 5, chap. 26, in NPNF, Second Series, Vol. XI, p. 243. CF. *Institutes,* book 3, chap. 2, and Conferences, part 1, conf. 3, chap. 1, in NPNF, Second Series, Vol. XI, pp. 213, 319.

[8] "Shabbath," 7.2, in Herbert Danby, trans., *The Mishnah* (London, 1933), p. 106.

[9] *Ibid.,* 17.6, in Danby, op. cit., p. 115.

[10] *Ibid.,* 11.1-6, in Danby, op. cit., pp. 110, 111.

[11] The earliest clear patristic source is Clement of Alexandria. See, e.g., his *Miscellanies,* book 5, chap. 14, in ANF, Vol. II, p. 469.

[12] *The Epistle of Barnabus,* chap. 15, in ANF, Vol. I, pp. 146, 147.

[13] *Apology I,* chap. 67, in ANF, Vol. I, p. 186.

[14] *Dialogue,* chap. 23, in ANF, Vol. I, p. 206. Several other statements in the Dialogue reveal a similar feeling.

[15] J. van Goudoever, *Biblical Calendars,* 2d rev. ed. (Leiden, 1961), pp. 19, 20, 23, 25, 26, 29. The Boethusians and Essenes actually chose Sundays a week apart because of a difference in their understanding of whether the Sabbath of Leviticus 23:11 was the Sabbath during or the Sabbath after the Feast of Unleavened Bread. Moreover, they used a solar calendar in contrast to the lunar calendar of the Pharisees.

[16] Eusebius, *Ecclesiastical History,* book 5, chaps. 23-25 (NPNF, Second Series, Vol. I, pp. 241-244), provides the details.

[17] *Ibid.,* chaps. 23.1 and 24.2, 3, in NPNF, Second Series, Vol. I, pp. 241, 242; Sozomen, *Ecclesiastical History,* book 7, chap. 19, in NPNF, Second Series, Vol. II, p. 390.

[18] The fact that Victor of Rome could not successfully excommunicate the Asian Christians (see Eusebius, *Ecclesiastical History,* book 5, chap. 24, in NPNF, Second Series, Vol. I, pp. 242-244) provides further substantiation of this view. If Rome could earlier have influenced almost the entire Christian world, both East and West, to give up an apostolic practice in favor of a Roman innovation, why was she now incapable of stamping out the last remaining vestige of this practice? The only reasonable explanation of all the data seems to be that the Sunday-Easter was not a late Roman innovation, but that both it and Quartodecimanism (observance of Nisan 14) stemmed from apostolic times. For further details, see my "John as Quartodecimanism: A Reappraisal," *Journal of Biblical Literature,* 84 (1965), pp. 251-258.

[19] See Tertullian, *The Chaplet,* chap. 3; *On Baptism,* chap. 19, in ANF, Vol. III, p. 678; and *On Fasting,* chap. 14, in ANF, Vol. IV, p. 112.

[20] Van Goudoever, op. cit., p. 167.

[21] Philip Carrington, *The Primitive Christian Calendar* (Cambridge, England, 1952), p. 38, has made this suggestion: Since crops could hardly have been ripe everywhere on the two Sundays especially set aside (day of barley firstfruits and Pentecost day), may it not have been implied that any Sunday within the fifty days was a proper day for the offering of the firstfruits? For an excellent discussion of the whole question of Easter in relation to the weekly Sunday, see Lawrence T. Geraty, "The Pascha and the Origin of Sunday Observance," Andrews University Seminary Studies (hereafter cited as AUSS) III (1965), pp. 85-96.

[22] See Dio Cassius, *Roman History,* book 68, chap. 32, and book 69, chaps. 12-14, in Loeb Classical Library, Vol. VIII, pp. 394-397, 420-423, 446-451; Eusebius, *Ecclesiastical History,* book 4, chap. 2, in NPNF, Second Series, Vol. I, pp. 174, 175.

[23] Comment on Galatians 1:7 in Commentary on Galatians, in NPNF, First Series, Vol. XIII, p. 8.

[24] In *On Fasting,* chap. 14 (ANF, Vol. IV, p. 112), Tertullian indicates that the Sabbath is "a day never to be kept as a fast except at the passover season, according to a reason elsewhere given." He also indicates his opposition to the Sabbath fast in *Against Marcion,* book 4, chap. 12 (*ibid.,* Vol. III, p. 363).

[25] Hippolytus mentions some who "give heed to doctrines of devils" and "often appoint a fast on the Sabbath and on the Lord's day, which Christ has, however, not ap-

pointed" (from his *Commentary on Daniel,* iv. 20; the Greek text and French translation are given by Maurice Lefevre [Paris, 1947], pp. 300-303).

[26] See Augustine's Epistles 36 (to Casulanus), 54 (to Januarius), and 82 (to Jerome), in NPNF, First Series, Vol. I, pp. 265-270, 300, 301, 353, 354. They are dated between A.D. 396 and 405. It is Epistle 36 that gives rebuttal to the Roman advocate of the Sabbath fast.

[27] English trans. in ANF, Vol. VII, p. 504. This canon is numbered 66 in the Hefele edition (see note 37, below).

[28] *Pseudo-Ignatius, To the Philippians,* chap. 13, in ANF, Vol. I, p. 119.

[29] *Institutes,* book 3, chap. 10, in NPNF, Second Series, Vol. XI, p. 218.

[30] The first statement appears in Epistle 36, par. 27 (NPNF, First Series, Vol. I, p. 268), and a similar remark is made in Epistle 82, par. 14 (*ibid.,* p. 353). References to Milan are found in Epistle 36, par. 32, and in Epistle 54, par. 3 (*ibid.,* pp. 270, 300, 301).

[31] See R. L. Odom, "The Sabbath in the Great Schism of A.D. 1054," AUSS I (1963), pp. 77, 78.

[32] Codex Justinianus, 1. iii., Tit. 12, 3, trans. in Philip Schaff, *History of the Christian Church,* 5th ed. (New York, 1902), Vol. III, p. 380, note 1.

[33] Theodosian Code, 11. 7. 13, trans. by Clyde Pharr (Princeton, N.J., 1952), p. 300.

[34] See Jerome, Epistle 108, par. 20, in NPNF, Second Series, Vol. VI, p. 206.

[35] Migne, op. cit., vol. 23, col. 1169.

[36] *S. Ephraem Syri humni et sermones,* ed. by T. J. Lamy (1882), vol. 1, pp. 542-544.

[37] Charles J. Hefele, *A History of the Councils of the Church,* trans. by Henry N. Oxenham (Edinburgh, 1896), Vol. II, p. 316. Canon 16 (*ibid.,* p. 310) refers to lections; and the fact that Saturday as well as Sunday had special consideration during Lent, as indicated in Canons 49 and 51 (*ibid.,* p. 320), also reveals that regard for the Sabbath was not entirely lacking.

[38] *Ibid.,* Vol. IV, pp. 208, 209.

[39] *Ibid.,* pp. 407-409, 422.

[40] *Ibid.,* p. 409.

[41] W. W. Hyde, *Paganism to Christianity in the Roman Empire* (Philadelphia, 1946), p. 261. *These Times,* May 1982.

Kenneth Strand was professor of church history, Theological Seminary, Andrews University, Berrien Springs, Michigan, and editor of Andrews University Seminary Studies when this article was written. He edited, compiled, or authored many books, including *Interpreting the Book of Revelation, A Panorama of the Old Testament World,* and *A Brief Introduction to the Ancient Near East.* He aided in school planning for several overseas colleges. Copyright © 1978 by Kenneth A. Strand.

CHAPTER 5

The World's Columbian Exposition of 1893

The second half of the 19th century was an age of fairs and expositions held in London, Paris, and other great cities throughout the world. The World's Columbian Exposition, held in Chicago in 1893, was the first critically and economically successful world's fair in the United States. Conceived as a celebration of the 400th anniversary of Columbus' landing in the new world, the exposition held a near-mythological appeal at the time.

The exposition showcased a cityscape just 60 years old; magnificently reborn just 22 years after the great Chicago fire. The exposition was officially dedicated on October 21, 1892, to coincide with the 400th anniversary of Columbus' voyage to the Americas, but it did not open for business until May 1, 1893, because of delays in getting everything ready. By the time it closed 6 months later on October 30th, 1893, more than 27,000,000 visitors had paid the 50-cent admission price to see the great sight. According to the U.S. Census Bureau there were only 62,000,000 people in the U.S. at that time, which means that almost half of them saw the fair. This number is even more significant when we recognize that all came either by horse and buggy or train! At the time, the fair was considered the greatest event of its kind in history.

So what does all this have to do with Sunday? Surprisingly, a lot. Apparently because of the delay in construction, workers preparing for the fair were encouraged to work seven days a week. And those countries, companies, and churches wishing to have an exhibition in the fair were also encouraged to set up on Sunday. The Presbyterians refused to unpack their boxes or utilize the space given them on Sunday and declined all contact with the "sacrilegious and Sabbathbreaking Exhibition." The Presbyterians and other church groups took their case to Congress by circulating thousands of petitions to churches across

the country. These petitions were signed by millions of people expressing opposition to the fair being open on Sunday. Though many people
opposed the idea of the government getting involved in this religious
matter, Congress capitulated to the demands of the religious groups,
and passed an act under which the appropriation of funds to support the
fair was contingent on the Great Exposition being closed to the public
on Sundays. The resulting law, which I found in the Law Library of the
Library of Congress, reads as follows:

*"Be it enacted by the Senate and House of Representatives of the
United States of America in Congress assembled.* . . . SEC. 4. That it
is hereby declared that all appropriations herein made for, or pertaining to, the World's Columbian Exposition are made upon the condition
that the said Exposition shall not be opened to the public on the first
day of the week, commonly called Sunday; and if the said appropriations be accepted by the corporation of the state of Illinois, known as
the World's Columbian Exposition, upon this condition, it shall be,
and it is hereby, made the duty of the World's Columbian
Commission, created by the act of Congress of April twenty fifth, eighteen hundred and ninety, to make such rules or modification of the
rules of said corporation as shall require the closing of the Exposition
on the said first day of the week commonly called Sunday.

"Approved, August 5, 1892"[1]

This law, recognized by many to be unconstitutional on its face,
was passed anyway because the majority of those contacting Congress
demanded it. The reason I have used this chapter to highlight these unusual circumstances is that we know that the big end-time Sunday law
will come about the exact same way. It will be urged by religious leaders, demanded by the people, and yielded to by Congress. Now back to
the story. The passage of this law began an unusual and historical
chain reaction.

SABBATHKEEPERS ENTER THE FRAY

In a response to the Congressional action to legislate in favor of
Christians, the International Religious Liberty Association published a
special edition called an "extra" of the monthly journal, "The
Religious Liberty Library," dated February 24, 1893. The title of the
21-page booklet was "Appeal and Remonstrance" and stated on the
cover that it was composed of "Resolutions Adopted by the General

Conference of Seventh-day Adventists." I was able to find an original copy of this booklet and made a photocopy for use in preparing this chapter. The document begins:

"WHEREAS, The Supreme Court of the United States, contrary to the principles upon which our government was established, and contrary to the Constitution of the same, has declared, this to be a Christian nation; and—

"WHEREAS, the Congress of the United States, following in the same course that the Supreme Court has taken, has violated the Constitution and invaded the dearest rights of the people by legislating upon the subject of religion, deciding a religious controversy and establishing a religious institution, in the matter of closing the World's Fair on Sunday; therefore, be it—

"Resolved, That we do hereby submit to the government and people of the United States this, our appeal and remonstrance:—"As Christians, we appeal on the ground of the divine right which Jesus Christ has recognized and declared—the right of every man to dissent even from the words of and the religion of Christ, in the words: 'If any man hear my words and believe not, I judge him not; for I came not to judge the world, but to save the world'" (John 12:47).

"As Protestants, we appeal on the ground of the historical right to protest against every interference of civil government in the affairs of religion; the grand charter of Protestantism, the Augsburg Confession, declaring:—'The civil administration is occupied about other matters than the gospel. The magistracy does not defend the souls, but the bodies, and bodily things, against manifest injuries, and coerces men by the sword and corporal punishment, that it may uphold *civil* justice and peace. Wherefore, the ecclesiastical power has its own command, to preach the gospel and administer the sacraments. Let it not by force enter into the office of another; let it not transfer worldly kingdoms; . . . let it not prescribe laws to the magistrate touching the form of the State; as Christ says, 'My kingdom is not of this world.' "—*Article 28*.

"As American Citizens, we appeal on the ground of the specifically declared constitutional right to the free exercise of religion according to the dictates of the individual conscience, totally free and exempt from all government connection, interference, or control.

"As men, we appeal on the ground of the natural right of mankind to render to the Creator such homage and such only as each believes to be acceptable to him; which right men possess by virtue of being men, and not by virtue of government; which was theirs before government was, and which would be theirs though there were no earthly government at all; which is their own in the essential meaning of the term; which is precedent to all the claims of civil society, and which would be the same to each man, though there were not another person on the earth; which they do not hold by any sub-infeudation, but by direct homage and allegiance to the Owner and Lord of all.

"And whether as Christians, as Protestants, as American citizens, or as men, what we mean by religion always and everywhere is 'the duty which we owe to our Creator, and the manner of discharging it.'

"Finally, in this our appeal from this action of the government of the United States, and our remonstrance against the principle and all the consequences of the action, we adopt and adapt the words of Madison, Jefferson, the Presbyterians, the Baptists, the Quakers, and the other good people of Virginia, in their memorable defense, from 1776 until 1785, against the establishment of the 'Christian religion' there, and the making of that 'a Christian State.'

"We would humbly represent that the only proper objects of civil government are the happiness and protection of men in the present state of existence, the security of life, liberty, and property of the citizens, and to restrain the vicious and encourage the virtuous by wholesome laws, equally extending to every individual. But religion, or the duty which we owe our Creator, *and the manner of discharging it,* can be directed only by reason and conviction, and is *nowhere* cognizable but at the tribunal *of the universal Judge.*"

And then follows 16 pages of statements regarding the history of the establishment of the United States with its separation of powers and the rights of the individual. When this document was circulated in the public domain the editors of the *Catholic Mirror* in Baltimore, Maryland, responded with four consecutive editorials in their weekly publication. This was during the heart of the tenure of James Cardinal Gibbons, the Archbishop of Baltimore. Cardinal Gibbons lived from 1834 to 1921 and was a cardinal the last 34 years of his life, including the year during which these editorials were printed in the Catholic *Mirror.* The *Mirror*'s name was changed to *Catholic Review* in 1913, and it continues to be the publication of the Baltimore Archdiocese.

In the paragraphs that follow I will record the text of these four editorials. You will note an almost cynical note in the articles, that blast the Protestant churches for claiming to believe the Bible only, yet they continue to worship on Sunday, which is not scriptural, but rather is "The genuine offspring of the union of the Holy Spirit and the Catholic Church, His spouse."

These editorials are posted on the Internet at several locations and were on the Catholic Web site, Maryonline, where the articles were prefaced with the following note: "Keep in mind that in 1893, political correctness had not been invented yet. Some readers may wince at the tone of the articles. It would do well to note that having principles and the convictions to articulate them was a more admired characteristic in those days, than a concern for those who might take offense. The tone, if anything, reflects the Church Militant prior to its late 20th century feminization, and older readers may recognize the Church of their childhood in the manner in which the convictions are so firmly held."

These four editorials in the *Catholic Mirror* were so significant at the time that the International Religious Liberty Association printed them in a booklet titled *Rome's Challenge,* and the *Catholic Mirror* responded by printing them in their own booklet titled *The Christian Sabbath.* The Catholic booklet was so popular that it was printed in at least five editions. My copy is a fifth edition. There may have been more. It is from the Catholic edition that I will reproduce the articles below. To save any editorializing on my part during the reproduction, it would be well for the reader to note that the Catholic Church refutes all attempts by the Protestants to any use of Scripture in the change of the Sabbath. All the texts that are commonly used by Protestants are systematically discussed and eliminated as biblical support for the change of the day of rest. The following is a verbatim transcript of the Catholic booklet *The Christian Sabbath:*

THE CHRISTIAN SABBATH

THE GENUINE OFFSPRING OF THE UNION
OF THE HOLY SPIRIT, AND THE

CATHOLIC CHURCH,
HIS SPOUSE.

THE CLAIMS OF PROTESTANTISM TO ANY PART THEREIN PROVED TO BE GROUNDLESS, SELF-CONTRADICTORY AND SUICIDAL.

CONSISTING OF FOUR EDITORIALS ON THE ABOVE SUBJECT PUBLISHED IN THE ISSUES OF THE *CATHOLIC MIRROR* OF 2D, 9TH, 16TH, AND 23D OF SEPTEMBER, 1893.

FIFTH EDITION

PUBLISHED BY THE
CATHOLIC MIRROR
BALTIMORE, MD.

PREFACE.

The contents of this pamphlet embrace four editorials which appeared in the columns of the *Catholic Mirror* in four successive issues of the paper, viz: on the 2d, 9th, 16th, and 23d of September, 1893. The unprecedented demand for copies of the above dates soon exhausted the issues, whilst to meet all further requests for an adequate supply we published in our columns a reprint of them for the benefit of our subscribers, availing ourselves of the opportunity to furnish them to all applicants in the present form.

A reprint of these articles has been issued by the International Religious Liberty Association, in Michigan, in a pamphlet of thirty-two pages, available in London, England; Australia; Cape Town, Africa; Toronto, Ontario; and in Michigan, New York, California and Tennessee.

Whilst the Protestant world evinces so profound an interest in these Catholic productions, we feel that the Catholics of the country should have within their reach arguments unanswerable by the opponents of our religion, placing it in an impregnable position, whilst they expose the utterly indefensible condition to which they have reduced Protestantism. With this view of the matter, we respectfully place its pages before our readers, anticipating both profit and pleasure to them in their perusal.

THE CATHOLIC MIRROR, PUBLISHERS.

[THE FIRST ARTICLE]

THE CHRISTIAN SABBATH

THE GENUINE OFFSPRING OF THE UNION OF THE HOLY

SPIRIT, AND THE CATHOLIC CHURCH HIS SPOUSE.

THE CLAIMS OF PROTESTANTISM TO ANY PART

THEREIN PROVED TO BE GROUNDLESS, SELF-

CONTRADICTORY AND SUICIDAL.
(From the *Catholic Mirror* of Sept. 2, 1893.)

Our attention has been called to the above subject in the past week by the receipt of a brochure of twenty-one pages, published by the International Religious Liberty Association, entitled "Appeal and Remonstrance," embodying Resolutions adopted by the General Conference of Seventh-Day Adventists (February 24th, '93). The resolutions criticize and censure, with much acerbity, the action of the United States Congress, and of the Supreme Court, for invading the rights of the people by closing the World's Fair on Sunday.

The Adventists are the only body of Christians with the Bible as their teacher, who can find no warrant in its pages for the change of day from the Seventh to the First. Hence their appellation, "Seventh-Day Adventists." Their cardinal principle consists in setting apart

Saturday for the exclusive worship of God, in conformity with the positive command of God Himself, repeatedly reiterated in the Sacred Books of the Old and New Testament, literally obeyed by the Children of Israel for thousands of years to this day, and endorsed by the teaching and practice of the Son of God whilst on earth.

Per contra, the Protestants of the world, the Adventists excepted, with the *same* Bible as their cherished and sole infallible teacher, by their practice, since their appearance in the Sixteenth century, with the time-honored practice of the Jewish people before their eyes, have rejected the day named for His worship by God, and assumed, in apparent contradiction of His command, a day for His worship never once referred to for that purpose, in the pages of the Sacred Volume.

What Protestant pulpit does not ring almost every Sunday with loud and impassioned invectives against Sabbath violation? Who can forget the fanatical clamor of the Protestant ministers throughout the length and breadth of the land, against opening the gates of the World's Fair on Sunday? The thousands of petitions, signed by millions, to save the Lord's Day from desecration? Surely, such general and widespread excitement and noisy remonstrance, could not have existed without the strongest grounds for such animated protests.

And when quarters were assigned at the World's Fair to the various sects of Protestantism for the exhibition of articles, who can forget the emphatic expression of virtuous and conscientious indignation exhibited by our Presbyterian brethren, as soon as they learned of the decision of the Supreme Court not to interfere in the Sunday opening? The newspapers informed us that they flatly refused to utilize the space accorded them, or open their boxes, demanding the right to withdraw the articles, in rigid adherence to their principles, and thus decline all contact with the sacrilegious and Sabbath-breaking Exhibition.

Doubtless, our Calvinistic brethren deserved and shared the sympathy of all the other sects, who, however, lost the opportunity of posing as martyrs in vindication of the Sabbath observance.

They thus become "a spectacle to the world, to angels and to men," although their Protestant brethren, who failed to share the monopoly, were uncharitably and enviously disposed to attribute their steadfast adherence to religious principle, to Pharisaical pride and dogged obstinacy.

Our purpose in throwing off this article, is to shed such light on this all important question (for were the Sabbath question to be removed from the Protestant pulpit, the sects would feel lost, and the preachers be deprived of their "Cheshire cheese") that our readers may be able to comprehend the question in *all its bearings,* and thus reach a clear conviction.

The Christian world is, morally speaking, united on the question and practice of worshiping God on *the first day* of the week.

The Israelites, scattered all over the earth, keep *the last day* of the week sacred to the worship of the Deity. In this particular, the Seventh-Day Adventists (a sect of Christians numerically few) have also selected the same day.

The Israelites and Adventists both appeal to the Bible for the Divine command, persistently obliging the strict observance of Saturday.

The Israelite respects the authority of the Old Testament only, but the Adventist, who is a Christian, accepts the New Testament on the same ground as the Old, viz: an inspired record also. He finds that the Bible, his teacher, is consistent in both parts; that the Redeemer, during His mortal life, never kept any other day than Saturday. The Gospels plainly evince to Him this fact; whilst, in the pages of the Acts of the Apostles, the Epistles and the Apocalypse, not the vestige of an act canceling the Saturday arrangement can be found.

The Adventists, therefore, in common with the Israelites, derive their belief from the Old Testament, which position is confirmed by the New Testament, endorsing fully by the life and practice of the Redeemer and His apostles the teaching of the Sacred Word for nearly a century of the Christian era.

Numerically considered, the Seventh-Day Adventists form an insignificant portion of the Protestant population of the earth, but, as the question is not one of numbers, but of truth, fact and right, a strict sense of justice forbids the condemnation of this little sect without a calm and unbiased investigation; this is none of our funeral.

The Protestant world has been, from its infancy, in the Sixteenth century, in thorough accord with the Catholic Church, in keeping "holy" not Saturday, but Sunday. The discussion of the grounds that led to this unanimity of sentiment and practice for over 300 years, must help towards placing Protestantism on a solid basis in this particular, should the arguments in favor of its position overcome those furnished by the Israelites and Adventists, the Bible, the sole recognized teacher of both litigants, being the umpire and witness. If, however, on the other hand, the latter furnish arguments, incontrovertible by the great mass of Protestants, both classes of litigants, appealing to their common teacher, the Bible, the great body of Protestants, so far from clamoring, as they do with vigorous pertinacity for the strict keeping of Sunday, have no other resource left than the admission that they have been teaching and practicing *what is Scripturally false for over three centuries,* by adopting the teaching and practice of what they have always pretended to believe an apostate church, contrary to every warrant and teaching of Sacred Scripture. To add to the intensity of this Scriptural and unpardonable blunder, it involves one of the most positive and emphatic commands of God to His servant, man: "Remember the Sabbath Day to keep it holy."

No Protestant living today has ever yet obeyed that command, preferring to follow the apostate church referred to than his teacher, the Bible, which, from Genesis to Revelation, *teaches no other doctrine,* should the Israelites and Seventh-Day Adventists be correct. Both sides appeal to the Bible as their "infallible" teacher. Let the Bible decide whether Saturday or Sunday be the day enjoined by God. One of the two bodies must be wrong, and, whereas a false position on this all-important question involves terrible penalties, threatened by God Himself, against the transgressor of this "perpetual covenant." We shall enter on the discussion of the merits of the arguments wielded by both sides. Neither is the discussion of this paramount subject above the capacity of ordinary minds, nor does it involve extraordinary study. It resolves itself into a few plain questions easy of solution:

1st. Which day of the week does the Bible enjoin to be kept holy?

2nd. Has the New Testament, modified by precept or practice, the original command?

3rd. Have Protestants, since the Sixteenth century, obeyed the command of God by keeping "holy" the day enjoined by their infallible guide and teacher, the Bible, and if not, why not?

To the above three questions we pledge ourselves to furnish as many intelligent answers, which cannot fail to vindicate the truth and uphold the deformity of error.

SENEX.

(From the *Catholic Mirror* of September 9, 1893.)
> *"But faith, fanatic faith, once wedded fast,*
> *to some dear falsehood, hugs it to the last."*—Moore.

Conformably to our promise in our last issue, we proceed to unmask one of the most flagrant errors and most unpardonable inconsistencies of the Biblical rule of faith. Lest, however, we be misunderstood, we deem it necessary to premise that Protestantism recognizes no rule of faith, no teacher save the "Infallible Bible." As the Catholic yields his judgment in spiritual matters implicitly, and with unreserved confidence, to the voice of his Church, so, too, the Protestant recognizes *no teacher but the Bible*. All his spirituality is derived from its teachings. It is to him the voice of God addressing him through His sole inspired teacher. It embodies his religion, his faith and his practice. The language of Chillingworth: "The Bible, the whole Bible, and nothing but the Bible, is the religion of Protestants," is only one form of the same idea multifariously convertible into other forms, such as "The Book of God," "The Charter of Our Salvation," "The Oracle of Our Christian Faith," "God's Text-Book to the race of Mankind," etc., etc. It is, then, an incontrovertible fact that *the Bible alone* is the teacher of Protestant Christianity. Assuming this fact, we will now proceed to discuss the merits of the question involved in our last issue.

Recognizing what is undeniable, the fact of a direct contradiction between the teaching and practice of Protestant Christianity—the Seventh-Day Adventists excepted—on the one hand, and that of the Jewish people on the other; both observing different days of the week for the worship of God, we will proceed to take the testimony of the only available witness in the premises, viz: the testimony of the teacher common to both claimants, the Bible. The first expression with which we come in contact in the Sacred Word, is found in Genesis 2d chapter, 2d verse: "And on the seventh day He (God) rested from all His work which He had made." The next reference to this matter is to be found in Exodus, 20th chapter, where God commanded the seventh day to be kept, *because* He had Himself rested from the work of creation on that day; and the sacred text informs us that *for that reason* He desired it kept, in the following words: *"Wherefore,* the Lord blessed the seventh day and sanctified it." Again, we read in the 31st chapter, 15th verse: "Six days you shall do work; in the seventh day is the

Sabbath, the rest holy to the Lord." Sixteenth verse: *"It is an everlasting covenant,"* "and a perpetual sign," "for in six days the Lord made Heaven and earth, and in the seventh He ceased from work." [2]

In the Old Testament reference is made one hundred and twenty-six times to the Sabbath, and all these texts conspire harmoniously in voicing the will of God, commanding the seventh day to be kept, because God Himself *first kept it,* making it obligatory on all as *"a perpetual covenant."* Nor can we imagine any one foolhardy enough to question the identity of Saturday with the Sabbath or seventh day, seeing that the people of Israel have been keeping the Saturday from the giving of the Law, A.M., 2514 to A.D. 1893, a period of 3,383 years. With the example of the Israelites before our eyes to-day, there is no historical fact better established than that referred to, viz: that the chosen people of God, the guardians of the Old Testament, the living representatives of the only Divine religion hitherto, had for a period of 1490 years anterior to Christianity, preserved by weekly practice the living tradition of the correct interpretation of the special day of the week, Saturday, to be kept "holy to the Lord," which tradition they have extended by their practice to an additional period of 1893 years more, thus covering the full extent of the Christian dispensation. We deem it necessary to be perfectly clear on this point, for reasons that will appear more fully hereafter. The Bible —the Old Testament—confirmed by the living tradition of a weekly practice for 3383 years by the chosen people of God, teaches, then, with absolute certainty, that God had, Himself, named the day to be "kept holy to Him,"—that the day was Saturday, and that any violation of that command was punishable with death. "Keep you my Sabbath, for it is holy unto you; he that shall profane it shall be put to death; he that shall do any work in it, his soul shall perish in the midst of his people."— Exodus 31 chapter, 14th verse.

It is impossible to realize a more severe penalty than that so solemnly uttered by God Himself in the above text, on all who violate a command referred to no less than one hundred and twenty-six times in the Old Law. The ten commandments of the Old Testament are formally impressed on the memory of the child of the Biblical Christian as soon as possible, but there is not one of the ten made more emphatically familiar, both in Sunday-school and pulpit, than that of keeping "holy" the Sabbath day.

Having secured with absolute certainty the will of God as regards the day to be kept holy, from His sacred word, *because* He rested on that day, which day is confirmed to us by the practice of His chosen people for thousands of years, we are naturally induced to inquire *when and where* God changed the day for His worship, for it is patent to the world that a change of day has taken place, and inasmuch as no indication of such change can be found within the pages of the Old Testament, nor in the practice of the Jewish people who continue for nearly nineteen centuries of Christianity obeying the written command, we must look to the Christian dispensation, viz: the New Testament, for the command of God cancelling the old Sabbath, Saturday.

We now approach a period covering little short of nineteen centuries, and proceed to investigate whether the supplemental Divine teacher—the New Testament—contains a decree canceling the mandate of the Old Law, and, at the same time, substituting a day for the Divinely instituted Sabbath of the Old Law, viz: Saturday; for, inasmuch as Saturday was the day kept and ordered to be kept by God, *Divine authority alone,* under the form of a canceling decree, could abolish the Saturday covenant, and another Divine mandate, appointing by name another day to be kept "holy," other than Saturday, is equally necessary to satisfy the conscience of the Christian believer. The Bible being the only teacher recognized by the Biblical Christian, the Old Testament failing to point out a change of day, and yet another day than Saturday being kept "holy" by the Biblical world, it is surely incumbent on the reformed Christian to point out in the pages of the New Testament the new Divine decrees repealing that of Saturday and substituting that of Sunday, kept by Biblicals since the dawn of the Reformation.

Examining the New Testament from cover to cover, critically, we find the Sabbath referred to sixty-one times. We find, too, that the Saviour invariably selected the Sabbath (Saturday) to teach in the synagogues and work miracles. The four Gospels refer to the Sabbath (Saturday) fifty-one times.

In one instance, the Redeemer refers to Himself as "the Lord of the Sabbath," as mentioned by Matthew and Luke, but, during the whole record of His life, whilst invariably keeping and utilizing the day, (Saturday), *He never once hinted at a desire to change it.* His Apostles and personal friends afford to us a striking instance of their scrupulous observance of it *after His death,* and, whilst His body was yet in the tomb, St. Luke, 23d chapter, 56 verse, informs us: "And they returned and prepared spices and ointments, *and rested on the Sabbath-day according to the Commandment.*" "But on the first day of the week, very early in the morning, (Easter Sunday) bringing the spices they had prepared." The "spices" and "ointments" had been prepared Good Friday evening, because "the Sabbath drew near." 54th verse. This action on the part of the personal friends of the Savoiur, proves beyond contradiction, that, *after His death,* they kept "holy" the Saturday, *and regarded the Sunday as any other day of the week.* Can anything, therefore, be more conclusive than that the Apostles and the holy women never knew any Sabbath, but Saturday, up to the day of Christ's death?

We now approach the investigation of this interesting question for the next thirty years, as narrated by the Evangelist, St. Luke, in his Acts of the Apostles. Surely some vestage of the canceling act can be discovered in the practice of the Apostles during that protracted period.

But, alas! We are once more doomed to disappointment. *Nine times* do we find the Sabbath referred to in the "Acts," but it is the *Saturday,* (the old Sabbath). Should our readers desire the proof, we refer them to chapter and verse in each instance. Acts, 13c., 14v.; again, same chapter, 27v., again, 42v.; again, 44v. Once more, 15c., 31v. Again, 17c., 2v.; again, 18c., 4v. "And he (Paul) reasoning in the Synagogue *every Sabbath,* and persuaded the Jews and the Greeks." *Thus the Sabbath (Saturday) from Genesis to Revelation!!!* Thus, it is impossible to find in the New Testament the slightest interference by the Saviour, or His Apostles, with the original Sabbath, but, on the contrary, an entire acquiescence in the original arrangement; nay a *plenary endorsement* by Him, whilst living; and an unvaried, active participation *in the keeping of that day and no other by the Apostles,* for thirty years after His death, as the Acts of the Apostles have abundantly testified to us.

Hence, the conclusion is inevitable, viz: that of those who follow the Bible as their guide, the Israelites and Seventh-Day Adventists have the exclusive weight of evidence on their side, whilst the Biblical Protestant has not a word in self-defense for his substitution of Sunday for Saturday.

SENEX.

---

[1] *United States Statutes at Large,* vol. 27, chapter 381, pp. 389, 390.

[2] Note: Scriptures quoted in these editorials are taken from the Douay or Catholic version of the Bible.

CHAPTER 6

The Catholic Church Refutes Biblical Sundaykeeping

T his chapter contains the last two editorials from the *Catholic Mirror* that refute the Protestant claim to biblical support for Sundaykeeping. You will note in this chapter that the church condemns Martin Luther and states that he was working with Satan to tear down "the Church." However, their conclusion remains, that if you follow the Bible only as your guide to faith and practice you will be a seventh-day Sabbathkeeper, since the only authority for keeping Sunday is that of the Catholic Church. Now follow articles three and four.

(From the *Catholic Mirror* of Sept. 16, 1893.)

When his Satanic Majesty, who was "a murderer from the beginning," "and the father of lies," undertook to open the eyes of our first mother, Eve, by stimulating her ambition, "you shall be as gods, knowing good and evil," his action was but the first of many plausible and successful efforts employed later, in the seduction of millions of her children. Like Eve, they learn too late, alas! the value of the inducements held out to allure her weak children from allegiance to God. Nor does the subject-matter of this discussion form an exception to the usual tactics of his sable majesty.

Over three centuries since he plausibly represented to a large number of discontented and ambitious Christians the bright prospect of the successful inauguration of a "new departure," by the abandonment of the Church instituted by the Son of God, as their teacher, and the assumption of a new teacher—*the Bible alone*—as their newly-fledged oracle.

The sagacity of the evil one foresaw but the brilliant success of this maneuver. Nor did the result fall short of his most sanguine expectations.

A bold and adventurous spirit was alone needed to head the expedition. Him his Satanic Majesty soon found in the apostate monk, Luther, who, himself repeatedly testifies to the close familiarity that

80

existed between his master and himself, in his "Table Talk," and other works published in 1558 at Wittenberg, under the inspection of Melancthon. His colloquies with Satan on various occasions, are testified to by Luther himself—a witness worthy of all credibility. What the agency of the Serpent tended so effectually to achieve in the Garden, the agency of Luther achieved in the Christian world.

"Give them a pilot to their wandering fleet,
Bold in his art, and tutored to deceit;
Whose hand adventurous shall their helm misguide
To hostile shores, or 'whelm them in the tide."

As the end proposed to himself by the Evil One in his raid on the Church of Christ was the destruction of Christianity, we are now engaged in sifting the means adopted by him to insure his success therein. So far, they have been found to be misleading, self-contradictory and fallacious. We will now proceed with the investigation of this imposture.

Having proved to a demonstration that the Redeemer, *in no instance,* had, during the period of His life, deviated from the faithful observance of the Sabbath, (Saturday), referred to by the four Evangelists fifty-one times, although He had designated Himself "Lord of the Sabbath," He never having *once,* by command or practice, hinted at a desire on His part to change the day by the substitution of another; and having called special attention to the conduct of the Apostles and the holy women, the very evening of His death, securing beforehand spices and ointments "to be used in embalming His body the morning after the Sabbath (Saturday), as St. Luke so clearly informs us; (Luke 24ch. 1v.) thereby placing beyond peradventure, the Divine action and will of the Son of God during life by keeping the Sabbath steadfastly; and having called attention to the action of His living representatives after His death, as proved by St. Luke; having also placed before our readers *the indisputable fact* that the Apostles for the following thirty years (Acts) never deviated from the practice of their Divine Master in this particular, as St. Luke (Acts 18ch., 4v.) assures us: "And he (Paul) reasoned in the synagogues *every Sabbath* (Saturday), and persuaded the Jews and the Greeks." The Gentile converts were, as we see from the text, equally instructed with the Jews, to keep the Saturday, having been converted to Christianity on that day, "the Jews and the Greeks" collectively.

Having also called attention to the texts of the Acts (9), bearing on the exclusive use of the Sabbath by the Jews and Christians for thirty years after the death of the Saviour as the *only* day of the week observed by Christ and His Apostles, which period *exhausts the inspired record,* we now proceed to supplement our proofs that the Sabbath (Saturday) enjoyed this exclusive privilege, by calling attention *to every instance* wherein the Sacred Record refers to the first day of the week.

The *first* reference to Sunday after the resurrection of Christ is to be found in St. Luke's Gospel, 24ch., from 33 to 40 vs., and in St. John's, 20ch., 19v.

The above texts themselves refer to the sole motive of this gathering on the part of the Apostles. It took place on the day of the resurrection (Easter Sunday), not for the purpose of inaugurating "the new departure" from the old Sabbath (Saturday) by keeping "holy" the new day, for there is not a hint given of prayer, exhortation, or the reading of the Scriptures, but it indicates the utter demoralization of the Apostles by informing mankind that they were huddled together in that room in Jerusalem *"for fear of the Jews,"* as St. John, quoted above, plainly informs us.

The second reference to Sunday is to be found in St. John's Gospel, 20th chapter, 26 to 29th verses: "And after eight days, the Disciples were again within, and Thomas with them." The resurrected Redeemer availed Himself of this meeting of all the Apostles to confound the incredulity of Thomas, who had been absent from the gathering on Easter Sunday evening. This would have furnished a golden opportunity to the Redeemer to change the day in the presence of all His Apostles, but we state the simple fact that, on this occasion, as on Easter Day, not a word is said of prayer, praise, or reading of the Scriptures. The third instance on record, wherein the Apostles were assembled on Sunday, is to be found in Acts, 2d chapter, 1st verse: "The Apostles were all of one accord in one place." (Feast of Pentecost—Sunday.) Now, will this text afford to our Biblical Christian brethren a vestige of hope that Sunday substitutes, at length, Saturday? For when we inform them that the Jews had been keeping *this Sunday* for 1500 years, and have been keeping it eighteen centuries after the establishment of Christianity, at the same time keeping the weekly Sabbath, there is not to be found either consolation or comfort in this text. Pentecost is the 50th day after Passover, which was called the Sabbath of weeks, consisting of seven times seven days; and the day after the completion of the seventh weekly Sabbath Day, was the chief day of the entire Festival, necessarily Sunday. What Israelite would not pity the cause that would seek to discover the origin of the keeping of the first day of the week to his Festival of Pentecost, that has been kept by him yearly for over 3,000 years? <u>Who but the Biblical Christian, driven to the wall for a pretext to excuse his sacreligious desecration of the Sabbath, always kept by Christ and His Apostles, should have resorted to the Jewish Festival of Pentecost for his act of rebellion against his God, and his teacher, the Bible?</u>

Once more, the Bible apologists, for the change of day, call our attention to the Acts, 20th chapter, 6th and 7th verses: "And upon *the first day of the week,* when the disciples came together to break bread," etc. To all appearances, the above text should furnish some consolation to our disgruntled Biblical friends, but being a Marplot, we cannot allow them even this crumb of comfort. We reply by the axiom: "*Quod probat nimis, probat nihil.*" "What proves too much, proves nothing." Let us call attention to the same Acts, 2d chapter, 46th verse: "And they, continuing *daily* in the Temple, and breaking bread from house to house," etc. Who does not see at a glance, that the text produced to prove the exclusive prerogative of Sunday, vanishes into thin air—an *ignis fatuus*—when placed in juxtaposition with the 46th verse of the same chapter? What the Biblical Christian claims by this text *for Sunday alone,* the same authority, Saint Luke, informs us was *common to every day of the week:* "And they, continuing *daily* in the Temple, and breaking bread from house to house."

One text more presents itself, apparently leaning towards a substitution of Sunday for Saturday. It is taken from St. Paul's, 1 Ep. Cor., 16th chapter, 1st and 2nd verses.

"Now concerning the collection for the saints." "On the first day of the week, let every one of you lay by him in store," etc. Presuming that the request of St. Paul had been strictly attended to, let us call attention to what had been done each Saturday during the Saviour's life, and continued for thirty years after, as the Acts informs us.

The followers of the Master met *"every Sabbath day."* "And Paul, as his manner was to reason in the Synagogue *every Sabbath,* interposing the name of the Lord Jesus," etc., Acts 18th chapter, 4th verse. What more absurd conclusion than to infer that reading of the Scriptures, prayer, exhortation, and preaching, which *formed the routine duties of every Saturday,* as has been abundantly proved, were overslaughed by a request to take up a collection on *another day of the week?*

In order to appreciate fully the value of this text now under consideration, it is only needful to recall the action of the Apostles and holy women on Good Friday before sundown. They bought the spices and ointments after He was taken down from the cross; they suspended all action until the Sabbath "holy to the Lord" had passed, and then took steps on Sunday morning to complete the process of embalming the sacred body of Jesus.

Why, may we ask, did they not proceed to complete the work of embalming on Saturday? Because they knew well that the embalming of the sacred body of their Master would interfere with the strict observance of the Sabbath, the keeping of which was paramount, and until it can be shown that the Sabbath day *immediately preceding the Sabbath of our text* had not been kept (which would be false, inasmuch as *every Sabbath had been kept*) the request of St. Paul to make the collection *on Sunday* remains to be classified with the work of the embalming of Christ's body, which could not be effected on the Sabbath, and was consequently deferred to the next convenient day, viz.: Sunday, or the first day of the week.

Having disposed of every text to be found in the New Testament referring to the Sabbath (Saturday), and to the first day of the week (Sunday), and having shown conclusively from these texts, that, so far, not a shadow of pretext can be found in the sacred volume for the Biblical substitution of Sunday for Saturday; it only remains for us to investigate the meaning of the expressions "Lord's Day" and "Day of the Lord," to be found in the New Testament, which we propose to do in our next article, and conclude with apposite remarks on the incongruities of a system of religion which we shall have proved to be indefensible, self-contradictory and suicidal.

SENEX.

(From the *Catholic Mirror* of September 23, 1893.)

"Halting on crutches of unequal size,
One leg by truth supported, *one by lies,*
Thus sidle to the goal with awkward pace,
Secure of nothing but to lose the race."

In the present article we propose to investigate carefully a new (and the last) class of proofs assumed to convince the Biblical Christian that God had substituted Sunday for Saturday for His worship in the New Law, and that the Divine will is to be found recorded by the Holy Ghost in Apostolic writings.

We are informed that this radical change has found expression, over and over again, in a series of texts in which the expression, "The day of the Lord" or, "The Lord's day" is to be found.

The class of texts in the New Testament, under the title "Sabbath," numbering 61 in the Gospels, Acts and Epistles, and the second class, in which "the first day of the week," or Sunday, having been critically examined (the latter class numbering nine), and having been found not to afford the slightest clue to a change of will on the part of God as to His day of worship by man, we now proceed to examine the third and last class of texts relied on to save the Biblical system from the arraignment of seeking to palm off on the world, in the name of God, a decree for which there is not the slightest warrant or authority from their teacher, the Bible.

The first text of this class is to be found in the Acts of the Apostles, 2d chapter, 20th verse: "The sun shall be turned into darkness, and the moon into blood, before that great and notable *day of the Lord* shall come." How many Sunday have rolled by since that prophecy was spoken? So much for that effort to pervert the meaning of the sacred text from the Judgment Day to Sunday!

The second text of this class is to be found in 1st Epistle Cor., 1st chapter, 8th verse: "Who also shall confirm you, unto the end that you may be blameless *in the day of Our Lord Jesus Christ.*" What simpleton does not see that the Apostle here plainly indicates the Day of Judgment? The next text of this class that presents itself, is to be found in the same Epistle, 5th chapter, 5th verse: "To deliver such a one to Satan for the destruction of the flesh, that the spirit may be saved *in the day of the Lord Jesus.*" The incestuous Corinthian was, of course, saved on the *Sunday next following!!* How pitiable such a make-shift as this! The fourth text, 2nd Cor., 1st chapter, 13th and 14th verses: "And I trust ye shall acknowledge even to the end, even as ye also are ours in the day of our Lord Jesus."

Sunday, or the Day of Judgment, which? The fifth text is from St. Paul to the Philippians, 1st chapter, 6th verse: "Being confident of this very thing, that He who hath begun a good work in you, will perfect it *until the day of Jesus Christ.*" The good people of Philippi, in attaining perfection *on the following Sunday,* could afford to laugh at our modern rapid transit!

We beg leave to submit our sixth of the class, viz. Philippians, first chapter, tenth verse. "That he may be sincere without offense unto *the day of Christ.*" That day was *next Sunday,* forsooth! not so long to wait after all. The seventh text, 2 Ep. Peter, third chapter, tenth verse. "But *the day of the Lord* will come as a thief in the night," The application of this text to Sunday passes the bounds of absurdity.

The eighth text, 2 Ep. Peter, third chapter, twelfth verse: "Waiting for and hastening unto *the coming of the day of the Lord,* by which the heavens being on fire, shall be dissolved" etc. This day of the Lord is the same referred to in the previous text, the application of both of which to *Sunday next* would have left the Christian world sleepless the next Saturday night.

We have presented to our readers, eight of the nine texts relied on to bolster up by text of Scripture the sacrilegious effort to palm off the "Lord's Day" for Sunday, and with what result? Each furnishes *prima facie* evidence of the last day; referring to it directly, absolutely and unequivocally.

The ninth text wherein we meet the expression "the Lord's day," is the last to be found in the Apostolic writings. The Apocalypse or Revelations, first chapter, tenth verse, furnishes it in the following words of St. John: "I was in the spirit on the Lord's day;" but it will afford no more comfort to our Biblical friends than its predecessors of the same series. Has St. John used the expression previously in his Gospels or Epistles? Emphatically *no.* Has he had occasion to refer to Sunday hitherto? Yes, twice. How did he designate Sunday on these occasions? Easter Sunday was called by him, chapter twenty, first verse, (St. John's Gospel), *"The first day of the week."*

Again, chapter twenty, nineteenth verse: "Now when it was late that same day, *being the first day of the week."* Evidently, although inspired, both in his Gospels and Epistles, he called Sunday "the first day of the week." On what grounds, then, can it be assumed that he dropped that designation? Was he *more inspired* when he wrote the Apocalypse, or did he adopt a new title for Sunday, because it was now in vogue?

A reply to these questions would be supererogatory especially to the latter, seeing that the same expression had been used eight times already, by St. Luke, St. Paul and St. Peter, *all under Divine inspiration,* and surely the Holy Spirit would not inspire St. John to call Sunday the Lord's day, whilst He inspired Sts. Luke, Paul and Peter collectively to entitle the day of Judgment "the Lord's day." Dialecticians reckon amongst the infallible motives of certitude, the moral motive of analogy or induction, by which we are enabled to conclude with certainty from the known to the unknown; being absolutely certain of the meaning of an expression uttered eight times, we conclude that the same expression can have the same meaning only, especially when we know that on the nine occasions the expressions were *inspired by the Holy Spirit.*

Nor are the strongest intrinsic grounds wanting to prove that this, like its sister texts, contains the same meaning. St. John (Apoc. first chapter, tenth verse) says: "I was in the spirit on the Lord's day;" but he furnishes us the key to this expression, chapter four, first and second verses. "After this I looked and beheld a door was opened in Heaven." A voice said to him: "Come up hither and I will show you *the things which must be hereafter."* Let us ascend in spirit with John. Whither? Through that "door in Heaven," to Heaven. And what shall we see? "The things that must come to pass hereafter," chapter four, first verse. He ascended in spirit to Heaven. He was ordered to write, in full, his vision of what is to take place antecedent to and concomitantly with "the Lord's day" or the day of Judgment; the expression, "Lord's day" being confined in Scripture to the day of Judgment exclusively.

We have studiously and accurately collected from the New Testament every available proof that could be adduced in favor of a law cancelling the Sabbath day of the Old Law, or one substituting another day for the Christian dispensation. We have been careful to make the above distinction, lest it might be advanced that the 3rd

Commandment was abrogated under the New Law. Any such law has been overruled by the action of the Methodist Episcopal Bishops in their Pastoral 1874, and quoted in the New York *Herald* of same date, of the following tenor: "The Sabbath instituted in the beginning and confirmed again and again by Moses and the Prophets, *has never been abrogated.* A part of the moral law, not a part or tittle of its sanctity has been taken away." The above official pronunciamento has committed that large body of Biblical Christians to the permanence of the 3rd Commandment under the New Law.

Again we beg leave to call special attention of our readers to the 20th of "the 39 articles of religion" of the Book of Common Prayer, "It is not lawful for the church to ordain anything that is contrary to *God's written word.*"

CONCLUSION.

We have in this series of articles, taken much pains for the instruction of our readers to prepare them, by presenting a number of *undeniable facts* found in the word of God, to arrive at a conclusion absolutely irrefragable. When the Biblical system put in an appearance in the 16th century, it not only seized on the temporal possessions of the Church, but in its vandalic crusade stripped Christianity, as far as it could, of all the sacraments instituted by its founder, of the Holy Sacrifice, &c., &c., retaining nothing but the Bible, which its exponents pronounced *their sole teacher* in Christian doctrine and morals.

Chief amongst their articles of belief was, and is today, the permanent necessity of keeping the Sabbath holy. In fact, it has been for the past 300 years *the only article* of the Christian belief in which there has been a plenary consensus of Biblical representatives. The keeping of the Sabbath constitutes the sum and substance of the Biblical theory. The pulpits resound weekly with incessant tirades against the lax manner of keeping the Sabbath in Catholic countries, as contrasted with the proper, Christian, self-satisfied mode of keeping the day in Biblical countries. We can ever forget the virtuous indignation manifested by the Biblical preachers through the length and breadth of our country, from every Protestant pulpit, as long as the question of opening the World's Fair on Sunday was yet undecided, and who does not know to-day, that one sect, to mark its holy indignation at the decision, has never yet opened the boxes that contained its articles at the World's Fair?

These superlatively good and unctuous Christians, by conning over their Bible carefully, can find their counterpart in a certain class of unco-good people in the days of the Redeemer, who haunted Him night and day, distressed beyond measure, and scandalized beyond forbearance, because He did not keep the Sabbath in as straight-laced manner as themselves.

They hated Him for using common sense in reference to the day, and He found no epithets expressive enough of His supreme contempt for their pharisaical pride. And it is very probable that the Divine mind has not modified its views to-day, anent the blatant outcry of their followers and sympathizers at the close of this 19th century. But when we add to all this, the fact that whilst the Pharisees of old kept the *true Sabbath,* our modern Pharisees counting on the credulity and simplicity of their dupes, *have never once in their lives kept the true Sabbath* which their Divine Master kept to His dying day, and which His Apostles kept, after His example, for thirty years afterwards, according to the Sacred Record.

This most glaring contradiction, involving a deliberate sacrilegious rejection of a most positive precept is presented to us to-day in the action of the Biblical Christian world. The Bible and the Sabbath constitute the watchword of Protestantism; but we have demonstrated that it is *the Bible versus their Sabbath.* We have shown that no greater contradiction ever existed than their theory and practice. We have proved that neither the Biblical ancestors nor themselves have ever kept one Sabbath day in their lives.

The Israelites and Seventh-Day Adventists are witnesses of their weekly desecration of the day named by God so repeatedly, and whilst they have ignored and condemned their teacher, the Bible, they have adopted a day kept by the Catholic Church. What Protestant can, after perusing these articles, with a clear conscience, continue to disobey the command of God, enjoining *Saturday to be kept,* which command his teacher, the Bible, from Genesis to Revelation, records as the will of God?

The history of the world cannot present a more stupid, self-stultifying specimen of dereliction of principle than this. The teacher demands emphatically in every page that the Law of the Sabbath be observed every week, by all recognizing it as "the only infallible teacher," whilst the Disciples of that teacher have not once for over 300 years observed the Divine precept! That immense concourse of Biblical Christians, the Methodists, have declared that the Sabbath has never been abrogated, whilst the followers of the Church of England, together with her daughter, the Episcopal Church of the United States, are committed to the 20th article of Religion, already quoted, to the ordinance that the Church cannot lawfully ordain anything *contrary to God's word written.*" God's written word enjoins His worship to be observed on Saturday absolutely, repeatedly, and most emphatically, with a most positive threat of death to him who disobeys. All the Biblical sects occupy the same self-stultifying position which no explanation can modify, much less justify.

How truly do the words of the Holy Spirit apply to this deplorable situation! "Iniquitas mentita est sibi."—"*Iniquity hath lied to itself.*" Proposing to follow *the Bible only* as teacher, yet, before the world, *the sole teacher,* is ignominiously thrust aside, and the teaching and practice of the Catholic Church—"the mother of abominations," when it suits their purpose to so designate her—adopted, despite the most terrible threats pronounced by God Himself against those who disobey the command, "Remember to keep holy the Sabbath."

Before closing this series of articles, we beg to call our readers' attention once more to our caption, introductory of each, viz.: 1st—The Christian Sabbath, the genuine offspring of the union of the Holy Spirit, with the Catholic Church, His spouse. 2nd—The claim of "Protestantism to any part therein proved to be groundless, self-contradictory and suicidal."

The first proposition needs little proof. The Catholic Church for over one thousand years before the existence of a Protestant, by virtue of her Divine mission, changed the day from Saturday to Sunday. We say by virtue of her Divine mission because He has so called Himself "the Lord of the Sabbath," and whom all Christians pretend to believe, commanded all, without exception, "to hear His Church, under penalty of being classed by Him as "the heathen and the publican." The command is: "Let him hear the Church," not, let him read the Bible, for the Bible as such did not exist when the Saviour spoke these words; but the Church, His own creation, already existed on earth before His death, for He says; "On this rock I will build My Church." The

Protestant world gives these words, to use a nautical phrase, "a wide berth;" they take no stock in them. Their notion of Christianity does not include a divinely ordained teacher, and they shut out from their minds any arrangement made by the Redeemer even, that may happen to clash with their preconceived notions. Their Gospel leaves them free to accept or reject all and every truth, even though Christ had said: "He that believeth not, shall be damned."

But the Protestant says: How can I receive the teachings of an apostate Church? How, we ask, have you managed to receive her teaching all your life, *in direct opposition* to your recognized teacher, the Bible, on the Sabbath question? "Out of your mouth I judge you," says Jesus Christ. But *every one* says that His Church has gone astray, teaching error. This assertion is untrue. The large majority of Christians pronounce it false. You are included in the minority. Did Jesus Christ, her founder, the Creator of all things, ever make a blunder in any of His creations? If so, let the world learn in which. Is not His Church the last of His creations, and has He acknowledged it to be a failure? Did He not promise to be with it, teaching to the end of the world? Has He broken that promise? Did He not declare most positively that "the gates of hell should not prevail against it?" Have they? If you believe that they have, then you do believe Him to be neither truthful nor omnipotent, and therefore, not God. *Your God* is, by your own position and admission, a fraud. Your situation is an anomaly and contradiction. Don't allow your wrath to fall on the Church; she is no better, no worse, than when He created her your teacher. His pledges, which are numerous, that she could never teach error; that she should be protected by Him and His Holy Spirit to the end of time in teaching "all truth," are the pledges of Him who is "the way, the truth, and the life," who cannot deceive nor be deceived.

Hearkening to the language of men who are liable to be deceived, and whose interest it may be to deceive, are you willing to accept their word before the repeated pledges and promises made you by the Omnipotent Himself? Read St. Paul to the Ephesians 5c. 25v., and ask whether Christ, whom St. Paul holds up to all husbands as their Divine model, permitted His spouse, for whom He had "delivered Himself," that she might be "holy and unspotted," to fall from her high estate. To harbor such an idea would be blasphemy, and yet every Protestant breathes this very atmosphere, who charges the Church of Christ with teaching error, and her Divine Spouse with treacherous abandonment of her, whom St. Paul represents (29v.), as being "loved and cherished" by Jesus Christ. Not only is she His spouse but His mouth-piece and teacher to mankind, interpreting His doctrines and voicing the Divine will with infallible certainty. She holds her charter as teacher from Him—a charter as infallible as perpetual. The Protestant world at its birth found the Christian Sabbath too strongly entrenched to run counter to its existence; it was therefore placed under the necessity of acquiescing in the arrangement, thus implying the Church's right to change the day, for over 300 years. The Christian Sabbath is therefore *to this day* the acknowledged offspring of the Catholic Church, as spouse of the Holy Ghost, without a word of remonstrance from the Protestant world.

Let us now, however, take a glance at our second proposition, with *the Bible alone* as the teacher and guide in faith and morals. This teacher *most emphatically forbids any change in the day for paramount reasons.* The command calls for a *"perpetual covenant."* The day commanded to be kept by the teacher *has never once been kept,* thereby developing an apostasy from an assumedly fixed principle, as self-contradictory, self-stultifying, and consequently as suicidal as it is within the power of language to express. Nor are the limits of demoralization yet reached. Far from it. *Their pretense* for leaving the bosom of the Catholic Church was for apostasy from the truth *as taught in the written word.* They adopted the written word as their sole teacher, which they had no sooner done than they abandoned it promptly as these articles have abundantly proved, and by a perversity as willful as erroneous, they accept the teaching of the Catholic Church in direct opposition to the plain, unvaried and constant teaching of their sole teacher in the most essential doctrine of their religion, thereby emphasizing the situation in what may be aptly designated "*a mockery, a delusion and a snare.*"

Should any of the Rev. Parsons, who are habituated to howl so vociferously over every real or assumed desecration of that pious fraud, *the Bible Sabbath,* think well of entering a protest against our logical and scriptural dissection of their mongrel pet, we can promise them that any reasonable attempt on their part to gather up the "disjecta membra" of the hybrid, and to restore to it a galvanized existence, will be met with genuine cordiality and respectful consideration on our part. But we can assure our readers that we know these reverend howlers too well to expect a solitary bark from them in this instance.

And they know us too well to subject themselves to the mortification which a further dissection of this anti-scriptural question would necessarily entail. Their policy now is to "lay low," and they are sure to adopt it.

SENEX.

And so ends this interesting and enlightening challenge to Protestants. Most significant is the statement that from a "Bible alone perspective," Saturday, the seventh day of the week is the Sabbath of the Lord. Also admitted is that the church changed the day from Saturday to Sunday by its own authority, which they say was granted to them by the Creator. This is the same "Sunday origin" perspective that was given in the Augsburg Confession and the Council of Trent. So we must conclude, as the articles do, that if one takes the Bible as his standard of faith and practice, he will honor the seventh day, Saturday, as the Sabbath of the Lord.

Most members of Protestant churches do not have a clue about the historical record revealed in this chapter. Most sincerely believe, as they have been erroneously taught, that Jesus or His disciples changed the day to honor the resurrection. These sincere believers will one day soon be confronted with the truth about the change of the Sabbath. They will then be placed in a position where they must decide whether they will obey God or men.

CHAPTER 7

Church and State

L ife will never be the same again—especially in America." These words are repeated over and over again when individuals talk and write about the effects of the terrorist attacks on the United States in New York City and Washington, D.C. From a prophetic/end time perspective, events seem to be running at a more intense level and at a faster speed.

TERRORISM PREDICTED?

In his description of the last days, Paul stated, "But know this, that in the last days perilous times will come: For men will be . . . without self-control, brutal . . ." (2 Timothy 3:1-3). A relevant description of end-time activities by Ellen White seems right on point. "The Lord is removing His restrictions from the earth, and soon there will be death and destruction, increasing crime, and cruel, evil working against the rich who have exalted themselves against the poor. Those who are without God's protection will find no safety in any place or position. Human agents are being trained and are using their inventive power to put in operation the most powerful machinery to wound and to kill" (*Testimonies,* vol. 8, p. 50).

Just 45 days after the September 11, 2001, terrorist attacks on the United States, with virtually no debate, Congress passed the U.S.A. Patriot Act. The debate was limited because of the urgency to respond to the attacks and the fact that the halls of Congress were virtually empty during the time when the debate would have normally taken place because of the anthrax scare. Many parts of this sweeping legislation take away checks on law enforcement and threaten the very rights and freedoms that have made America great. For example, without a warrant and without probable cause, the FBI now has the power to access your most private medical records, your library records, and your student records— and can prevent anyone from telling you it was done.

The Patriot Act jeopardizes many of the basic rights afforded under the U.S. Constitution and the Bill of Rights. For example, the First Amendment—Freedom of religion, speech, assembly, and the press; The Fourth Amendment—Freedom from unreasonable searches and seizures; The Fifth Amendment—No person to be deprived of life, liberty, or property without due process of law; The Sixth Amendment —Right to a speedy public trial by an impartial jury, right to be informed of the facts of the accusation against you; The Eighth Amendment—No excessive bail or cruel or unusual punishment shall be imposed; and The Fourteenth Amendment—All persons within the U.S. are entitled to due process and the equal protection of the laws. It should be common knowledge to most readers that all of the above mentioned rights have been curtailed since 9/11 and the passage of the Patriot Act. And what is the people's reaction? Most people seem all too willing to trade freedoms for an elusive "security."

Roman Catholic attorney Alberto Gonzales was confirmed as the Attorney General during President Bush's second term. He was one of the architects of the Patriot Act. He has also stated that Al Qaeda and Taliban fighters are not prisoners of war but enemy combatants, with no legal rights under the Geneva Convention. Gonzales contended that "the ability to quickly obtain information from captured terrorists and their sponsors in order to avoid further atrocities against American civilians . . . renders obsolete Geneva's strict limitations on the questioning of enemy prisoners" (*Time,* November 22, 2004).

FEAR IN MEN'S HEARTS

The Bible says that men's hearts would be filled with fear as they see the things coming on the earth (see Luke 21:26). On September 20, 2001, just nine days after the terrorist attacks, President Bush announced the creation of a cabinet-level office of Homeland Security and named the Roman Catholic governor of Pennsylvania, Tom Ridge, as its first director. Since that time, literally millions of dollars have been spent to help prevent terrorists from inflicting more harm on Americans. Barriers have been placed around public buildings and a whole new agency, the Transportation Security Administration (TSA), has been organized to screen airline passengers for threats to safety. People say they are willing to put up with the long lines at airports, but they still cringe at the fact that a perfect stranger can riffle through their personal luggage.

On Friday, June 11, 2004, the late President Ronald Reagan's body lay in state in the rotunda of the U.S. Capitol. Long lines of people had come to pay respects. Without any warning, the police quickly evacuated everyone, including the members of Congress, from the entire building, including the members of Congress. People were running in all directions. A small twin-engine plane was observed approaching Washington D.C. Jet fighters, already in the air, were alerted. It turned out to be a false alarm, but the Defense Department has admitted that they came closer to shooting it down than at any other previous incident. The plane was carrying the governor of Kentucky, Ernie Fletcher, to the Reagan funeral and had actually been cleared to land by the FAA at Reagan National Airport. But the FAA had failed to notify the other relevant Homeland Security departments!

The fear factor could also be observed with the January 2004 inauguration of President George W. Bush. There was an unprecedented level of security with police lined up shoulder to shoulder on both sides of the parade route that utilized thousands of police from across the country. There was also a new high-tech screening of all the inaugural guests and a military contingent that included an entire combat brigade of nearly 4,000 troops.

A RELIGIOUS AWAKENING

Christian booksellers report that since September 11 there has been an 80 percent increase in sales of books on prophecy. *Newsweek* magazine featured authors Tim LaHaye and Jerry B. Jenkins on its May 24, 2004, cover with the following headline in bold letters across their pictures: "*The New Prophets of Revelation—Why Their Biblical 'Left Behind' Novels Have Sold 62 Million Copies—And Counting.*" The accompanying article stated that "After September 11, 2001, there was such a run on the latest 'Left Behind' volume, *Desecration,* that it became the best-selling novel of the year."

America's 50 million Evangelicals as represented by the National Association of Evangelicals released a 12-page draft document on June 21, 2004, titled "*For the Health of the Nation: An Evangelical Call to Civic Responsibility.*" The declaration, which encourages Christians to get into the political arena, begins by saying, "Since the atrocities of September 11, 2001, the spiritual and religious dimensions of global conflict have been sharpened." The document goes on to state, "Our goal in civic engagement is to bless our neighbors by making good laws." Much is promoted that benefits "the common good."

Time magazine's cover story for its June 21, 2004, issue was "*Faith, God & the Oval Office.*" The article states that after September 11 the President's focus changed to "America's destiny and Bush's view of God's plan for him and for the U.S." Mr. Bush states that there has been a significant change in the way people respond to him. Now when he works the rope line talking with average citizens, a large number say, "Mr. President, we pray for you."

Many individual Christians have taken the events of 9/11 as a wake-up call and are seriously involved with personal and group Bible studies. More people are volunteering for short-term mission experiences. Adventist evangelists report a better response to invitations to meetings. And many more are making decisions for baptism. I see more people at camp meetings and more people at church. A study done by the Barna Research Group reported that since 9/11 in the age group of 35 and younger nearly nine out of ten said they are concerned about the future. What an opportunity this gives us to share hope!

A DECLINE IN MORAL VALUES

Unfortunately, at a time when church members should be eager to seek the counsel of their pastors, many in the Christian world are now afraid to let their children be alone in the presence of their pastor or priest. Pedophilia has rocked the moral authority of the Christian church and left people confused and angry. To make matters worse, several high profile cases have been in the news regarding the ordination of openly gay and practicing homosexual "ministers." At a time when all should be concerned about family values, we are bombarded with demands for recognition of gay "marriages."

Violence, vulgarity, nudity, and just plain rottenness have become commonplace in art, music, and film. At the same time that many are turning to God and seeking spiritual renewal, there is an opposite trend to move away from God and toward Satan.

What is the response of religious leaders to these two factors? They are working together on an unprecedented scale to integrate moral values into the political process. When Karl Rove, President Bush's primary political strategist and counselor, went to Liberty University in Lynchburg, Virginia, in May of 2004, his personal visit with Jerry

Falwell was photographed and the picture appeared in *World* magazine August 7, 2004, and in *Newsweek* November 22, 2004. They were accompanied by a full-page story regarding the fact that the "Religious Right" was being courted to help reelect the President. The *Newsweek* article came out after the election and was headlined: "Of Prayer and Payback—The Religious Right Strongly Believes It Helped Bush Seal Re-election. So What Does It Want in Return?"

Jerry Falwell, in a speech at the Christian Coalition's Road to Victory Conference in October 2004, stated that following the meeting with Rove, he (Falwell) had personally spoken to 39 gatherings of Evangelical pastors of at least 500 in each group! Following the re-election of President Bush, Jerry Falwell posted his plan to become even more active in the political process on the Moral Majority Web site. In his words: "Following the sweeping re-election of President Bush and a new generation of conservative lawmakers nationwide, a new organization, The Moral Majority Coalition, has been launched. The group's central premise is to utilize the momentum of the November 2 elections to maintain an evangelical revolution of voters who will continue to go to the polls to "vote Christian." Essentially, TMMC is a 21st century resurrection of the Moral Majority.

"At age 71, I am committing to a four-year stint as national chairman of The Moral Majority Coalition (TMMC). In addition, Mathew Staver, founder and general counsel of the Orlando, Fla.-based Liberty Counsel, will serve as vice-chairman, while my son, Jonathan Falwell, will serve as executive director. Additionally, renowned author and theologian Dr. Tim LaHaye will serve as the Coalition's board chairman.

"One of our primary commitments is to help make President Bush's second term the most successful in American history. He will certainly need the consistent prayer and support of the evangelical community as he continues to spearhead the international war on terror and the effort to safeguard America.

THE FOUR-PRONGED TMMC PLATFORM
"Our four-fold platform is:

"(1) TMMC will conduct an intensive four-year "Voter Registration Campaign" through America's conservative churches, para-church ministries, pro-life and pro-family organizations.

"(2) TMMC will conduct well organized "Get-Out-the-Vote

Campaigns" in 2006 and 2008.

"(3) TMMC will engage in the massive recruitment and mobilization of social conservatives through television, radio, direct mail (U.S.P.S. and Internet) and public rallies.

"(4) TMMC will encourage the promotion of continuous private and corporate prayer for America's moral renaissance based on 2 Chronicles 7:14.

"My new leadership role in TMMC reminds me of a similar commitment I made more than a quarter-century ago. It was April 1979. I had just founded the Moral Majority and agreed to devote five years to its leadership. I actually gave ten years of my life before disbanding the organization in 1989 to focus on the expansion of Liberty University.

"At that time, God burdened my heart to mobilize religious conservatives around a pro-life, pro-family, strong national defense and pro-Israel platform, designed to return America to her Judeo-Christian heritage.

"And I distinctively feel that burden again. Our nation simply cannot continue as we know it if we allow out-of-control lawmakers and radical judges—working at the whims of society—to alter the moral foundations of America.

"During Moral Majority's heyday, we registered millions of new voters and re-activated millions more. More than 100,000 pastors, priests and rabbis and nearly seven million families joined hands and hearts to reclaim America for God. Many historians believe the result was the election of Ronald Reagan in 1980 and the genesis of what the media calls the 'Religious Right.'

VOTE CHRISTIAN! A NEW REVOLUTION

"On November 2, my wife Macel and I watched the election returns until early the next morning. President Bush was reelected (despite apparent manipulation of the early exit polling). Eleven family initiatives passed overwhelmingly in favor of traditional marriage, and opposing same-sex marriage. Unprecedented victories in the Senate and the House strengthened the President's hand for future congressional action.

"Tom Daschle, the Senate Minority Leader who had consistently obstructed President Bush's efforts to appoint constructionist judges, was defeated. His defeat should serve as a powerful indicator that we have the power to effectively take on politicians who are under the spell of the potent abortion-rights organizations across this nation.

"On election night, I actually shed tears of joy as I saw the fruit of a quarter century of hard work. Nearly 116 million Americans voted. More than 30 million were evangelical Christians who, according to the pollsters, voted their moral convictions. I proudly say . . . they voted Christian!!

"Christian giants like Dr. James Dobson, founder of Focus on the Family, provided energetic and courageous leadership. Dr. Donald Wildmon of the American Family Association, Dr. D. James Kennedy of Coral Ridge Ministries, Dr. John Hagee of Cornerstone Church in San Antonio, the many national leaders of the Arlington Group, the upstart alternative Internet news sites, and more than 225,000 evangelical pastors helped turn out the largest electorate ever. And, I repeat, they all voted Christian!!

"We must now diligently work to multiply our turnout for the 2006 and 2008 elections.

"As national chairman of TMMC, I am committed to lending my influence to help send out at least 40 million evangelical voters in 2008. The thought of a Hillary Clinton or John Edwards presidency is simply unacceptable (and quite frightening).

" 'FINISH WHAT YOU STARTED 25 YEARS AGO' "

"Over the past few days, I have been inundated with requests from across America to 'finish what you started 25 years ago.'

"With more than seven decades now in the rearview mirror, I can honestly say that I feel the leading of the Holy Spirit to answer that call and to once again mobilize people of faith to reclaim this great country as 'one nation under God.' My primary 'light of the world' calling is to continue serving as pastor of Thomas Road Baptist Church and chancellor of Liberty University.

"But I am praying for the strength and wisdom to also successfully complete my 'salt of the earth' ministry. America is worth saving. Our children and children's children will hold us accountable if we fail.

"We will be organizing in all 50 states and enlisting and training millions of Americans to become partners in this exciting task of bringing this nation back to the moral values of faith and family on which it was founded. My National Liberty Journal newspaper will serve as a springboard for this great effort.

"I urge my friends around the country to immediately get involved and join me in this four-year commitment, which is really an investment in America, in our children and in our children's children."

JAMES DOBSON THE POLITICIAN

In its January 17, 2005, edition, *U.S. News and World Report* featured a nine-page report highlighting the political power of Dr. James Dobson. The headline read, **"An Evangelical Leader Steps Squarely Into the Political Ring."** The article states that Dobson is "the best-known leader among America's 50 million-strong evangelical Christians." Dobson is the helmsman of a multimedia empire. "His radio show reaches nearly 2 million listeners daily, and the volume of constituent mail to his organization requires a separate zip code." Dobson says, "Our strategy has been to let people who see things the way we do know what's at stake and encourage them to hang on until change occurs." And in response to this statement the article reports, "For Dobson, his followers, and many American Evangelicals—who made up nearly a quarter of the electorate in the last Election Day and who voted for President Bush by a factor of almost 4 to 1—change might finally be in the offing." In fact "it's grown from hope to confidence that something will change."

The Evangelicals have three basic expectations from the government now: (1) new curbs on abortion; (2) a constitutional amendment banning gay marriage; and (3) a more conservative federal judiciary, including the Supreme Court.

Politics aside, "Dobson is unrivaled as an evangelical leader. 'Given Billy Graham's advanced age,' says Richard Land, president of the 16 million-strong Southern Baptist Convention's Ethics and Religious Liberty Commission, 'it's James Dobson who's stepped in to fill the void.'"

READY TO PLAY HARDBALL

"Dobson, for his part, is ready to play hardball, having already sent letters to 1.2 million supporters in which he threatens to challenge six 'red' and 'purple' state Democratic senators up for re-election in 2006 if they filibuster Bush's conservative judicial nominees." *U.S. News* has learned that "Focus, a network of 36 'state policy councils' associated with the group, and other Christian organizations are planning to capitalize on the success of the 11 state ballot initiatives outlawing same-sex marriage that passed in November [2004] to promote similar measures in up to 15 more states." In an interview granted to *U.S. News,* Dobson said, "There is a window which may remain open only a short time to make critical changes. If Republicans . . . in the White House and Senate squander this opportunity, I believe they will pay a price for it in four years—and maybe in two."

Dobson has moved more deeply into politics. "Before the election [November 2004], he stepped down from the presidency of Focus (he's still chairman) to launch Focus on the Family Action, a fund-raising and grassroots organizing engine free of the political spending limits imposed on the nonprofit Focus. The move allowed Dobson to make his first presidential endorsement (for President Bush), to write hundreds of thousands of Focus constituents in states with tight Senate races with political advice, and to appear in ads to unseat Senate Minority Leader Tom Daschle in South Dakota. Last fall [2004], Dobson hosted huge 'stand for the family' rallies—widely seen as supportive of Republican candidates—in close Senate race states, while Focus helped distribute an eye-popping 8 million voting guides. 'I can't think of anybody who had more impact than Dr. Dobson on social conservatives this election,' says Richard Viguerie, the GOP direct-mail pioneer. 'He was the 800-pound gorilla.'"

"'[James] Dobson is more prominent and popular right now than Pat Robertson, Ralph Reed, or Gary Bower were at their highpoints,' says John Green, director of the Ray C. Bliss Institute of Applied Politics at the University of Akron."

There is much more detail regarding the political contacts of Dr. Dobson. "Although much of Dobson's political power derives from his ability to connect with the grass roots, he is more plugged into Washington than he lets on. 'I have a very close relationship with Jim,' Pennsylvania Sen. Rick Santorum, the Senate's No. 3 Republican, tells *U.S. News.* 'I consider him to be a friend.' Indeed, 'his influence is huge,' says Land, who is widely seen as closer to the White House than Dobson. 'He may not be an insider, but he can shut down the phone lines in Congress.'"

COURT CASES GOING AGAINST RELIGIOUS LIBERTY

The book *Evangelism* predicted: "In our land of boasted freedom, religious liberty will come to an end" (*Evangelism*, p. 236).

"Zellman v. Harris—Supreme Court, 5-4, Upholds Voucher System That Pays Religious School's Tuition" (New York *Times*, Friday, June 28, 2002). Thus read the front page headlines of this prestigious newspaper. The case was so significant that the paper printed the entire decision, including the dissenting opinions.

In this landmark case, Justice Steven's dissent sounds an alarm to those who value religious liberty. He wrote, "Whenever we remove a brick from the wall that was designed to separate religion and government, we increase the risk of religious strife and weaken the foundation of our democracy. I respectfully dissent."

In 1990 Supreme Court Associate Justice, Scalia, stated in *Employment Division v. Smith* (494 U.S. 872, 1990): "Subsequent decisions have consistently held that the right of free exercise does not relieve an individual of the obligation to comply with a valid and neutral law of general application . . . [for example] we upheld Sunday-closing laws against the claim that they burdened the religious practices of persons whose religions compelled them to refrain from work on other days."

A recent review of state laws found that all U.S. states except one currently have some form of Sunday laws on the books. And according to the courts, these laws do not violate the federal or state constitutions. The only state free of Sunday laws is Alaska.

And it is not only Sunday laws that we have to worry about. Every year in the U.S. more than a thousand Seventh-day Sabbathkeepers are fired from their jobs for no crime other than obeying God rather than men. This may seem like a small thing, but imagine the fidelity it takes to lose your income, your health insurance, and all the other benefits that come with employment. It is no easy matter.

We cannot afford to be apathetic about this. Speaking during the early days of our church Ellen White stated: "We are not doing the will of God if we sit in quietude, doing nothing to preserve liberty of conscience" (*Testimonies for the Church*, vol. 5, p. 714).

HOW SHOULD WE THEN LIVE?

I am impressed that Romans 13:11-14 is timely counsel: "Now it is high time to awake out of sleep; for now our salvation is nearer than when we first believed.

"The night is far spent, the day is at hand. Therefore let us cast off the works of darkness, and let us put on the armor of light.

"Let us walk properly, as in the day, not in revelry and drunkenness, not in licentiousness and lewdness, not in strife and envy.

"But put on the Lord Jesus Christ, and make no provision for the flesh, to fulfill its lusts."

Many years ago, when those on the "religious right" were pushing for a Sunday law, Ellen White shared these amazing insights: "We as a people have not accomplished the work which God has committed to us. We are not ready for the issue to which the enforcement of the Sunday law will bring us. It is our duty, as we see the signs of approaching peril, to arouse to action. Let none sit in calm expectation of the evil, comforting themselves with the belief that this work must go on because prophecy has foretold it, and that the Lord will shelter His people. We are not doing the will of God if we sit in quietude, doing nothing to preserve liberty of conscience. Fervent, effectual prayer should be ascending to heaven that this calamity may be deferred until we can accomplish the work which has so long been neglected. Let there be most earnest prayer, and then let us work in harmony with our prayers. It may appear that Satan is triumphant and that truth is overborne with falsehood and error; the people over whom God has spread His shield, and the country which has been an asylum for the conscience-oppressed servants of God and defenders of His truth, may be placed in jeopardy. But God would have us recall His dealings with His people in the past to save them from their enemies. He has always chosen extremities, when there seemed no possible chance for deliverance from Satan's workings, for the manifestation of His power. Man's necessity is God's opportunity. It may be that a respite may yet be granted for God's people to awake and let their light shine. If the presence of ten righteous persons would have saved the wicked cities of the plain, is it not possible that God will yet, in answer to the prayers of His people, hold in check the workings of those who are making void His law? Shall we not humble our hearts greatly before God, flee to the mercy seat, and plead with Him to reveal His mighty power?

"If our people continue in the listless attitude in which they have been, God cannot pour upon them His Spirit. They are unprepared to cooperate with Him. They are not awake to the situation and do not realize the threatened danger. They should feel now, as never before, their need of vigilance and concerted action.

"The peculiar work of the third angel has not been seen in its importance. God meant that His people should be far in advance of the position which they occupy today. But now, when the time has come for them to spring into action, they have the preparation to make. When the National Reformers began to urge measures to restrict religious liberty, our leading men should have been alive to the situation and should have labored earnestly to counteract these efforts. It is not in the order of God that light has been kept from our people—the very present truth which they needed for this time. Not all our ministers who are giving the third angel's message really understand what constitutes that message. The National Reform movement has been regarded by some as of so little importance that they have not thought it necessary to give much attention to it and have even felt that in so doing they would be giving time to questions distinct from the third angel's message. May the Lord forgive our brethren for thus interpreting the very message for this time.

"The people need to be aroused in regard to the dangers of the present time. The watchmen are asleep. We are years behind. Let the chief watchmen feel the urgent necessity of taking heed to themselves, lest they lose the opportunities given them to see the dangers. . . .

"We have been looking many years for a Sunday law to be enacted in our land; and, now that the movement is right upon us, we ask: Will our people do their duty in the matter? Can we not assist in lifting the standard and in calling to the front those who have a regard for their religious rights and privileges? The time is fast approaching when those who choose to obey God rather than man will be made to feel the hand of oppression. Shall we then dishonor God by keeping silent while His holy commandments are trodden underfoot?

"While the Protestant world is by her attitude making concessions to Rome, let us arouse to comprehend the situation and view the contest before us in its true bearings. Let the watchmen now lift up their voice and give the message which is present truth for this time. Let us show the people where we are in prophetic history and seek to arouse the spirit of true Protestantism, awaking the world to a sense of the value of the privileges of religious liberty so long enjoyed.

"God calls upon us to awake, for the end is near. Every passing hour is one of activity in the heavenly courts to make ready a people upon the earth to act a part in the great scenes that are soon to open upon us. These passing moments, that seem of so little value to us, are weighty with eternal interests. They are molding the destiny of souls for everlasting life or eternal death. The words we utter today in the ears of the people, the works we are doing, the spirit of the message we are bearing, will be a savor of life unto life or of death unto death.

"My brethren, do you realize that your own salvation, as well as the destiny of other souls, depends upon the preparation you now make for the trial before us? Have you that intensity of zeal, that piety and devotion, which will enable you to stand when opposition shall be brought against you? If God has ever spoken by me, the time will come when you will be brought before councils, and every position of truth which you hold will be severely criticized. The time that so many are now allowing to go to waste should be devoted to the charge that God has given us of preparing for the approaching crisis" (*Testimonies,* vol. 5, pp. 713-717).

Don't take life for granted. Remember that, as Christians, our real home is in heaven. We are pilgrims and strangers here. Be faithful to God and His commands. Store up treasure in heaven. Memorize Scripture passages. Memorize some old hymns or gospel songs. Have confidence in the prophecies. God knows what is going on. He will be with us. "The Word of God portrays the wickedness and corruption that would exist in the last days. As we see the fulfillment of prophecy, our faith in the final triumph of Christ's kingdom should strengthen; and we should go forth with renewed courage to do our appointed work" (*Gospel Workers,* pp. 26, 27).

CHAPTER 8

Full Diplomatic Relations

T he timing was calculated. The result is prophetic. The consequences are serious. On January 10, 1984, upon the orders of United States President Ronald Reagan and the "Holy See," the central government of the Roman Catholic Church, represented by "The Holy Father," Pope John Paul II, full diplomatic relations were established between these two entities.

"This cordial and cooperative framework did not always exist. In fact it took 208 years for the United States to enter into full diplomatic relations with the oldest international personality in the community of nations" (Thomas P. Melady, *The Ambassador's Story—The United States and the Vatican in World Affairs,* p. 41).

In the first few weeks after his election in November of 1980, President Ronald Reagan appointed William Wilson, his friend from California, as his personal representative to the Vatican. Then something happened that changed the course of history in this regard. President Reagan had a private meeting with the pope in the Vatican on June 7, 1982. Many modern historians use this date as the beginning of the "Holy Alliance" between the U.S. and the Vatican. (See my book *Even at the Door,* p. 232, for more details of this meeting and its aftermath.)

Following this historic meeting with the pope, in the last year of his first term as president of the United States, Ronald Reagan initiated a process for doing what had never been done before—sending a full "ambassador," not just to the Vatican City State but to the "Holy See"—the central government of the Roman Catholic Church!

FROM PERSONAL REPRESENTATIVE TO AMBASSADOR—THE PROCESS

President Reagan's staff, aware of what had happened to potential "ambassadors" in the past, made an extensive study of the subject. This review included looking at Section 2, article 2 of the Constitution that defines the president's authority to nominate diplomatic officials and the responsibility of the Senate to give its consent. The staff felt convinced that they could defend the proposed ambassadorship with their interpretation of the Constitution. In addition, though the legal situation had not changed (remember Congress had passed a law in 1868 that had prohibited funding for an embassy to the Vatican), the domestic political climate had changed significantly! Popular Protestant evangelist Billy Graham had stated publicly that he saw a significant difference in the national Protestant attitude. There would still be some opposition, but not of the magnitude as 30 years before.

Ambassador Melady states, "Once he [Reagan] was convinced that the nomination of an Ambassador to the Holy See was constitutional and in the national interest of the country, President Reagan approved a move to void the 1868 law which prohibited the expenditure of public funds for an Embassy to the Vatican. This action was successful. The relative ease with which this action took place reassured the Reagan White House about proceeding with their project" (Melady, p. 52).

Melady adds these very significant statements: "On January 10, 1984, President Ronald Reagan announced the establishment of formal diplomatic relations with the Holy See . . . The announcement gave full recognition to the unique international sovereign role of the Pope and his government, not only in Vatican City State but throughout the world where the Pope and his government exercised their spiritual and political authority. There was no equivocation. **The United States was extending full recognition for the first time to the government of the Holy Catholic and Apostolic Church.**

"The announcement implied the acceptance of the international law principle that the Holy See is a bona fide international personality. Thus the announcement by President Reagan acknowledged the papacy as a religious organ with international rights and duties. This was not a qualified recognition of Vatican City State. In previous times it would have caused a firestorm of protest. But it immediately became evident, both in tone and substance, that there had been a major change in domestic U.S. political opinion" (Melady, pp. 50, 53).

UNDERSTANDING THE HOLY SEE

To the average Protestant layman the term "Holy See" has no meaning whatsoever. It is probably not even in common usage among

Catholic laymen. The reason for this uncertainty is the unusual "nature of the beast." It would be best, I believe, to get the definition of the Holy See from someone who ought to know. Back again to Thomas Patrick Melady, a Roman Catholic career diplomat and formerly the official Ambassador of the United States of America to the Holy See. His explanation is as follows: "The Government of the United States has diplomatic relations with the government of the Roman Catholic Church; that is, the Holy See.

"The Holy See is the composite of the authority, jurisdiction, and sovereignty vested in and exercised by the Pope and his advisers in the temporal and spiritual direction and guidance of **the Roman Catholic Church throughout the world. The Holy See,** consequently, **is a moral entity;** in modern terms, **it is the central government of the Roman Catholic Church"** (Melady, p. 178).

The Holy See is not just the small city-state of 110 acres called the Vatican within the City of Rome, Italy. It is the worldwide body of over one billion Roman Catholic members with the pope at its head. The Holy See has formal diplomatic relations with 174 nations including the United States. This is more than three fourths (76 percent) of all the nations on earth as recognized as sovereign nations by the United Nations (228). This represents an increase of 29 new nations with full diplomatic relations with the Holy See in the last nine years—an increase of 20 percent! The Vatican claims that during the pontificate of John Paul II he tripled the number of nations with full diplomatic relations with the Holy See.

"The Pope's Ambassador [the individual representatives of the Holy See to the 174 nations] has two functions. One is diplomatic as an ambassador of the Holy See to the government where he is accredited. The other is religious, as a representative to the local church of the Pope to assure that canonical regulations are being followed. He also recommends appointments of new bishops. When there are no diplomatic relations, the Pope's representative has solely a religious role. . . . Vatican City State is the physical seat of the Holy See. The Holy See is a sovereign entity that has this unique universal sovereignty because of the role of the Pope of the Catholic Church in the world" (Melady, p. 179).

THE HOLY SEE NOT DEMOCRATIC

In the summer of 1995 I visited the Vatican, the museum, the treasury, St. Peter's Basilica and related facilities. There in the Vatican treasury I saw the famous triple crown of the pope. It appears to be made of pure gold with large jewels attached to it.

In the treasury gift shop I purchased the official full-color directory and gift book of the treasury printed by the Vatican press. I noted that the triple crown photo has this caption: "The Triple Crown—papal tiara comprising the three crowns which symbolize the Pope's three-fold power as Father of Kings, Rector of the World, and Vicar of Christ." Thomas Melady stated that upon arrival in Rome he presented his credentials to the pope as "Vicar of Christ, head of the Universal Catholic Church, and sovereign of Vatican City State."

In his explanation of how the government of the Holy See functions Ambassador Melady states, **"The Pope exercises supreme legislative, executive, and judicial power over the Holy See. He is the equivalent of an absolute monarch.** This authority is not restricted to the State of Vatican City. The sovereignty of the Holy See is a universal historical fact accepted by international society. The Holy See has sent and received diplomatic missions since the fourth century. The Pope rules the Holy See through the Roman Curia and the Papal Civil Service which staffs it" (Melady, p. 179).

The pope is elected for life, and there is no such thing as a deputy pope. Consequently, no one is "a heartbeat away from the papacy." In the only electoral process in the Roman Catholic Church the pope is "elected" by the cardinals who have been appointed by a pope. "Cardinals" are medieval creations with no scriptural foundation. The cardinals will choose the next pope, "the 265th successor of Saint Peter," from among their own number. By current canon law there can be only 120 eligible cardinals. Once they reach the age of 80 years they are no longer eligible to vote.

Noted Roman Catholic journalist Peter Hebblethwaite, who was widely respected as a commentator on events and trends in the Catholic Church, gave some insight into the papacy's political process. In his book *The Next Pope,* printed in 1995, just a few months after his death, he states many interesting things about the papal electoral process. For example, "There is a great difficulty in speaking honestly and directly about popes, for as soon as a man becomes pope a process of mythologization sets in that transforms overnight the mediocre into a genius and the merely talented into a superluminary" (*The Next Pope,* p. 89).

All this about the politics of the papacy underlines the irony of the Holy See talking loudly about human rights and religious freedom in its affairs with nations. Ambassador Melady goes into considerable detail in his book about the Holy See's efforts to bring about democracy and religious freedom in Poland, the Baltic States, Czechoslovak Federal Republic, Hungary, Romania, Bulgaria, Albania, Cuba, Central and South America, and in Africa. Yet it is not democratic in its own process nor is it interested in religious freedom for anyone but Roman Catholics and the Holy See. For example, Ambassador Melady, when commenting on his work of getting the U.S. and Holy See officials together to discuss the situation in China, states, "Both the Holy See and the United States were confronted by the same human-rights and religious-freedom concerns in China . . . When I arranged for a meeting of Secretary [of State James] Baker with Cardinal Angelo Sodano [Secretary of State of the Holy See—newly appointed] on November 8, 1991, the promotion of human rights and religious freedom in China was on the agenda.

"This was the first meeting of Cardinal Sodano, first with Secretary Baker, then with President Bush . . . The exchange with Secretary Baker focused on how to accelerate the process of change in China that could reduce the current abuses. <u>Cardinal Sodano brought up the matter of the right of the Catholic Church to carry out its mission in China</u>" (Melady, p. 92). The Holy See has since established full diplomatic relations with China.

THE SENATE HEARINGS

To reverse the current situation in which the United States has a full and formal diplomatic relationship with the Holy See would quite literally take the proverbial "act of Congress." The Congressional Records give a word-by-word transcript of the hearing before the Committee on Foreign Relations of the United States Senate regarding the nomination of William A. Wilson to be the U.S. ambassador to the Holy See on February 2, 1984. The committee met, pursuant to notice, at 2:31 p.m., in room SD-419, Dirksen Senate Office Building, with the Hon. Richard Lugar presiding. The committee announced before the hearings that their deliberations would focus on the question Should the United States have diplomatic relations with the Holy See? However, as the record states, several speakers noted that the Senate had already settled that question and they were just now going to consider the qualifications of Mr. Wilson for the post. Since he had already served at the Vatican as President Reagan's personal representative for the past three years no one was more qualified than he to be named as ambassador. The vote of the committee was 15 in favor and 1 opposed.

The nominee, Mr. William Wilson, was introduced to the committee by the Hon. Pete Wilson, then U.S. Senator from California. His remarks were, in part, as follows:

"Thank you very much, Mr. Chairman, for giving me the privilege of introducing to you a fellow Californian, a very distinguished American . . . Mr. Chairman, in the interest of the committee's time and that of the nominee, I will try to come quickly to the point. There will, I assume, be witnesses who follow me and who follow the nominee wishing to address the committee with respect to what they term the propriety or lack of propriety of <u>an action that I would point out is an accomplished fact. Diplomatic relations were established between the United States and the Vatican as of January 10 of this year.</u>

"I mention that not to excite counter argument. That probably will not be necessary. But I would point out that the action has been taken. <u>That debate has occurred in Congress and the decision has been taken.</u> So what we are concerned with, quite properly, today, Mr. Chairman, is not the propriety of this relationship. <u>The relationship exists.</u>"

Senator Richard Lugar, the presiding chairman of the Committee on Foreign Relations for this hearing, then gave an opening statement in which he said, in part, "I believe the President has made a wise decision in establishing diplomatic relations with the Holy See and in nominating William Wilson to conduct those relations at the ambassadorial level.

"The Holy See maintains a diplomatic presence and has wide influence and unique access in areas of great concern to the foreign policy of the United States. . . .

"Vatican officials and diplomats are not simply observers or moral guides but play an active role in international affairs. . . .

"Over the past two years, the President, the Vice President, the Secretary of State, and other Cabinet officers have had audiences with the Pope to discuss a wide range of political and moral problems which confront the world. Every President of the United States in recent memory has indicated his respect for the prominent international standing of the Papacy by meeting with the pope. . . . Pope John Paul II is a powerful force for the political and moral values which we in the United States cherish and which are so important to the dignity of men and women everywhere. . . .

"I will not argue the case further today. I will simply say I believe the burden of proof lies upon those who would argue that there is a special reason to abrogate the President's clearly stated constitutional authority to name Ambassadors. The President established diplomatic relations with the Holy See on January 10, 1984. Strictly speaking, Senators will be called upon not to judge this action but to judge the suitability of Mr. Wilson for the post for which he has been nominated."

The die was cast before the "hearing" was ever held. The action had already been taken! Another major step had been taken to form the image to the beast.

WHERE TO FROM HERE?

This is only half of the story, of course, because when we are dealing with the Holy See we must consider not just the political side but also the religious side. In his book *Keys of This Blood,* the late Malachi Martin noted that there would be a struggle for world dominion between the three great powers on earth—Communism, Capitalism, and Catholicism. Martin predicted, in essence, that by the year 2000 only one would remain—that being the Roman Catholic Church with the pope as its leader.

Ambassador Melady outlines how this struggle played out with a "common enemy" factor. "Both the United States and the Holy See faced the same powerful opponent. The years following World War II (when the then Soviet Union acquired superpower status) were especially difficult for the United States and the Holy See. Both the United States and the Holy See were deeply involved—from 1945 to the late 1980s—in efforts to thwart the advance of atheistic communism. . . . Senior Vatican officials told me on several occasions that the world owed a great thanks to the United States for having orchestrated and played a leading role in this collapse [of the Soviet Union] and having done this in a non-violent way. . . ."

Melady goes on to say, "With the arrival of Gorbachev on the scene in 1985, <u>the Holy See sensed that **the time was approaching when significant changes could take place**</u>" (Melady, pp. 74, 75). This statement reminds one of Ellen White's statement in *The Great Controversy*, page 580: "Marvelous in her shrewdness and cunning is the Roman Church. She can read what is to be. She bides her time . . ."

So what will the future bring? Ambassador Melady concludes, **"I believe that the U.S., as the world's only superpower, and the Holy See, as the only world-wide moral-political sovereignty, have significant roles to play in the future. Their actions will impact the lives of people in all parts of the globe"** (Melady, p. 10). Surely, he doesn't realize how "prophetic" his words are.

Early in his first term as president, George W. Bush named James Nicholson as U.S. Ambassador to the Holy See. Nicholson had been the chairman of the Republican National Committee from 1996 to 2000 and had orchestrated the election of the president. And so this top-ranking politician represented the United States to the central government of the Roman Catholic Church. *Inside the Vatican* reported in an interview with James Nicholson: "Several times he uses the word 'convergence' in explaining the link between the interests of the Church and the American government. <u>'The values of this [the Bush] administration and those of the Vatican line up hand in glove,' he said</u>" (*Inside the Vatican,* December 2001, pp. 24, 25).

As President George W. Bush began his second term, Jim Nicholson was recalled from the Holy See and now heads the Office of Veterans' Affairs.

CHAPTER 9

"And All the World Wondered"

After nearly a decade of declining health, Karol Wojtyla, known as Pope John Paul II, died in his apartment in Rome on April 2, 2005. He had "held the chair of St. Peter," or "reigned" as Supreme Pontiff for more than 26 years. He was the most photographed public figure of his era, having appeared on the cover of *Time* magazine a record 16 times.

Newsweek, April 11, 2005, in a special report by Kenneth L. Woodward, noted that "John Paul transformed the See of Peter into a fulcrum of world politics—his politics. The papal voice—his voice—was heard and often heeded in major capitals like Moscow and Washington. Above all he took the papacy—which only a century earlier was locked inside the ecclesiastical confines of Vatican City—on the road. He visited Africa four times, Latin America five, managing altogether an astounding 104 pilgrimages to 129 countries around the globe. In doing so, he transformed the figure of the pope from a distant icon to a familiar face. His face."

The same issue of *Newsweek* stated in a picture caption, "All the World His Stage. Under John Paul II, who helped bring down the Iron Curtain, the Holy See gained more political clout than it had enjoyed since the Renaissance." It is also significant from a political perspective that during his years as pope, likely in response to his many travels, he actually tripled the number of nations with diplomatic relations with the Holy See. By the time John Paul II died, the church, the Holy See, had a list of 174 countries with which it had established full diplomatic relations. That astounding number represents more than 75 percent of all the 228 sovereign nations recognized by the United Nations!

When it was announced that the pope had died, the White House released the following statement by President Bush:

"Laura and I join people across the earth in mourning the passing of Pope John Paul II. The Catholic Church has lost its shepherd, the world has lost a champion of human freedom, and a good and faithful servant of God has been called home.

"Pope John Paul II left the throne of St. Peter in the same way he ascended to it—as a witness to the dignity of human life. In his native Poland, that witness launched a democratic revolution that swept Eastern Europe and changed the course of history. Throughout the West, John Paul's witness reminded us of our obligation to build a culture of life in which the strong protect the weak. And during the Pope's final years, his witness was made even more powerful by his daily courage in the face of illness and great suffering.

"All Popes belong to the world, but Americans had special reason to love the man from Krakow. In his visits to our country, the Pope spoke of our 'providential' Constitution, the self-evident truths about human dignity in our Declaration, and the 'blessings of liberty' that follow from them. It is these truths, he said, that have led people all over the world to look to America with hope and respect.

"Pope John Paul II was, himself, an inspiration to millions of Americans, and to so many more throughout the world. We will always remember the humble, wise and fearless priest who became one of history's great moral leaders. We're grateful to God for sending such a man, a son of Poland, who became the Bishop of Rome, and a hero for the ages."

Not long after the above statement was released by the White House, President Bush issued the following executive order:

"PRESIDENT BUSH ORDERS FLAGS FLOWN AT HALF STAFF IN HONOR OF POPE JOHN PAUL II

"A Proclamation by the President of the United States of America:

"As a mark of respect for His Holiness Pope John Paul II, I hereby order, by the authority vested in me by the Constitution and laws of the United States of America, that the flag of the United States shall be flown at half staff at the White House and on all public buildings and grounds, at all military posts and naval stations, and on all naval vessels of the Federal Government in the District of Columbia and throughout the United States and its Territories and possessions until sunset on the day of his interment. I also direct that the flag shall be flown at half staff for the same period at all United States embassies, legations, consular offices, and other facilities abroad, including all military facilities and naval vessels and stations.

IN WITNESS WHEREOF, I have hereunto set my hand this second day of April, in the year of our Lord two thousand five, and of the Independence of the United States of America the two hundred and twenty ninth.

GEORGE W. BUSH"

Accolades praising the pope came in from all around the world including the many nations that the pope had granted diplomatic relations.

At the pope's funeral, kings, queens, prime ministers, and presidents from more than 100 nations were in attendance. Prince Charles of Great Britain postponed his wedding in order to attend. For the first time in history a sitting president of the United States attended a papal funeral. Due to security and space constraints, the papacy limited the U.S. delegation to 5 members. The five were President George W. Bush, First Lady Laura Bush, Former President George H. W. Bush, Former President Bill Clinton, and U.S. Secretary of State Condoleezza Rice. When the U.S. delegation went to St. Peter's Basilica to view the remains of the pope the day before the funeral, they knelt before the body of the pope in prayer, with hands folded and heads bowed.

Viewing the picture taken by Getty Images of the U.S. delegation kneeling before the pope, we are struck by how obviously the prophetic picture of Revelation 13 is coming into focus. With an estimated 4 million visitors to Rome—which included many trainloads, more than 700 passenger buses, and hundreds of cars just from Poland alone—the pope's funeral was the largest ever conducted in the history of the world. It was also estimated that more than 2 billion people watched the event on television. The estimate was a result of the fact that between 3:00 a.m. and 9:00 a.m. Eastern Time on April 8, 2005, the pope's funeral was almost all that was on television!

The publication *Inside the Vatican* produced a Special Commemorative Issue in memory of John Paul II. The 100-page full-color document featured the life, the pontificate, and the final journey of the late pope. It featured prominently the U.S. Presidents kneeling before the pope and noted that "many of the world's most powerful political leaders gathered to pay their last respects to the spiritual figure of John Paul II, whose body lay before them during the funeral in a simple wooden coffin. Five kings, four queens, and at least 70 presidents and prime ministers were surrounded by their entourages, with many of the women wearing black lace head coverings or black hats as a sign of respect. Some analysts considered it the largest gathering ever of world leaders."

The fact that the U.S. presidents and the largest gathering of world leaders ever, attended the funeral is not just evidence of the formation of an image to the beast; it is also a fulfillment of Revelation 13:3: "And all the world marveled and followed the beast." The KJV puts it: "And all the world wondered after the beast."

"IN MARY'S HANDS"

Pope John Paul II was the most "Marian" pope in modern times. He had dedicated himself and the world to Mary on several occasions. In his last will and testament that was released by the Vatican during the funeral the pope declared to Mary, "I am completely in your hands." And Cardinal Ratzinger closed his funeral homily with these words: "We entrust your dear soul to the Mother of God, your Mother, who guided you each day and who will guide you now to the eternal glory of her Son, our Lord Jesus Christ. Amen." You will note that both the pope and Cardinal Ratzinger (now Pope Benedict XVI) committed the pope to Mary and not to Jesus. This spiritualistic influence is very pervasive in Roman Catholic leadership and church life.

A GREAT MORAL LEADER

As noted above, President Bush stated that "we will always remember the humble, wise and fearless priest who became one of history's great moral leaders. Evangelist Billy Graham, "whose own ministry and growing frailty has paralleled that of the pope, called John Paul 'unquestionably the most influential voice for morality and peace in the world during the last 100 years'" (*Christian Century*, April 19, 2005). Graham also called the pope "the moral conscience of the West" (*Newsweek*, April 11, 2005). It is true that the pope spoke publicly against abortion and homosexuality and even, in the case of Terri Schiavo, stated that life should be sustained if necessary by artificial means as part of "the Culture of life." But in actual practice the story is quite different. For example, in Poland, the pope's native homeland, which is 98 percent Catholic, post-Communist Poland "was reporting more abortions than live births" (*ibid.*). This means that for every 1,000 live births, there were more than 1,000 abortions!

Under John Paul II's leadership, he was confronted by one of the church's greatest scandals: revelations of widespread child sex abuse by Catholic priests in the United States and around the world. At first the church tried to downplay the problem by stating that the press was making a big deal out of an isolated incident. It later came out that in every one of the church's 170 plus dioceses in the United States there had been multiple cases of child sexual abuse and that the church has paid out over $900,000,000.00 (That's right—$900 million) in the U.S. alone in court judgments against the church. This reflects only those cases in which the victims took the church to court!

In the most notable case, that of the Boston archdiocese, Cardinal Bernard Law, who was found guilty of aiding and abetting pedophilia, instead of going to jail was welcomed back to the Vatican, where he was given a cushy job and actively participated in the papal funeral by conducting one of the funeral masses and was involved in the conclave that elected the next pope! What does this say about the pope's moral leadership and his outspokenness on homosexuality and pedophilia? In addition, though homosexuality is stated to be sinful by the church, a very high percentage of active priests are homosexual, and studies show that a high percentage of Catholic seminary students (priests in training) are also homosexual.

Medical doctors and psychologists point out that the forced celibacy of the priests unnaturally curtails the normal sexual desires of the men. Consequently many priests find their sexual expression with innocent little children, young women, or the wives of other men. In spite of this phenomenon and the fact that forced celibacy is totally un-biblical, "John Paul's most decisive early act was to reaffirm the discipline of priestly celibacy" (ibid.). Time, May 2, 2005, printed a letter to the editor that speaks the sentiments of many: "I am an ex-Catholic, ex-seminarian who walked the slums of South America, teeming with devout Roman Catholics, after Pope John Paul II's visit in the 1980s. I know he saw the same poverty I saw. I was appalled and wished I could help. The Pope had the power to mitigate the worldwide overpopulation problem, yet he chose to continue the policy banning contraception, which, like the foolish rule of celibacy for priests, has no convincing basis in Scripture. I hold John Paul II accountable for millions of children who roam the earth unloved and unwanted, leading lives of abject poverty, hunger and persistent misery." GC—*Sherborn, Mass.*

It is also significant to note that though the pope publicly stated that life should be artificially sustained in connection with the Schiavo case in the early years, he and/or his medical staff allowed him to die a natural death in his apartment rather than being kept alive artificially in a hospital!

AWAITING WHITE SMOKE

The "conclave" has been described as a blend of prayer, piety, politics, and intrigue. "When the white smoke cleared over the Vatican on April 9, 2005, German theologian Joseph Ratzinger had been elected to replace Pope John Paul II as supreme pontiff of the world's 1.2 billion Roman Catholics" (*World,* April 30, 2005).

Cardinal Ratzinger was for 24 years the prefect [director] of the Office of the Sacred Congregation for the Doctrine of the Faith—formerly known as the Office of the Inquisition. His nicknames coined by fellow Catholics include: God's Rottweiler, The Pope's Enforcer, The Panzer Cardinal, and so forth. His strict adherence to Catholic theology cost many people their jobs. For example: "Ratzinger helped spearhead a church investigation that culminated in the 1979 revocation of Swiss theologian Hans Kung's license to teach Catholic theology. Largely responsible for inspiring the Vatican II reforms, Kung was fired because of his works challenging papal infallibility" (*U.S. News and World Report,* May 2, 2005, p. 36). So we know what his attitude will be regarding papal infallibility.

We have known that "the papal church will never relinquish her claim to infallibility. All that she has done in her persecution of those who reject her dogmas she holds to be right; and would she not repeat the same acts, should the opportunity be presented? Let the restraints now imposed by secular governments be removed and Rome be reinstated in her former power, and there would speedily be a revival of her tyranny and persecution" (*The Great Controversy,* p. 564).

After the election of Cardinal Ratzinger there was apparently some negative response from Europe and the United States. So the New York *Times* reported (April 20, 2005) that "all seven American cardinal-archbishops appeared at an unusual news conference at the Pontifical North American College in Rome and tried to introduce the world to a man they revered enough to elevate to the papacy. They acknowledged their concern that some American Catholics might prejudge the new pope by his reputation as Cardinal." On April 21, 2005, the Washington *Post* reported the same story and interviewed Cardinal Theodore McCarrick from Washington, D.C. "Although the 115 cardinals vowed to not reveal the inner workings of their brief conclave in the Sistine Chapel, <u>Cardinal McCarrick did describe his amazement at seeing a fellow cardinal transformed into, under Catholic doctrine, an infallible pope.</u>

"'You're in a group of 115 people and you're saying "your eminence this" and "your eminence that," and suddenly he's the Holy Father,' he said."

It is interesting that before Cardinal Ratzinger was elected pope, *Time* (April 11, 2005) issued a Commemorative Issue of their magazine dedicated to Pope John Paul II. In it they featured an article on the history of the popes from St. Peter all the way to John Paul II—all 264 of them were listed. In a sidebar they noted some of the unusual papal statistics such as who had the longest and shortest "reigns." They noted that Benedict IX had been pope three different times. "He became pope in 1032, 1045, and 1047. He was the nephew of his two immediate predecessors and became notorious for selling the papacy and maneuvering to reclaim it." After reading this news item, I was surprised that the new pope also took the name Benedict.

Pope Benedict XVI's first speech was a simple four sentences: "Dear brothers and sisters, after the great Pope, John Paul II, the cardinals have elected me, a simple and humble worker in the Lord's vineyard. The fact that the Lord can work and act even with insufficient means consoles me, and above all I entrust myself to your prayers. In the joy of the resurrected Lord, we go on with His help. He is going to help us and <u>Mary will be on our side.</u> Thank you."

In a surprise to many, Benedict XVI has named an American Cardinal to take his place as the prefect for the Congregation for the Doctrine of the Faith. He is San Francisco Archbishop William J. Leveda. At first blush it appears to be another link between the U.S. and the Vatican.

I will conclude this chapter with two relevant quotes from Ellen White.

"I have been shown that Satan is stealing a march upon us. The law of God, through the agency of Satan, is to be made void. In our land of boasted freedom, religious liberty will come to an end. The contest will be decided over the Sabbath question, which will agitate the whole world" (*Evangelism,* p. 236).

"While the Protestant world is by her attitude making concessions to Rome, let us arouse to comprehend the situation and view the contest before us in its true bearings. Let the watchmen now lift up their voice and give the message which is present truth for this time. Let us show the people where we are in prophetic history and seek to arouse the spirit of true Protestantism, awaking the world to a sense of the value of the privileges of religious liberty so long enjoyed" (*Testimonies,* vol. 5, p. 716).

CHAPTER 10

The New Evangelicals

American Evangelicalism—with its home-schooling Fundamentalists and PTA-attending megachurch moms, its neo-Calvinists and Pentecostals, its multiple denominations and thousands of unaffiliated churches—seems to defy unity, let alone hierarchy. There is no pope, no central ruling body. Yet its members share basic commitments: to the divinity and saving power of Jesus, to personal religious conversion, to the Bible's authority, and to the spreading of the gospel. Those understandings unite a generation of influential leaders who channel conservative Christianity's overflowing energies.

We have already mentioned the Religious Right and the role of Jerry Falwell and James Dobson in mixing religion and politics. There are, of course, other very active "Evangelicals" with significant influence in American religion and politics. The cover story of the February 7, 2005, issue of *Time* highlighted thc 25 most influential Evangelicals in America. The feature asked, "What does Bush owe the Religious Right? They helped reelect the President, and Christian Conservatives want payback." The Evangelicals see President Bush as "one of us." They feel that this is now the golden opportunity to achieve their agenda. Three of their primary goals are: overturning *Roe vs. Wade;* the election of conservative judges for the Supreme Court and other Federal Courts; and a constitutional amendment banning gay marriage.

THE RICK WARREN PHENOMENON

When the White House wanted advice on how to observe the first anniversary of the September 11 attacks, aides called Rick Warren to meet with the President and First Lady and West Wing staff members, many of whom have dog-eared copies of his best-selling book *The Purpose Driven Life.*

According to *Time*, February 7, 2005, "These are heady times for Rick Warren. His *The Purpose Driven Life,* which says that meaning in life comes from following God's purposes, has sold more than 20 million copies over the past two years and is the best-selling hardback in U.S. history. When he took the podium to pray on the final night of Billy Graham's Los Angeles crusade at the Rose Bowl in November [2004], the 82,000 congregants cheered as if Warren had scored the winning touchdown. And on the eve of the presidential inauguration, Warren, who pastors the 22,000-member Saddleback megachurch in Lake Forest, California, delivered the invocation at the gala celebration. Later he met with 15 Senators, from both parties, who sought his advice and heard his plan to enlist Saddleback's global network of more than 40,000 churches in tackling such issues as poverty, disease, and ignorance. And when 600 senior pastors were asked to name the people they thought had the greatest influence on church affairs in the country, Warren's name came in second only to Billy Graham's. Although Franklin Graham is heir to the throne of the Billy Graham organization, many believe that Warren, 51, is the successor to the elder Graham for the role of America's minister."

Warren's brand of Christianity is called by many critics as "Christianity lite" because of the lack of emphasis on obedience in the lifestyle. He also portrays a "dumbing down" of the position of minister by his emphasis on casual dress. He is known for his floral or "Hawaiian" style sport shirts that he wears as he preaches or in other "ministerial" functions. In his recent photos he has changed the floral pattern for all-black, open-collar, sport shirts. He has also cut his hair and now wears it "spiked"—that is, sticking straight out/up—and has also grown a mustache and goatee. Generally, how a man dresses demonstrates the importance he places in his job and who he represents. For example, over the past several years I have been invited to a special dinner on Capitol Hill sponsored by *Liberty* magazine and the North American Religious Liberty Association. Senators and Congressmen attend and are frequently speakers. In addition, ambassadors and other representatives attend. It has been my observation that all of the men present wear dark suits with white shirts and ties—all this to pay respect to government leaders in a meeting that is held in the Russell Senate Office Building. Do you really think we should dress more casually when we come before our awesome God in church?

We have been told, <u>"the God of heaven, whose arm moves the world, who gives us life and sustains us in health, is honored or dishon-</u>

ored by the apparel of those who officiate in His honor. To Moses He gave special instruction regarding everything connected with the tabernacle service, and He specified the dress that those should wear who were to minister before Him. 'Thou shalt make holy garments for Aaron thy brother for glory and for beauty,' [Ex. 28:2] was the direction given to Moses. Everything connected with the apparel and deportment of the priests was to be such as to impress the beholder with a sense of the holiness of God, the sacredness of His worship, and the purity required of those who came into His presence" (*Gospel Workers*, p. 173).

As a wake-up call to those pastors and others who have gone through Warren's "40 Days of Purpose" study group, note the following evangelism strategy developed and promoted by Warren: "For Purpose-Driven church leaders, he [Warren] has developed an 'evangelism strategy' that includes casual dress code, convenient parking, bright lights, live bands, short prayers and sermons that accentuate the positive" (*Time*, March 29, 2004). Is this the kind of church service you want? Or does it remind you of what is happening to your church? Whatever you may think of the Warren worship style, you must remember that the devil's false revival, that immediately precedes the true latter-rain revival, will appear to be genuine to the casual observer. But you will know that it is part of Apostate Protestantism as they teach the natural immortality of the soul (which sets one up for the deceptions of spiritualism) and Sunday sacredness (which is a child of the papacy). Rick Warren certainly teaches both of these errors. You decide to which star you will hitch your wagon.

CATHOLIC EVANGELICALS?

Two of the "Evangelicals" listed in the *Time*, February 7, 2005, feature were Catholic priest Richard John Neuhaus and Catholic Senator Rick Santorum. It is difficult for one to include Catholics in the evangelical camp. Well before the Reformation—even going back some 1,500 years—Catholics have placed the authority of the church above Scripture. Evangelicals, on the other hand, elevate the Bible as the Word of God and their ultimate authority! The fact is that "politics makes strange bedfellows" and that is exactly what we have here.

Here is what the *Time* feature said about these two "Evangelicals."

"Richard John Neuhaus **Bushism Made Catholic**. When Bush met with journalists from religious publications last year, the living authority he cited most often was not a fellow Evangelical but a man he calls Father Richard, who, he explained, 'helps me articulate these [religious] things.' A senior Administration official confirms that Neuhaus 'does have a fair amount of under-the-radar influence' on such policies as abortion, stem-cell research, cloning and the defense-of-marriage amendment.

"Neuhaus, 68, is well prepared for that role. As founder of the religion-and-policy journal *First-Things,* he has for years articulated toughly conservative yet nuanced positions on a wide range of civic issues. A Lutheran [for 19 years a Lutheran minister] turned Catholic priest, he can translate conservative Protestant arguments couched tightly in Scripture into Catholicism's broader language of moral reasoning, more accessible to a general public that does not regard chapter and verse as final proof. And there is one last reason for Bush to cherish Neuhaus, who has worked tirelessly to persuade conservative Catholics and Evangelicals to make common cause. It's called the conservative Catholic vote, and it played a key role last November."

The second "evangelical" Catholic is "Rick Santorum, **the Point Man on Capitol Hill.** The Senate's third-ranking Republican may be Catholic, but he's the darling of Protestant Evangelicals. Pennsylvania's Rick Santorum, chairman of the Senate Republican Conference Committee, is the standard-bearer of social conservatives on the Hill, regularly and vocally taking the point position against gay marriage, abortion rights, and judges who defend either. [Remember these are the three goals of the Evangelicals.] He speaks monthly with evangelical leaders, hearing their concerns and briefing them on the status of legislation, while his staff regularly taps evangelical broadcasters and activists to help mobilize support for their common agenda. . . . Santorum, 46, is said to have presidential ambitions. 'Never say never,' he says—music to evangelical ears."

These influential evangelical leaders have one thing in common. They are using their considerable influence as religious leaders to work with and for political leaders. They are pressuring political leaders to pass laws that benefit their agenda! Senator Santorum is, obviously, already a politician, but he is being used by the Religious Right.

Quoting again from *Time,* Feb. 7, 2005: "Luis Cortes **Bringing Latinos to the Table.** [Note: This means bringing Latino Christians to the political table.] In the summer of 2000, a fleet of dark, unmarked vehicles pulled up to the North Philadelphia office of the Rev. Luis Cortes, Jr. As neighbors watched in amazement, armed men hustled a mysterious visitor inside. What happened next launched the remarkable ascent of a Hispanic Baptist minister until then little known outside Philadelphia. The visitor was G.O.P. presidential candidate George W. Bush, on a low-profile visit to woo Cortes and other Hispanic leaders. Over the next few hours, Cortes and Bush formed a bond that has vaulted the minister to the top tier of the fast-growing Hispanic Protestant community. With grants from Bush's Faith-Based Initiative and the cachet that comes from the Bush connection, Cortes, now 47, has expanded his two-decade-old organization, Nueva Esperanza (New Hope) nationwide, building houses in poor communities, offering start-up loans to Hispanic businesses and launching an AIDS-awareness program. In 2002 Cortes established the National Hispanic Prayer Breakfast, addressed annually by Bush and attended by a bi-partisan slate of political heavyweights."

And the list goes on—"David Barton **The Lesson Planner.** Even before he got directly involved in politics, David Barton was a major voice in the debate over church-state separation. His books and videotapes can be found in churches all over the U.S., educating an evangelical generation in what might be called Christian counter-history. The 51-year-old Texan's thesis: that the U.S. was a self-consciously religious nation from the time of the Founders until the 1963 Supreme Court school-prayer ban (which Barton has called 'a rejection of divine law'). Many historians dismiss his thinking, but Barton's advocacy organization, Wallbuilders, and his relentless stream of publications, court amicus briefs and books like *The Myth of Separation,* have made him a hero to millions—including some powerful politicians. He has been a co-chair of the Texas Republican Party for eight years, is friends with House majority leader Tom DeLay and was tapped by the Republican National Committee during its election sprint as a liaison to social conservatives."

And now, "Richard Land **God's Lobbyist.** You can chart Richard Land's clout by his phone log. The 58-year-old Texan, the Southern Baptist Convention's main man in Washington, recalls that the Reagan Administration returned his calls promptly; the first Bush White House less so and Clinton's staff (eventually) not at all. Now? The men around his longtime friend George W. Bush don't sit around waiting for Land's call. They reach out to him, individually and as part of a weekly teleconference with other Christian conservatives, to plot strategy on such issues as gay marriage and abortion.

"Land, who helped engineer his 16-million-member convention's 1979 shift from moderacy to hard-line conservatism, has a hand in most of its key policies, from its 1995 apology for having supported slavery to its 1998 statement that wives should submit to the leadership of their devout husbands. Since arriving in Washington in 1987, Land has cultivated dozens of sympathetic members of Congress. Princeton- and Oxford-educated, he is as formidable a public spokesman as he is in Washington's corridors and regularly battles culture-war foes on venues such as Meet the Press. 'People think they're going to be dealing with some bootstrap preacher,' says Larry Eskridge, associate director of the Institute for the Study of American Evangelicals at Wheaton College. 'But he can match pedigree and training with the best of them.'"

And finally, **"Ted Haggard Opening Up the Umbrella Group.** At a meeting with President Bush in November 2003, after nearly an hour of jovial Oval Office chat, the Rev. Ted Haggard, 48, got serious. He argued against Bush-imposed steel tariffs on the grounds that free markets foster economic growth, which helps the poor. A month later, the White House dropped the tariffs. Haggard wasn't alone in faulting the policy, and he doesn't claim to be the impetus, but as president of the National Association of Evangelicals, he gets listened to. He represents 30 million conservative Christians spread over 45,000 churches from 52 diverse denominations. Every Monday he participates in the West Wing conference call with evangelical leaders. The group continues to prod the President to campaign aggressively for a federal marriage amendment. 'We wanted him to use the force of his office to actively lobby the Congress and Senate, which he did not adequately do,' says Haggard. He is also working to broaden his group's agenda. A document issued last fall offered a theological justification for civic activism by U.S. Evangelicals."

So why is the civic activism by Evangelicals so significant? Here is the answer: "In the movements now in progress in the United States to secure for the institutions and usages of the church the support of the state, Protestants are following in the steps of papists. Nay, more, they are opening the door for the papacy to regain in Protestant America the supremacy which she has lost in the Old World. And that which gives greater significance to this movement is the fact that the principal object contemplated is the enforcement of Sunday observance—a custom which originated with Rome, and which she claims as the sign of her authority. It is the spirit of the papacy—the spirit of conformity to worldly customs, the veneration for human traditions above the commandments of God—that is permeating the Protestant churches and leading them on to do the same work of Sunday exaltation which the papacy has done before them" (*The Great Controversy,* p. 573).

THE TERRI SCHIAVO SAGA

"Terri Schiavo grew up in a middle-class subdivision outside Philadelphia as the oldest of three kids. An animal lover who was shy and insecure about her weight, she had more hamsters and birds than friends. By 1981, in her senior year at an all-girls Roman Catholic high school, she had reached as much as 250 pounds—at which point she went on a NutriSystem diet and quickly lost about 100 pounds. Soon thereafter, she met Michael Schiavo at a community college, and he asked her out. . . . After dating for five months, the couple got engaged. They married in 1984 and eventually moved to Florida, where Michael worked as a restaurant manager and Terri as an insurance claims clerk. . . . When they decided to start a family, Terry had trouble getting pregnant, and sought help from an obstetrician. By that time, Terri weighed [a mere] 110 pounds, and had a figure she proudly flaunted by wearing bikinis for the first time. No one suspected that she had an eating disorder, though in hindsight, her friend Diane Meyer remembers the meagerness of Terri's typical lunch: a bagel chopped into tiny triangular pieces, with minute dabs of cream cheese.

"Doctors blame her eating disorder for the tragedy that befell her in the early hours of Feb. 25, 1990. Awakened by a thud, Michael found Terri, then 26, lying in the hallway, making a gurgling sound. She had suffered cardiac arrest, probably provoked by bulimic purging that generated a severe potassium deficiency. The loss of oxygen to her brain caused permanent damage. With her cerebral cortex degenerated into scar tissue and spinal fluid, Terri fell into a 'persistent vegetative state.' Retaining the capacity for reflexes like coughing or grimacing but lacking any cognitive ability" (*Newsweek,* April 4, 2005).

Each day, as all health professionals know, families across the country suffer private anguish over the decision to remove a loved one from life support. Their stories rarely make news, or prompt urgent action from lawmakers. So what made Terri Schiavo's case unique? The basic facts seem uncontested. For several years after Terri's heart attack and disability her parents and husband worked together to make sure she received every possible therapy and medical treatment available in an effort to reverse her condition. Terri's husband, Michael, was fastidious about her appearance, spraying her with Picasso perfume and outfitting her in stirrup pants and matching tops from The Limited. To better care for Terri, Michael even enrolled in nursing school. In 1994, after consulting with doctors, Michael concluded that his wife would not recover. All of the public accounts agree that all of the physicians that Michael consulted and almost all of those that were appointed by the courts concluded that Terri was in a persistent vegetative state and could not and would not ever "wake up" or get well. It was also clear that all 19 judges who heard the facts regarding Terri's situation agreed with her husband that she would not want to live that way and that the feeding tube should be removed.

However, Terri's Roman Catholic parents, Bob and Mary Schindler, were motivated by the pope's "Culture of Life" concept from his 1995 encyclical. The Vatican had spoken out on this case and, in fact, energized the Religious Right to pressure legislative and executive leaders to intervene on Terri's behalf. Florida's Roman Catholic governor, Jeb Bush, the president's brother, took up the case and encouraged the Florida Legislature to pass "Terri's Law" to allow him as governor to order that the feeding tube be reinstated. The Florida State Court ruled that law unconstitutional and the Florida Supreme Court agreed in a unanimous decision.

Having failed at the state level, the Religious Right pressured leaders at the federal level. Tom DeLay, the powerful Majority Leader in the U.S. House of Representatives, was so bold in supporting the Religious Right in the Schiavo matter that he even embarrassed them. For example, he insisted that keeping Schiavo and patients like her alive was more important than "the sanctity of marriage." DeLay told a group of Christian conservatives: "One thing that God brought us is Terri Schiavo, to help elevate the visibility of what is going on in

America" (The Washington *Post,* March 23, 2005, page A15).

Senate Majority Leader, Doctor Bill Frist, went to the Senate Floor and produced maybe the most galvanizing moment in the political debate. A renowned heart and lung transplant surgeon, Frist was elected to the Senate in 1994. He played up his medical credentials from the beginning, asking that he be called "Doctor" instead of "Senator." But pressured by the Religious Right, Frist went outside his medical specialty, and without ever seeing or examining Terri Schiavo—after inspecting some videotapes made by her parents—the doctor announced that the examinations by the court-appointed physicians were erroneous in concluding that Schiavo had been in a persistent vegetative state for the past 15 years! The "Doctor" announced on the floor of the United States Senate, "There seems to be insufficient information to conclude that Terri Schiavo is in a persistent vegetative state. I don't see any justification in removing hydration and nutrition" (*U.S. News & World Report,* April 4, 2005). Following Frist's appeal, the House and Senate agreed on a bill that let Terri's case be heard in Federal Court. Congress convened a special session during its Easter recess to pass this bill that was crafted for just one family!

President Bush cut short a rest at his Texas ranch to return to Washington to be available to sign the bill. The president keeps a very rigid personal schedule and is almost always in bed by 10:00. A White House source said he was awakened from his sleep for the signing at 1:11 a.m.! The Washington *Post* reported that the entire episode in Washington smacked of political opportunism. "For George W. Bush, too, Terri Schiavo came along at a propitious time. All is not well in Bushland. The more the American people hear about the president's Social Security scheme, the more they reject it—lately by margins approaching 2 to 1. The Bush bills that have been moving through Congress—tightening up bankruptcy regulations, authorizing drilling for oil in the Arctic National Wildlife Refuge, limiting consumer lawsuits—do nothing for the Christian conservatives who helped reelect him. . . . If signing a bill in his pajamas meant he could rekindle their support, why, that was worth even interrupting his sleep" (The Washington *Post,* Wednesday, March 23, page A15).

The Schiavo case points out the growing power and influence of the Religious Right, which is composed of conservative Catholics and evangelical Protestants. It is likely that this powerful coalition will eventually push for Sunday legislation. The rhetoric of the religious and political leaders show how unpopular it will be to oppose those who are doing what they think is best for America. Pat Robertson called the removal of Terri Schiavo's feeding tube "Judicial murder," and House Majority Leader Tom DeLay described it as an "act of medical terrorism." Brother Paul O'Donnell, a Franciscan monk and spiritual adviser to Robert and Mary Schlindler, Schiavo's parents, called the case a "modern-day crucifixion."

Terri Schiavo died March 31, 2005, after 15 years in a vegetative state. Ironically, polls taken during the religio/political saga indicate that more than 70 percent of Americans opposed governmental interference in this private family matter, and even the majority of Evangelicals felt it was inappropriate. "Despite sincere and altruistic motivation, the Legislative and Executive branches of our government have acted in a manner demonstrably at odds with our Founding Fathers' blueprint for the governance of a free people—our Constitution"—Stanley Birch, a conservative judge in Atlanta's federal appeals court, rebuking the President and Congress for behaving like "activist judges" in intervening in the Schiavo case (*Time,* April 11, 2005).

THE EVANGELICAL MARY

If the mixture of religion and politics and evangelical Protestant and Catholic wasn't ominous enough, now we learn that Protestants are getting excited about the virgin Mary. The evangelical journal *Christianity Today,* in the December 2003 issue, featured a cover story with a bold title: **"The Blessed Evangelical Mary**—Why we shouldn't ignore her any longer." The accompanying 6-page article states, in essence, that though the Catholic veneration of Mary is not biblically grounded or theologically sound, Protestants should not ignore her altogether. Though all that is said about Mary in the Bible could be written on one page, this full article encourages respect and honor for Mary because of her faithfulness in pointing others to Jesus. A song and a poem about Mary are included. This rather innocuous article simply starts Protestants thinking more about Mary and prepares them for the next step.

That step was taken by *Time,* March 21, 2005. The cover featured a portrait of Mary with the following caption: "Hail, Mary—Catholics have long revered her, but now Protestants are finding their own reasons to celebrate the mother of Jesus." The Table of Contents page noted: **"Something About Mary**—Once relegated to the Christmas season, the mother of Jesus is gaining a wider following among Protestants. Some now see her as His First Disciple." *Time* devoted the cover and a full eight-page article to Mary. Albert Mohler, president of the Southern Baptist Convention's Southern Seminary, charges that "those who use her full [biblical] record to justify new 'theological constructions' around her are guilty of 'overreaching,' 'wishful thinking' and effectively 'flirting with Catholic devotion.' Insofar as Evangelicals may have marginalized Mary's presentation in the Bible, it needs to be recovered," he concedes. "But the closer I look at the New Testament, the more convinced I am that it does not single her out for the kind of attention that is being proposed. We have not missed the point about her. To construct a new role for her is simply overreaching."

"He is most exasperated that 'Mary is held forth as the maternal face of God, some dimension that is fundamentally absent from Scripture. God's love is presented in Biblical terms without any need for Mary as intermediary. To suggest that need, even as "symbolic" instead of doctrinal' he pauses—'this is the Reformation in reverse. It's simply profoundly unbiblical, and it leads to the worst excesses of Marian devotion.'"

But Pastor Albert Mohler's traditional Protestant reserve is far outweighed by those pushing for more Marian adoration. For example, the article noted: "Mary is gaining popularity at Protestant divinity schools, where her icons adorn future pastor's walls. Even Evangelical publishing is interested."

Lutheran theologian Carl Braaten, coeditor of an essay collection on what might be called Marian upgrade, claims, "We don't have to go back to Catholicism. We can go back to our own roots and sources. It could be done without shocking the congregation. I can't predict how exactly it will happen. Some of it will be good, and some of it bad. But I think it's going to happen."

Donald Charles Lacy, a 72-year-old Methodist minister, following Vatican II, was inspired to join with other Protestants and Catholics to form a new group called the Ecumenical Society of the Blessed Virgin Mary. His writings about the virgin Mary were largely ignored by

Methodist publications "until four years ago, when a Methodist house suddenly printed his *Collected Works.* 'I stood alone for so many years,' Lacy says now. 'It's very gratifying to see [people] begin to come this way.'"

Mary Burks-Price is the manager of pastoral-care education at a Louisville, Kentucky, hospital. Though she is a Baptist, "her office is filled with Marys: porcelain statuettes, laminated prayer cards, icons. She keeps a Rosary for Catholic patients, and sometimes, she says, 'I know [the prayer] better than they do.'"

The Mel Gibson movie *The Passion of the Christ* was viewed by thousands and thousands of Evangelicals. Pastors such as Rick Warren rented entire theaters and chartered buses to take their members. "Conservative pastors interviewed by *Christianity Today* particularly lauded its treatment of Mary, which featured scenes not found in Scripture: Mary witnessing her son's scourging, sopping up his blood, kissing his bloody face—and her flashback, as Christ stumbles in carrying the Cross, to a moment in his boyhood when he fell and cried and she could cradle him in her arms."

The *Time* article concludes by saying, "In the end Mary's role may be less influenced by Mohler [the traditional Protestant view] than by a group only now beginning to make its considerable Protestant presence felt. A man stands at the lectern at the El Amor de Dios church on Chicago's South Side reading in Spanish, tears streaming down his cheeks. His text is a treatment of the Virgin Mary from one of the Bible's apocryphal books. Another congregant follows, reciting his own verses to the Virgin from a dog-eared notebook filled with tiny, precise printing. Flanking the altar are two Mary statues with fresh roses at their feet, and hanging from the hands of the baby Jesus is a Rosary. The altar cover presents the church's most stunning image: Mary again, this time totally surrounded by a multi-colored halo, in the traditional iconography of the Our Lady of Guadalupe. The church is Methodist." The article goes on to note that the Spanish Protestant churches that are "Marian" are growing rapidly.

This is one more step toward Rome as predicted in Scripture and the Spirit of Prophecy. The worship and adoration of Mary as practiced by Roman Catholicism is by definition pure spiritualism. Spiritualism has two elements. The first is the belief in conscious existence—life after death. The second is that people alive on the earth can communicate with the dead. Praying to Mary, as in the Rosary, includes both elements. Mariology is actually Spiritualism! Protestants' embrace of the cult of Mary is another major step toward union with Rome. We are witnessing another of the final events taking place. "The Protestants of the United States will be foremost in stretching their hands across the gulf to grasp the hand of spiritualism; they will reach over the abyss to clasp hands with the Roman power; and under the influence of this threefold union, this country will follow in the steps of Rome in trampling on the rights of conscience" (*The Great Controversy,* p. 588).

CHAPTER 11

"One Apostolic Faith"

November 17, 2004, marked another historic ecumenical event: the formation of a new Christian alliance called Christian Churches Together in the U.S.A. The Associated Press recorded: "The nation's Roman Catholic bishops voted Wednesday (November 17, 2004) to join a new alliance that would be the broadest Christian group ever formed in the United States, linking America's Evangelicals and Catholics in an ecumenical organization for the first time."

The Catholic News Service reported on November 18, 2004, "The U. S. Catholic bishops November 17 [2004] took a historic ecumenical step by joining the new national ecumenical forum Christian Churches Together in the USA.

"It marks the first time that the U.S. Catholic Church is a partner church in such a national body, although Catholic churches in about 70 other countries belong to national councils of churches or similar bodies. The bishops approved the proposal to join CCT by a vote of 151-73, slightly more than a 2-to-1 margin."

Roman Catholic bishop Stephen E. Blaire of Stockton, California, chairman of the Committee on Ecumenical and Interreligious Affairs, presented the proposal to the other bishops and urged their adoption. He noted that "The Holy See has also encouraged it."

"Bishop Blaire emphasized that for the Catholic Church the ultimate goal of ecumenism is the full, visible unity of all Christian churches in the one apostolic faith." In the discussion among the bishops about whether or not to join the organization "bishop Fabian W. Bruskewitz of Lincoln, Nebraska, asked if the other churches in the CCT are aware of the perspective from which the Catholic Church approaches the organization. Bishop Blaire said not only are the other churches aware of the Catholic view, but many of them also believe that full, visible unity is the ultimate goal and that organizations such as the CCT are only interim steps.

"Several bishops expressed concern whether there are sufficient safeguards in the organizational structure of the CCT to protect the Catholic Church from being associated with statements that contradict Catholic beliefs. Bishop Blaire said such safeguards are in place."

This new ecumenical organization has divided Christians in America into five "families" and will have representatives from each family group. The families are: (Roman) Catholic, Orthodox (Catholic), historical Protestant, historical racial and ethnic churches, and Evangelical/Pentecostal. With 67 million members in the U.S., the Catholics will be by far the largest denomination in the new organization.

The Vatican was eager for the Catholic bishops to become involved in CCT because Evangelicals and Pentecostals were joining and they wanted to have more contact with this group. The Catholic News Service reported: "Cardinal Walter Kasper, president of the Pontifical Council for Promoting Christian Unity, has encouraged USCCB [United States Conference of Catholic Bishops] membership in CCT. In a June [2004] letter to Bishop Blaire the cardinal said that 'one of its strongest points is the effort to bring into discussion those Christians such as Evangelicals and Pentecostals who are among the fastest growing Christian communities, and who have not been sufficiently involved in the ecumenical dialogue.' He [the Vatican Cardinal] suggested the new U.S. organization would likely contribute to the Vatican's own ongoing efforts to build stronger relations with Evangelicals and Pentecostals."

COMMON POINTS FOR UNITY

Years ago we were told that unity among Christian churches would be sought based on the barest points in common and that this unity would be used for political purposes. "When the leading churches of the United States, uniting upon such points of doctrine as are held by them in common, shall influence the state to enforce their decrees and to sustain their institutions, then Protestant America will have formed an image of the Roman hierarchy, and the infliction of civil penalties upon dissenters will inevitably result" (The Great Controversy, p. 445).

So what are the common points that have been established for membership in the Christian Churches Together organization? They are so basic that there are only three in number. As the CNS reported: "The CCT organizational plan says the organization 'welcomes churches, Christian communities [parachurch organizations] and national Christian organizations that:

'Believe in the Lord Jesus Christ as God and Savior according to the Scriptures.

'Worship and serve the one God, Father, Son and Holy Spirit.

'Seek ways to work together in order to present a more credible Christian witness in and to the world.'"

In its simplest terms the prerequisites for membership are that you believe in God and want to work with other Christian groups. In essence these groups are laying aside their doctrinal differences and uniting for common goals.

WHO IS BEHIND CCT?

The news items on November 17 and 18, 2004, headlined the fact that the U.S. Catholic Bishops had voted to join CCT—as if there had been some possibility that they wouldn't! However, when one researches the origin and history of CCT it is clear that the Catholic Church was the originator of the idea and, in fact, hosted most of the organizational meetings! I will underline a few key words in the following quotes to highlight these facts. The CNS news release stated: "CCT began with an invitation sent out to a number of church leaders in the summer of 2001 by Cardinal William H. Keeler of Baltimore; the Rev. Robert Edgar, National Council of Churches general secretary; the Rev. Wesley Granberg-Michaelson, general secretary of the Reformed Church in America; and Bishop Tod D. Brown of Orange, Calif., then-chairman of the bishop's Committee on Ecumenical and Interreligious Affairs."

And where did the first organizational meeting take place? "In response to the invitation 27 church leaders met Sept. 7-8, 2001, at St. Mary's Seminary and University in Baltimore to explore the idea of a broader structure under which the wide diversity of Christian churches could come together to strengthen their unity in Christ and empower their witness and mission."

MAIN ORGANIZATIONAL MEETING AT JESUIT RETREAT HOUSE

"Christian Churches Together in the USA (CCT) will hold its organizing meeting June 1-3, 2005, at El Retiro, the Jesuit Retreat House in Los Altos, California. Over 35 representatives of Christian Churches and

National Christian Organizations have already indicated they will attend the meeting. At the meeting those Churches and Christian organizations who have decided to become founding participants will select a Steering Committee and adopt Articles of Incorporation, Bylaws and Dues Structure. Together, they will pray, worship, and consider the future of CCT. Additionally, they will hear about plans for the September celebration launching CCT which marks the historical coming together of the major Christian Faith Families in the USA" (www.christianchurches together.org Web site, posted 3/7/2005).

The same Web site posted the following notice of the official launching of the CCT:

"CCT Will Worship and Celebrate Its Founding at the National Cathedral, Washington, D.C., September 18, 2005. The National Cathedral in Washington, D.C., has been designated as the site for the official launching of Christian Churches Together in the USA on September 18, 2005. Founding participants from the five faith families (Catholic, Evangelical and Pentecostal, Racial Ethnic, Orthodox and Protestant) and their guests will assemble for worship in celebration of the coming together of the Christian families and their growing closer in Christ in order to broaden and expand fellowship and strengthen Christian witness in the world."

When commenting about this new organization, the Associated Press reported on November 17, 2004: "It is considered a biblical imperative for Christians to find ways to build unity among their different denominations. Pope John Paul II has made such efforts a priority of his pontificate."

The National Council of Churches, which has never had Catholic members, hailed the new CCT and the Bishops' decision to join. It issued the following press release:

"November 18, 2004, NEW YORK CITY—National Council of Churches General Secretary Bob Edgar welcomed the U.S. Catholic Bishops' decision Nov. 17 to join Christian Churches Together in the U.S.A. (CCT, an effort to bring Catholics, Evangelicals and mainline Protestants, the Orthodox Christians around a common table for the first time)."

THE STATED PURPOSE OF CCT
In the organizational plan posted on their Web site CCT states that

"The purpose of Christian Churches Together is to enable churches and national Christian organizations to grow closer together in Christ in order to strengthen our Christian witness in the world. Participants in Christian Churches Together accomplish this purpose by:

Rejoicing in our faith in the Triune God;

Discerning the guidance of the Holy Spirit through prayer and theological dialogue;

Providing fellowship and mutual support;

Affirming our commonalities and understanding our differences;

Fostering Christian evangelism faithful to the proclamation of the gospel;

Speaking to society with a common voice whenever possible;

Promoting the common good of society.

"Christian Churches Together will sponsor in the name of Christian Churches Together, various Forums, national and regional, on diverse topics (e.g., evangelism, worship, public policy)."

NEW POPE CALLS FOR UNITY

Pope Benedict XVI announced in his first sermon that he has a "primary commitment to work without sparing energies for the reconstitution of the full and visible unity of all the followers of Christ." The pope's ecumenical commitment did not suddenly appear with his election, however. He was personally involved with the crafting and signing of the Lutheran-Roman Catholic Joint Declaration on the Doctrine of Justification (JDDJ). "He offers an unambiguous affirmation of Vatican II's assertion that the bishop of Rome is 'the perpetual and visible principle and foundation' of the unity of the bishops and the faithful throughout the world. . . . There was for Cardinal Ratzinger and there will be for Pope Benedict no doubt that the church of Christ is found in its fullness uniquely in the Catholic Church" (*Christian Century,* May 17, 2005).

PAPAL FUNERAL BRINGS A CALL FOR
UNITY WITH ROME

Following the worldwide attention on the Vatican in regard to the funeral of John Paul II and the election of Benedict XVI, Protestant leaders are calling for unity with Rome. Many were impressed with the pomp and majesty of the events in and around St. Peter's and realize that Protestants could never pull off an event in which the heads of state of over a hundred countries and millions of common people would come together for one event. Those who have written about this need for unity recognize that it must be Protestants that must return to the papacy and not the other way around. After all, the papacy has political clout and diplomatic relations with 75 percent of the nations of the world and boasts a worldwide membership of over 1 billion. Protestants, on the other hand, are totally unorganized, have little political influence outside the United States, and have a combined membership that is less than 10 percent of the Roman Church.

The May 17, 2005, issue of *Christian Century* featured an article on the topic of *Protestants and the Papacy.* "Do Protestants Need the Papacy?" the article begins. "Given the recent fascination with the pontificate of John Paul II and with the election of Benedict XVI, it would seem that the papacy is on the Protestant horizon in a way that would have been unthinkable even a generation ago. This may be the result of savvy marketing, the omnipresence of CNN, the celebrity status of John Paul II or a penchant for the exotic. But I think something more is going on. It is the papacy itself that fascinates us.

"Protestants find ourselves in the odd situation of seeing a need for the papacy. . . . The papacy offers an impressive visible manifestation of the church's unity. Christians must seek the unity of Christ's body in a visible way through the church. . . . When it comes to visible unity, it is time for us Protestants to admit that we have failed. We are disunified beyond repair and cannot solve our divisions through our traditionally Protestant resources. Perhaps it is time to look to the papacy for the necessary visible manifestation of Christian unity; perhaps it alone provides the necessary unity of the church through a subjective and personal reality that mirrors that of Jesus Christ himself."

The Protestant author concludes his article by saying, "The Catholic Church has acknowledged contributing to the ruptures that divide us, ruptures that are always sin. We Protestants must now reciprocate and name our sin in dividing Christ's body. Can we do this without rethinking its unity in the primacy of the bishop of Rome? I do not think so.

"At one point in history, to be a Protestant was explicitly or tacitly to will an end to the papacy. I think many Protestants can now confess that was a mistaken view. Both the church and the world would sorely lack a witness if there were no papacy. If being a Protestant means willing the end of the papacy, then I find myself no longer capable of willing such an act."

In actual practice very few Protestant churches protest the errors of the papacy anymore. Many mainline Protestant denominations are seeking union with Rome and the Evangelicals are cooperating with Rome in a common-cause agenda. The major steps of the ecumenical movement in the 1990s have paved the way for the overt actions of today. The picture portrayed in Revelation 13 continues to come into focus. The stage is set for the final movements.

CHAPTER 12

Countdown to Sunday

How do we know for certain that there will be a "Sunday Law" before the Second Coming as part of the final events scenario? God has provided prophetic guidance at the time of every major event in salvation history. The inspired Word records, "Surely the Lord God does nothing, unless He reveals His secret to His servants the prophets" (Amos 3:7).

When Jesus returned to heaven after His first advent the Bible says He "gave gifts to men" (Ephesians 4:8). Five places in the New Testament lists of these divine gifts to the Christian church are given. The lists are recorded in Romans 12:6-8; 1 Corinthians 12:4-11; 1 Corinthians 13:1-3; 1 Corinthians 14:1-40; and Ephesians 4:8-16. It is significant to note that only one gift occurs in all five lists. It is the gift of prophecy! Apparently our Lord Jesus recognized the need for continuing contact with His people—especially as the time of the end approached.

Knowing that God will send prophets to the Christian church is important. Knowing that the devil will send false prophets is also important. Four times in Matthew 24 Jesus warned His disciples not to be deceived. (See the chapter "Beware of False Prophets" in my book *Ready or Not.*) The bottom line is that we should all have a clear understanding of the four biblical tests of a prophet and apply them consistently to those who claim to have the gift of prophecy or who seek to interpret the words of Scripture.

I believe that Ellen G. White, who claimed to be a messenger of the Lord, meets the biblical tests of a prophet. I believe that God has used her to enlighten the end-time Christian community with details of prophetic significance. Accordingly, I will refer to her counsel in some detail to see the prophetic countdown.

The student of Daniel and the Revelation sees prophetic fulfillment in the papal church of the Middle Ages attempting to change times and laws in changing the Sabbath from Saturday, the seventh day of the week, to Sunday, the first day of the week. Particularly significant to us today is the fulfillment of Revelation 13. There we see a second beast arising out of the earth and forming an image to the first beast—the church of the Middle Ages, which has been revived for the final act in the great controversy.

SUNDAY IN PROPHECY

When one studies the mark of the beast and the seal of God (see appendix of this book) it is clear that at the end, the United States of America—the world's only remaining political superpower—will finally give its support to the papacy—the world's great superchurch. This is a well-established biblical understanding. However, Scripture does not give the details about just how this image to the beast will be formed around worship on the counterfeit Sabbath. Fortunately for us, this is where God's end-time prophetic communication fills in the details.

For example, in the Bible the word "Sunday" does not occur. We must look under "first day of the week" to find any comments about "Sunday." The first day of the week is mentioned only once in the full text of the 39 books of the Old Testament. That one reference is Genesis 1:5, used in connection with the Creation account. There are only eight New Testament references to "first day," most of which are in the Gospel accounts of events surrounding the crucifixion of Christ. A study of these nine biblical "first day" references gives no indication that God intended to change the fourth commandment and establish the Sabbath on the first day of the week. In fact, there is ample biblical evidence to the contrary. The *Catholic Mirror* articles pointed this out as we have noted in earlier chapters.

Though the Bible is virtually silent with regard to the significant role of Sunday worship in the end times, the Spirit of Prophecy (as Ellen White's prophetic writings are called in recognition of the Spirit which inspired them) is filled with information. The word "Sunday" is used 1,895 times in the writings of Ellen White. Many are simple references to what day of the week it was when a certain event took place in her life. The majority, however, deal with the change of the Sabbath by the papacy and the end-time significance of Sunday laws and worship.

In this chapter we will look at a ten-point countdown to the establishment of Sunday laws in the United States and eventually the entire world. Current events make it clear that the countdown has begun.

"The history which the great I AM has marked out in His word, uniting link after link in the prophetic chain, from eternity in the past to eternity in the future, tells us where we are today in the procession of the ages, and what may be expected in the time to come. <u>All that prophecy has foretold as coming to pass, until the present time, has been traced on the pages of history, and we may be assured that all which is yet to come will be fulfilled in its order</u>" (*Education,* p. 178). Yes—Sunday is coming!

God does not want us to have to face any surprises at the end. He has given information, that if heeded, will save us from a lot of stress and grief later on. "God has revealed what is to take place in the last days, that His people may be prepared to stand against the tempest of opposition and wrath. Those who have been warned of the events before them are not to sit in calm expectation of the coming storm, comforting themselves that the Lord will shelter His faithful ones in the day of trouble. We are to be as men waiting for their Lord, not in idle expectancy, but in earnest work, with unwavering faith. It is no time now to allow our minds to be engrossed with things of minor importance. While men are sleeping, Satan is actively arranging matters so that the Lord's people may not have mercy or justice. The Sunday movement is now making its way in darkness. The leaders are concealing the true issue, and many who unite in the movement do not themselves see whither the undercurrent is tending. Its professions are mild and apparently Christian, but when it shall speak it will reveal the spirit of the dragon" (*Testimonies for the Church,* vol. 5, p. 452). Then Ellen White outlines how to prepare:

"It is our duty to do all in our power to avert the threatened danger.

"We should endeavor to disarm prejudice by placing ourselves in a proper light before the people.

"We should bring before them the real question at issue, thus interposing the most effectual protest against measures to restrict liberty of conscience.

"We should search the Scriptures and be able to give the reason for our faith. Says the prophet [Daniel]: 'The wicked shall do wickedly: and none of the wicked shall understand; <u>but the wise shall understand</u>' " (*ibid.*).

Ellen White had a lot to say about Sunday laws when there was agitation for such near the turn of the last century.[1] Her comments apply very much today, as we face a similar challenge. "Sooner or later Sunday laws will be passed." She wrote in 1905, "But there is much for God's servants to do to warn the people" (*Review and Herald,* Feb. 16, 1905).

Many who become involved in the pro-Sunday law movement are apparently very sincere and conscientious Christians who are simply exasperated with world conditions. They believe with all their hearts that by "getting back to God" many of the problems that are evident in society will get better, and they will be able to offer hope for their children's future.

To His followers Jesus gave this warning, "They will put you out of the synagogues; yes, the time is coming that whoever kills you will think that he offers God service" (John 16:2). It was in such a setting that Saul, at the stoning of Stephen, thought he was doing God service. No doubt the testimony of Stephen's life and death helped convict "Paul," leading directly to his own martyrdom for the cause of God.

We are told that "there are many, even of those engaged in this movement for Sunday enforcement, who are blinded to the results which will follow this action. They do not see that they are striking directly against religious liberty" (*Testimonies for the Church,* vol. 5, p. 711).

Apparently the Sunday legislation will be encouraged from the grass roots up rather than being the work of bureaucrats in Washington trying to make it hard on civilians. In fact, we are told, "Plans of serious import to the people of God are advancing in an underhand manner among the clergymen of various denominations, and the object of this secret maneuvering is to win popular favor for the enforcement of Sunday sacredness. If the people can be led to favor a Sunday law, then the clergy intend to exert their influence to obtain a religious amendment to the Constitution, and compel the nation to keep Sunday" (*Review and Herald,* Dec. 24, 1889).

THE LAW WILL GET PROGRESSIVELY WORSE

Evidently those agitating for Sunday laws do not truly anticipate the reaction of those who choose to remain true to the law of God and honor the Bible Sabbath as the sign of their allegiance to God. Accordingly, the law at first is very mild with perhaps only fines for failure to comply. Then follow harsher penalties—loss of property, economic pressure (can't buy or sell), and finally the death sentence (see Revelation 13:15, 16).

"The time will come when men will not only forbid Sunday work, but they will try to force men to labor on the Sabbath. And men will be asked to renounce the Sabbath and to subscribe to Sunday observance or forfeit their freedom and their lives" (*The Southern Work,* p. 69).

"In the last conflict the Sabbath will be the special point of controversy throughout all Christendom. Secular rulers and religious leaders will unite to enforce the observance of the Sunday; and as milder measures fail, the most oppressive laws will be enacted. It will be urged that the few who stand in opposition to an institution of the church and a law of the land ought not to be tolerated" (*Maranatha,* p. 188).

POLITICAL PRESSURE

When discussing the Evangelicals and the Religious Right above we noted that currently they are putting tremendous pressure on members of Congress to vote in certain ways. Another interesting phenomenon has occurred with regard to the Catholic members of Congress. During the 2004 general election there was much talk in the press regarding whether or not presidential candidate John Kerry could receive communion in the Catholic Church where he is a member because of his proabortion stand. There are even letters being written to the Vatican and articles being printed in new magazines and papers encouraging Roman Catholic leaders to excommunicate members of Congress who do not vote according to Catholic teaching.

There are currently about 150 Catholic members of Congress. Some observers choose to believe that these individuals are not influenced by the church and therefore there is no significance in their large number. This may have been true in the past, but not now, as recent statements from Catholic leaders, including the pope, have indicated. Things have indeed changed.

Catholic attorney Keith Fournier, former executive director for the Christian Coalition's American Center for Law and Justice, says, "It is the role of the lay faithful, according to Catholic theology, to 'renew the temporal order.' This is why it was second nature for a devout Catholic such as [U.S. Representative] Henry Hyde to bring his Christian convictions into the political arena. It is simply *not Catholic* to privatize your faith. Thus, the modern aberrations being proposed by certain Catholic politicians about their private convictions versus their public life are not only nonsense, but un-Catholic" (Keith Fournier, *A House United,* p. 32).

In Pope John Paul II's encyclical *"Evangelium Vitae"* (The Gospel of Life), issued on April 6, 1995, the pope stated that the abortion culture is the "culture of death." He goes on to imply that Catholic politicians will be held responsible for their votes on the abortion question. "Catholic politicians who back abortion, even reluctantly, bear a greater responsibility before God than do women who undergo the procedure, Vatican leaders said. The question of whether they should be excommunicated is open to debate they suggested. They made their comments in a news conference in Rome after the release of Pope John Paul II's new encyclical *Evangelium Vitae* (The Gospel of Life). The 194-page document brands abortion and euthanasia as evils that no law can justify. It called for non-violent opposition to both. . . . The encyclical dismissed claims by politicians who say they oppose abortion, but are compelled by their position to uphold laws allowing it. 'Politicians cannot renounce their consciences when they take on legislative duties,' the pope said" (*National & International Religion Report,* April 17, 1995).

Even though there are those who may take a different view on some topics or issues than the pope, the bottom line is that very few feel so strongly about an issue that they are willing to risk excommunication.

According to Catholic theology, very few people, with the possible exception of a few popes and some saintly people, go straight to heaven when they die. Instead they go first to purgatory (not a biblical term or place) where they are "purged" of their sins. This may require a great deal of suffering by the one in purgatory and a great many prayers and much money from the living relatives to get the person out of purgatory.

An excommunicated person doesn't "get" to go to purgatory. He first of all loses all rights of church membership and is excluded from any fellowship with the church and cannot participate in the rites of the church. He cannot receive "last rights" before he dies or be buried in a church cemetery. At death he is simply banished straight to hell, to burn throughout the ceaseless ages of eternity—with no hope of ever going to heaven. How would you react to the possibility of such a fate?

Concerning this Ellen White stated, "The Roman Catholic Church, with all its ramifications throughout the world, forms one vast organization under the control, and designed to serve the interests, of the papal see. Its millions of communicants [now over 1 billion—that's a thousand million], in every country on the globe, are instructed to hold themselves as bound in allegiance to the pope. Whatever their nationality or their government, they are to regard the authority of the church as above all other. Though they may take the oath pledging their loyalty to the state, yet back of this lies the vow of obedience to Rome, absolving them from every pledge inimical to her interests" (*The Great Controversy,* p. 580).

What if a congressman wanted to just vote by secret ballot so no one would know how he voted on a particular issue? That is not a possibility as every vote is public—on the record. In fact, the Christian Coalition, Focus on the Family, and other groups print information as to how every member of Congress votes on issues of interest to them—i.e., family values. The higher percentage you have in votes to the liking of the Christian Coalition the greater are your chances of getting reelected.

The defeat of the powerful Senate minority leader, Tom Daschle, is an indication of the power of the Religious Right today. This group hopes to send a message to all politicians with the Daschle defeat of what to expect if they are opposed in their agenda.

It's certain that when the Sunday law is proposed many of the lawmakers will not personally be in favor of it, but apparently they vote in favor in order to keep their positions. "Political corruption is destroying love of justice and regard for truth; and even in free America, rulers and legislators, in order to secure public favor, will yield to the popular demand for a law enforcing Sunday observance. Liberty of conscience, which has cost so great a sacrifice, will no longer be respected" (*The Great Controversy,* p. 592).

Today many of the most powerful politicians seek the approval and support of the religious leaders. Ellen White might have been commenting directly from today's trends when she wrote: "To secure popularity and patronage, legislators will yield to the demand for Sunday laws. But those who fear God, cannot accept an institution that violates a precept of the Decalogue. On this battlefield will be fought the last great conflict in the controversy between truth and error" (*Prophets and Kings,* p. 606).

Legislators "will yield to the demand for Sunday laws." Now the statement in the new Catechism takes on greater significance, doesn't it? The command of the Roman Church is, "Christians should seek recognition of Sundays . . . as legal holidays." A groundswell of popular support will trigger the Sunday law. Apparently, fear of financial collapse, declining moral standards, and natural disasters motivate the people to ask for a law to appease "an angry God." Some folks talk about judicial action, others talk about constitutional amendment, others talk about executive orders. A personal study of the topic in the Spirit of Prophecy shows that the Sunday law will be enacted as a panic reaction to deteriorating world affairs. Much like the 1973 National Gas Station Sunday Closing law was a panic reaction to the Arab oil embargo, pressure tactics will be used by Satan to encourage Sunday law support.

COUNTDOWN TO SUNDAY

NUMBER 1

FINANCIAL PROBLEMS

Any thinking person recognizes the precarious economic situation in the United States today.[2] We have witnessed the collapse of major corporations and the loss of the investment portfolios of thousands. The news carries stories of the dangerous position of Social Security and Medicare. We are witnessing an alarming escalation in home prices—to say nothing about gas prices. Our government goes deeper and deeper into debt—now some 9 trillion! Many are expressing concern that the days of prosperity are over. Books are being sold that hype "How to profit from the coming economic crash."

In commenting on this aspect of life in America, Ellen White wrote, "Those who hold the reins of government are not able to solve the problem of moral corruption, poverty, pauperism, and increasing crime. They are struggling in vain to place business operations on a more secure basis" (*Testimonies for the Church,* vol. 9, p. 13). But what does this have to do with the Sunday law? Note the following: "It will be declared that men are offending God by the violation of the Sunday sabbath; that this sin has brought calamities which will not cease until Sunday observance shall be strictly enforced; and that those who present the claims of the fourth commandment, thus destroying reverence for Sunday, are troublers of the people, preventing their restoration to divine favor and **temporal prosperity**" (*The Great Controversy,* p. 590).

NUMBER 2

MORAL CORRUPTION

There is an almost complete breakdown of society in America

today. Ellen White described conditions in our day very precisely, "Those in the world, having lost their connection with God, are making desperate, insane efforts to make centers of themselves [mass murderers and hostage takers]. This causes distrust of one another, which is followed by crime. The kingdoms of the world will be divided against themselves [Bosnia]. Fewer and fewer will become the sympathetic cords which bind man in brotherhood to his fellow man. The natural egotism of the human heart will be worked upon by Satan. He will use the uncontrolled wills and violent passions which were never brought under the control of God's will.

"Every man's hand will be against his fellow man [every man for himself]. Brother will rise against brother, sister against sister, parents against children [Andrea Yates], and children against parents [the Menendez brothers]. All will be in confusion. Relatives will betray one another. There will be secret plotting to destroy life [the 9/11/2001 terrorist attacks]. Destruction, misery, and death will be seen on every hand" (*Selected Messages,* vol. 3, p. 418). I have given a few illustrations in brackets. The situation is much worse than a few illustrations can convey. During the Susan Smith trial (she drowned her two little boys) the Washington *Post* reported that for each of the past three years running, more than 2,000 children under the age of 5 were killed by their parents or guardians. Most were terribly abused before being killed!

As a reaction to the very obvious moral decay in society today, many people desire steps to be taken to "bring our nation back to God." "This very class [those who are sick and tired of the way things are going] put forth the claim that the fast-spreading corruption is largely attributable to the desecration of the so-called 'Christian sabbath,' and that the enforcement of Sunday observance would greatly improve the morals of society" (*The Great Controversy,* p. 587).

And just in case men have not thought of the moral corruption problem themselves, "Communications from the spirits will declare that God has sent them to convince the rejecters of Sunday of their error, affirming that the laws of the land should be obeyed as the law of God. They will lament the great wickedness in the world and second the testimony of religious teachers that the degraded state of morals is caused by the desecration of Sunday" (*The Great Controversy,* p. 591).

God's true followers will be blamed for the moral problems in society. "Those who honor the Bible Sabbath will be denounced as enemies of law and order, as breaking down the moral restraints of society, causing anarchy and corruption, and calling down the judgments of God upon the earth. Their conscientious scruples will be pronounced obstinacy, stubbornness, and contempt of authority" (*ibid.,* p. 592).

NUMBER 3

NATURAL DISASTERS

Who would argue against the increasing prevalence of natural disasters worldwide? Major volcanic eruptions, major earthquakes, devastating floods are an ever more common occurrence. The great tragedy of the December 26, 2004, great earthquake and resulting tsunami is etched in our minds. This tragedy cost the lives of nearly 300,000 people. It was one of the most deadly natural disasters in recent memory. Apparently the devil not only causes these disasters but he also blames them on those who keep God's Sabbath.

"Satan has control of all whom God does not especially guard . . . While appearing to the children of men as a great physician who can heal all their maladies, he will bring disease and disaster, until populous cities are reduced to ruin and desolation. Even now he is at work. In accidents and calamities by sea and by land, in great conflagrations, in fierce tornadoes, and terrific hailstorms, in tempests, floods, cyclones, tidal waves, and earthquakes, in every place and in a thousand forms, Satan is exercising his power. He sweeps away the ripening harvest, and famine and distress follow. He imparts to the air a deadly taint, and thousands perish by the pestilence. These visitations are to become more and more frequent and disastrous . . . And then the great deceiver will persuade men that those who serve God are causing these evils . . . It will be declared that men are offending God by the violation of the Sunday sabbath" (*The Great Controversy,* pp. 589, 590).

Many who are involved in the Sunday movement are convinced by Satan that they are doing God a service by establishing Sunday laws. "Satan puts his interpretation upon events, and they [leading men] think, as he would have them, that the calamities which fill the land are a result of Sunday-breaking. Thinking to appease the wrath of God, these influential men make laws enforcing Sunday observance. They think that by exalting this false rest-day higher, and still higher, compelling obedience to the Sunday law, the spurious sabbath, they are doing God service" (*Maranatha*, p. 176).

NUMBER 4

BRIBERY

The enforcement of Sunday worship by the state is directly contrary to the principles of our Constitution and religious liberty. And, since there is absolutely no scriptural support for Sunday exaltation, those who point out these major problems will be approached with bribes to comply. "The dignitaries of church and state will unite to bribe, persuade, or compel all classes to honor the Sunday. The lack of divine authority will be supplied by oppressive enactments. Political corruption is destroying love of justice and regard for truth; and even in free America, rulers and legislators, in order to secure public favor, will yield to the popular demand for a law enforcing Sunday observance" (*The Great Controversy*, p. 592).

In another statement Ellen White predicts, "As the movement for Sunday enforcement becomes more bold and decided, the law will be invoked against commandment keepers. They will be threatened with fines and imprisonment, and some will be offered positions of influence, and other rewards and advantages, as inducements to renounce their faith. But their steadfast answer is: 'Show us from the word of God our error.'. . . Those who are arraigned before the courts make a strong vindication of the truth, and some who hear them are led to take their stand to keep all the commandments of God. Thus the light will be brought before thousands [maybe on C-Span or courtroom TV coverage] who otherwise would know nothing of these truths" (*Maranatha*, p. 186). I must add here that once the Sunday agitation begins there is nothing we can do to stop it. The reason why we speak up is that those who are really open to following the Word of God will see the truth about the Sabbath.

NUMBER 5

APPEAL TO REASONING AND COMPROMISE

Since Sunday is "kept" by most Christians today it is the "logical" choice for a day of rest, worship, and family time. "We can't have two rest days," some say. "We must unite and work together to reverse the problems on society. Besides, aren't Christians supposed to be model citizens and uphold the law? How can you guys be right when the majority see things another way?" The real kicker is when the Sunday law is mixed with other good reforms such as temperance and morality. In fact, we can agree with most of what the Religious Right stands for. The problem is that they are preparing to "legislate" morality—which is contrary to scriptural principles. When this happened in the former Sunday law crisis, Ellen White counseled, <u>"The fact that a movement to establish error is connected with a work which is in itself good, is not an argument in favor of error.</u> We may disguise poison by mingling it with wholesome food, but we do not change its nature. On the contrary, it is rendered more dangerous, as it is more likely to be taken unawares. <u>It is one of Satan's devices to combine with falsehood just enough truth to give it plausibility. The leaders of the Sunday movement may advocate reforms which the people need, principles which are in harmony with the Bible; yet while there is with these a requirement which is contrary to God's law, His servants cannot unite with them.</u> Nothing can justify them in setting aside the commandments of God for the precepts of men" (*The Great Controversy,* pp. 587, 588).

Ellen White was given a vision of how ridicule and mockery would also be used to try to persuade God's people to conform to the Sunday law. "The time of trouble was upon us. I saw our people in great distress, weeping and praying, pleading the sure promises of God, while the wicked were all around us mocking us and threatening to destroy us. <u>They ridiculed our feebleness, they mocked at the smallness of our numbers,</u> and taunted us with words calculated to cut deep. They charged us with taking an independent position from all the rest of the world. They had cut off our resources so that we could not buy or sell, and they referred to our abject poverty and stricken condition. They could not see how we could live without the world. We were dependent on the world, and we must concede to the customs, practices, and laws of the world, or go out of it. If we were the only people in the world whom the Lord favored, the appearances were awfully against us" (*Selected Messages,* vol. 3, pp. 427, 428).

We are all under tremendous pressure to conform. We call it peer pressure. While most young people "know" that tobacco and drugs are bad for them and really don't want to spend the money and waste their lives, many get involved to be like their friends. Other young people drift into various kinds of sexual immorality because of the tremendous peer pressure.

This pressure to conform is evident in the Christian world as well. Many of us were startled by the January 1995 announcement by Joseph Tkach, Sr., the leader of the Worldwide Church of God, that "it was no longer mandatory to observe a seventh day sabbath, Old Testament Holy Days, or to tithe." *Christianity Today* welcomed the WCG into the mainstream of Protestantism, saying that the Protestant world applauded them for efforts to shift from Levitical legalism to evangelical orthodoxy. (See *Christianity Today,* April 24, 1995, p. 53, and July 17, 1995, p. 63.)

The *Adventist Review* (Jan. 16, 1996) in a follow-up report on this incident, commented that "Joseph Tkach, Sr., introduced doctrinal changes to bring the church more in line with the Protestant mainstream.

"The changes included dropping the Sabbath, observance of the annual feasts, and the distinction between clean and unclean meats. The WCG has declared the practices to be part of the old covenant and no longer obligatory for its members. As a result, nearly 50,000 members [out of a total of 100,000] and 500 pastors have left the denomination." As you can see there is tremendous pressure to conform.

NUMBER 6

MIRACLES AND MARIOLOGY

We are told that this will be one of the main avenues the devil uses to bolster support for the Sunday law.

Ellen White mentions that "Papists, who boast of miracles as a certain sign of the true church, will be readily deceived by this wonder-working power; and Protestants, having cast away the shield of truth, will also be deluded. Papists, Protestants, and worldlings will alike accept the form of godliness without the power, and they will see in this union a grand movement for the conversion of the world and the ushering in of the long-expected millennium" (*The Great Controversy,* pp. 588, 589). The most amazing fulfillment of this statement is that today Catholics believe that the miracles of God are happening now!

The late Malachi Martin, author of *Keys of This Blood,* wrote the foreword to *The Thunder of Justice,* a best-selling book in the Catholic bookstores. Here are his amazing words: "Only a very distracted and unaware Christian of today could have avoided receiving at least a fleeting impression . . . that for a number of years now there has been a steady build-up of events—in the broadest sense of that word—all of which indicate that <u>humanity as a whole and the Holy Roman Catholic Church in particular have reached a fateful threshold beyond which lies a new condition of human affairs.</u>

"Literally, every decade of this one century alone has piled one on the other, what Christ called 'the signs of the times.' (Matt. 16:1-4).

"In a general way of speaking, it is quasi-impossible to have totally escaped any awareness of these events, and the clamor of the claimant participants. Visions. Appearances. Messages. Predictions. Warnings. Interpretations. Weeping statues and bleeding icons. Miraculous spring waters. Spontaneous cures. Spinning dances of the sun, and eclipses of the moon. Little children telling the future. Uneducated men and women instructing popes and presidents. Nationwide publicity tours by bearers of special revelations. Throughout all of this, an obvious emphasis on the singular role of the Blessed Virgin Mary of Nazareth as the Queen of Heaven, Mother of All Living, and—not surprisingly—as the Mediatrix of All Graces is pervasive" (Malachi Martin, in the foreword to *The Thunder of Justice,* by Ted and Maureen Flynn).

What a list of <u>current</u> miracles and capped off by the exaltation of the virgin Mary. The whole of the 400-page book is devoted to the "Apparitions"—visits and messages—of the virgin Mary. And what is "Mary" saying? When "Our Lady appeared to a local farmer, Michael O'Donnell, she told him, '<u>preserve Sunday for prayer</u>'" (Flynn, *The Thunder of Justice,* p. 30).

This is even more significant with the growing acceptance of Mariology by many Protestants today. It's startlingly plain. It's a direct fulfillment of prophecy. Another indication that Sunday's coming!

NUMBER 7

MESSAGES FROM THE DEAD

As part of the continuing barrage of lying wonders Satan "will bring back the dead" in an attempt to seduce the faithful into dishonoring God and joining the Sunday movement. "Those who would stand in this time of peril must understand for themselves the testimony of the Scriptures. <u>Many will be confronted by the spirits of devils person-</u>

ating beloved relatives or friends and declaring the most dangerous heresies. These visitants will appeal to our tenderest sympathies and will work miracles to sustain their pretensions. We must be prepared to withstand them with the Bible truth that the dead know not anything and that they who thus appear are the spirits of devils" (*The Great Controversy,* pp. 559, 560). This statement doesn't mention what those who "return" say except that they declare "the most dangerous heresies." However, a few pages later we are told, "Through the two great errors [heresies], the immortality of the soul and Sunday sacredness, Satan will bring the people under his deceptions" (*ibid.,* p. 588).

Already the devil is preparing people to accept this dangerous deception of visits from the dead. *The Christian Ministry* magazine, published by the Christian Century Foundation, featured an article titled "Looking for Angels." In the article the author, a pastor, stated, "My advice is to keep a look out for angels, but not to be myopic [a narrow view of something]. Angels take many forms—the current interest is too focused on the two-winged, haloed sort. Here are some other places to look for them. [The author lists five places—only number four is relevant here.] . . . Fourth, look for angels in the form of loved ones who have died" (*The Christian Ministry,* May-June 1995, p. 9).

NUMBER 8

THE "RETURN OF THE APOSTLES"

The Scriptures are the primary source of support for God's people, giving the standard by which they live and determine truth. Naturally the devil works to undermine the Scriptures and therefore eliminate its defense against his heresies such as the Sunday law. "The apostles, as personated by these lying spirits, are made to contradict what they wrote at the dictation of the Holy Spirit when on earth. They deny the divine origin of the Bible, and thus tear away the foundation of the Christian's hope and put out the light that reveals the way to heaven. Satan is making the whole world believe that the Bible is a mere fiction, or at least a book suited to the infancy of the race, but now to be lightly regarded, or cast aside" (*The Great Controversy,* p. 557).

A similar statement in *Early Writings* gives an additional perspective. "He who is the father of lies, blinds and deceives the world by sending forth his angels to speak for the apostles, and to make it ap-

pear that they contradict what they wrote by the dictation of the Holy
Ghost when on earth. These lying angels make the apostles to corrupt
their own teachings and to declare them to be adulterated. By so doing,
Satan delights to throw professed Christians and all the world into uncertainty about the Word of God" (*Early Writings,* p. 264).

This revisionist view of the Bible is already current. Too many,
perhaps even some in our ranks, see the Bible as an archaic book, more
suited to, and shaped by, "the infancy of our race." What will be the
reaction from those who think this way when spirit visitants appear and
endorse their views?

NUMBER 9

EVIL ANGELS APPEAR AS GOOD ANGELS

In the increasing pressure to push acceptance of Sunday worship
the devil will send his angels to appear among men with the Sunday
message. "They [the wicked] declared that they had the truth, that
miracles were among them; that angels from heaven talked with
them and walked with them, that great power and signs and wonders
were performed among them, and that this was the temporal millennium they had been expecting so long. The whole world was converted and in harmony with the Sunday law, and this little feeble
people stood out in defiance of the laws of the land and the law of
God, and claimed to be the only ones right on the earth" (*Selected
Messages,* vol. 3, p. 428).

"The miracle-working power manifested through spiritualism will
exert its influence against those who choose to obey God rather than
men. Communications from the spirits [evil angels] will declare that
God has sent them to convince the rejecters of Sunday of their error,
affirming that the laws of the land should be obeyed as the law of God.
They will lament the great wickedness in the world and second the testimony of religious teachers that the degraded state of morals is caused
by the desecration of Sunday. Great will be the indignation excited
against all who refuse to accept their testimony" (*Maranatha,* p. 167).

Even the devil when he finally personates Christ "declares that
those who persist in keeping holy the seventh day are blaspheming his
name by refusing to listen to his angels sent to them with light and
truth" (*The Great Controversy,* p. 624).

NUMBER 10

THE ALMOST OVERMASTERING DELUSION

So far we have looked at nine aspects that put pressure on God's people to accept the Sunday law. Now Satan himself gets into the act by trying to make it appear that he is Christ—come again. Ellen White calls this the "strong, almost overmastering delusion."

"As the crowning act in the great drama of deception, Satan himself will personate Christ. The church has long professed to look to the Saviour's advent as the consummation of her hopes. Now the great deceiver will make it appear that Christ has come. In different parts of the earth, Satan will manifest himself among men as a majestic being of dazzling brightness, resembling the description of the Son of God given by John in the Revelation. Revelation 1:13-15. The glory that surrounds him is unsurpassed by anything that mortal eyes have yet beheld. The shout of triumph rings out upon the air: 'Christ has come! Christ has come!' The people prostrate themselves in adoration before him, while he lifts up his hands and pronounces a blessing upon them, as Christ blessed His disciples when He was upon the earth. His voice is soft and subdued, yet full of melody. In gentle, compassionate tones he presents some of the same gracious, heavenly truths which the Saviour uttered; he heals the diseases of the people, and then, in his assumed character of Christ, he claims to have changed the Sabbath to Sunday, and commands all to hallow the day which he has blessed. He declares that those who persist in keeping holy the seventh day are blaspheming his name by refusing to listen to his angels sent to them with light and truth. This is the strong, almost overmastering delusion" (*The Great Controversy,* p. 624).

And so he will look like Jesus, sound like Jesus, dress like Jesus, act like Jesus, and to most of the world he will be Jesus. How will the faithful ones realize that it isn't Jesus? There are only two ways.

The first identifying factor is the manner of his coming. The Bible says, "For as the lightning comes from the east and flashes to the west, so also will the coming of the Son of Man be" and "Behold He is coming with clouds, and every eye will see Him" (Matthew 24:27; Revelation 1:7). Ellen White adds, "This coming there is no possibility of counterfeiting. It will be universally known—witnessed by the whole world" (*ibid.,* p. 625). The second element to enable identification of the counterfeit is the sure Word of God. "Only those who have been diligent students of the Scriptures and who have received the love of the truth will be shielded from the powerful delusion that takes the world captive. <u>By the Bible testimony these will detect the deceiver in his disguise</u>" (*ibid., p.* 625).

Do we know and love the Bible so well that we will be able to trust it over our senses? Have we been too busy with life's burdens to take time to study and memorize Scripture? God's Messenger to the Remnant asks, "Are the people of God now so firmly established upon His word that they would not yield to the evidence of their senses? Would they, in such a crisis, cling to the Bible and the Bible only?" She warns, "Satan will, if possible, prevent them [God's people] from obtaining a preparation to stand in that day. He will so arrange affairs as to hedge up their way, entangle them with earthly treasures, cause them to carry a heavy, wearisome burden, that their hearts may be overcharged with the cares of this life and the day of trial may come upon them as a thief" (*ibid.,* pp. 625, 626).

After digesting the startling information presented so far, maybe you are beginning to see that things are in place for the very final events. My purpose is not to alarm you, but rather to help you prepare for the challenge ahead. Spiritual things are of the utmost importance—eternal life or death is the real issue here. We need to know what we may expect in the weeks and months ahead and realize that we have been told these things before they happen. We each need to be spiritually secure and prepared to remain faithful.

In one long sentence we read the final scenario. "When Protestantism shall stretch her hand across the gulf to grasp the hand of the Roman power, when she shall reach over the abyss to clasp hands with spiritualism, when, under the influence of this threefold union, our country shall repudiate every principle of its Constitution as a Protestant and republican government, and shall make provision for the propagation of papal falsehoods and delusions, <u>then we may know that the time has come for the marvelous working of Satan</u> [his personation of Christ discussed above] <u>and that the end is near</u>" (*Maranatha,* p. 190).

What an exciting time to be alive.

---

[1] Section 55 in volume 3 of *Selected Messages* contains 50 pages of very timely counsel. I would highly recommend the entire section. The chapter titles are: "Lessons

From Meeting the Sunday Law Crisis of the Late 1880's and Early 1890's"; "As We Near the End"; and "The Last Great Struggle." The trustees of the White Estate give a short introduction to this section in which they state: "Agitation for Sunday legislation gradually waned, but in succeeding years Ellen White kept the issues of the final conflict before church leaders. Times might have changed, so far as actual persecution for Sabbath observance was concerned, but the issues and the principles involved remained the same. Since Ellen White's death further changes have taken place, but we believe that the same principles and the same issues will be revived in the coming conflict, present appearances to the contrary not withstanding" (*Selected Messages,* vol. 3, p. 381).

[2] In *Even at the Door* I dedicated an entire chapter "Economic Armageddon" to this topic.

CHAPTER 13

Standing Firm Through Persecution

One cannot study the topic of end times and Sunday laws without discovering that difficult times are just ahead. A few biblical examples include Daniel 12:1: "At that time Michael shall stand up . . . and there shall be a time of trouble, such as never was since there was a nation, even to that time. And at that time your people shall be delivered, every one who is found written in the book." Another is Matthew 24:9-13: "Then they will deliver you up to tribulation and kill you, and you will be hated by all nations for My name's sake. And then many will be offended, will betray one another, and will hate one another. Then many false prophets will rise up and deceive many. And because lawlessness will abound, the love of many will grow cold. But he who endures to the end shall be saved." Matthew 5:11, 12 gives another insight: "Blessed are you when they revile and persecute you, and say all kinds of evil against you falsely for My sake. Rejoice and be exceedingly glad, for great is your reward in heaven, for so they persecuted the prophets who were before you." Revelation 2:10 encourages us, "Do not fear any of those things which you are about to suffer. Indeed, the devil is about to throw some of you into prison, that you may be tested, and you will have tribulation ten days. Be faithful until death, and I will give you the crown of life."

It is interesting to note that each of these verses has two parts: The prediction by God that persecution would come and then the promise of God's care for the faithful ones.

As He looked to the future and saw that His beloved disciples would suffer trials and persecution, Jesus said, "Remember the word that I said to you, 'A servant is not greater than his master.' If they persecuted Me, they will also persecute you" (John 15:20). Jesus suffered terribly at the hands of His creatures. So when we suffer we are in excellent company because Jesus suffered for us. This may be one of the reasons that we are counseled to study the life of Christ, especially the closing scenes of His life. "There was never one who walked among men more cruelly slandered than the Son of man. He was derided and mocked because of His unswerving obedience to the principles of God's holy law. They hated Him without a cause. Yet He stood calmly before His enemies, declaring that reproach is a part of the Christian's legacy, counseling His followers how to meet the arrows of malice, bidding them not to faint under persecution" (*Sons and Daughters of God,* p. 308).

CHRISTIAN AGAINST CHRISTIAN

To one not familiar with the issues in the great controversy it would seem reasonable that the persecution of God's faithful would come from the lower element—the real wicked—the hoodlums, criminals, gangs, drug dealers, and the mafia. But as history records in the past, the Bible predicts that the most severe persecution will come from other "Christians." "Christ forewarned His disciples of this, saying: 'These things have I spoken unto you, that ye should not be offended. They shall put you out of the synagogues; yea, the time cometh, that whosoever killeth you will think that he doeth God service. And these things will they do unto you, because they have not known the Father, nor Me. But these things I have told you, that when the time shall come, ye may remember that I told you of them.'[John 16:1-5] It is not the world, who make no profession, from whom the persecution comes. It is those who profess to be doing God service who manifest the most bitter hatred" (Ellen White, *Signs of the Times,* September 2, 1897).

The persecution predicted in the Bible and the Spirit of Prophecy is far more than just stress and anxiety. In some cases there will be torture and death. "As the defenders of truth refuse to honor the Sunday-sabbath, some of them will be thrust into prison, some will be exiled, some will be treated as slaves. To human wisdom all this now seems impossible; but as the restraining Spirit of God shall be withdrawn from men, and they shall be under the control of Satan, who hates the divine precepts, there will be strange developments. The heart can be very cruel when God's fear and love are removed" (*The Great Controversy,* p. 608).

The primary reason persecution will come is that God's faithful people will not conform to the command to violate the Sabbath of the Bible. "The time is coming when God's people will feel the hand of persecution because they keep holy the seventh day. . . . But God's people are to stand firm for Him. And the Lord will work in their behalf, showing plainly that He is the God of gods" (*Christian Service,* p. 156). We can see that this time is not far away when we consider the evidence of cooperation between the United States and the Vatican that has been given in this book. And we know that "When the churches of our land, uniting upon such points of faith as are held by them in common, shall influence the State to enforce their decrees and sustain their institutions, then will Protestant America have formed an image of the Roman hierarchy. <u>Then the true church will be assailed by persecution, as were God's ancient people</u>" (*The Spirit of Prophecy,* vol. 4, p. 278).

We are also told that this time of trouble will not last for a long time. "We are standing on the threshold of great and solemn events. Prophecies are fulfilling. <u>The last great conflict will be short, but terrible. . . . How long will it last? Only a little while</u>" (*Selected Messages,* vol. 3, p. 419).

WHY GOD ALLOWS PERSECUTION

A number of reasons could be cited for seeing the good side of persecution. It is actually turned back on the devil because of the positive effect it has on those who receive it and those who witness it. Note the following positive results.

Character building. "God, in His great love, is seeking to develop in us the precious graces of His Spirit. He permits us to encounter obstacles, persecution, and hardships, not as a curse, but as the greatest blessing of our lives. Every temptation resisted, every trial bravely borne, gives us a new experience, and advances us in the work of character building" (*Colporteur Ministry,* p. 67).

A witness to the world. "On every occasion when persecution takes place, those who witness it make decisions either for Christ or against Him" (*The Desire of Ages,* p. 630). As the movement for Sunday enforcement moves forward some will be arrested and brought before courts. "<u>Those who are arraigned before the courts make a strong vindication of the truth, and some who hear them are led to take their stand to keep all the commandments of God.</u> Thus light will be brought before thousands who otherwise would know nothing of these truths" (*The Great Controversy,* p. 607). Recent televised trials have gripped the attention of millions. When God's faithful are dragged into court it may result in far more free air time for God!

To reveal God's grace. "Through trial and persecution the glory—the character—of God is revealed in His chosen ones" (*God's Amazing Grace,* p. 280). It must have been very clear to onlookers that God was with the martyrs who were tortured and killed. Many, instead of cursing or screaming, prayed or sang as they died. "These examples of human steadfastness bear witness to the faithfulness of God's promises—of His abiding presence and sustaining grace" (*Reflecting Christ,* p. 357). Why would God allow aged, faithful Daniel to be thrown to the lions? Apparently, as a testimony to God's protection and sustaining grace.

To put us in a place of service or blessing. "By permitting John to be banished to the Isle of Patmos, Christ placed His disciple in a position where he could receive the most precious truth for the enlightenment of the churches. . . . The persecution of John's enemies became a means of grace. . . . Never had he learned so much of Jesus. Never had he heard such exalted truth" (*Our High Calling,* p. 315).

To spread the gospel. People have a tendency to gather around institutions in colonies. But "the Lord desires that His people shall be dispersed throughout the earth. They are not to colonize. Jesus said, 'Go ye into all the world, and preach the gospel to every creature.' Mark 16:15. When the disciples followed their inclination to remain in large numbers in Jerusalem, persecution was permitted to come upon them, and they were scattered to all parts of the inhabited world" (*Testimonies for the Church,* vol. 8, p. 215).

One of the most interesting statements I have found on this topic paints a very graphic picture of the great divide between the saved and the lost. "As trials thicken around us, both separation and unity will be seen in our ranks. Some who are now ready to take up weapons of warfare will in times of real peril make it manifest that they have not built upon the solid rock; they will yield to temptation. Those who have had great light and precious privileges, but have not improved them, will, under one pretext or another, go out from us. Not having received the love of the truth, they will be taken in the delusions of the enemy; they will give heed to seducing spirits and doctrines of devils, and will depart from the faith. But, on the other hand, when the storm of persecution really breaks upon us, the true sheep will hear the true Shepherd's voice. Self-denying efforts will be put forth to save the lost, and **many**

who have strayed from the fold will come back to follow the great Shepherd. The people of God will draw together and present to the enemy a united front. In view of the common peril, strife for supremacy will cease; there will be no disputing as to who shall be accounted greatest" (*Maranatha,* p. 202).

In a very vivid picture Ellen White described the separation that persecution will bring. "When the testing time shall come, those who have made God's word their rule of life will be revealed. In summer there is no noticeable difference between evergreens and other trees; but when the blasts of winter come, the evergreens remain unchanged, while other trees are stripped of their foliage. So the falsehearted professor may not now be distinguished from the real Christian, but the time is just upon us when the difference will be apparent. Let opposition arise, let bigotry and intolerance again bear sway, let persecution be kindled, and the half-hearted and hypocritical will waver and yield the faith; but the true Christian will stand firm as a rock, his faith stronger, his hope brighter, than in days of prosperity" (*The Great Controversy,* p. 602).

PREPARATION FOR PERSECUTION

Only the power of God will guide us through the trials ahead. Yet we can prepare by following His counsel to us. I have found a number of points we are encouraged to pay attention to.

Study God's Word. The Bible contains so many promises that should be committed to memory and claimed personally. My favorites are in the Psalms, Isaiah, the Gospels, and Philippians. Also Chapter 37 of *The Great Controversy,* "The Scriptures a Safeguard," gives good counsel. Two short statements there tell a lot. "None but those who have fortified the mind with the truths of the Bible will stand through the last great conflict" (p. 593). "It is the first and highest duty of every rational being to learn from the Scriptures what is truth, and then to walk in the light and encourage others to follow his example" (p. 598).

Spend time with God in prayer. Regular communion with God will enable one to maintain a relationship with Him. The chapter on prayer in *Steps to Christ* is very helpful. "What was the strength of those who in the past have suffered persecution for Christ's sake? It was union with God, union with the Holy Spirit, union with Christ. It is this fellowship with the Saviour that will enable God's people to endure to the end" (*The Faith I Live By,* p. 330).

Make friends with others. We need to get to know our neighbors and those of influence in our communities. This will help them to realize that we are sincere and honest people and not members of a cult or some wild-eyed kooks. It is also the best, grassroots way to witness to them. The counsel is: "As they approach the time of trouble, the followers of Christ should make every exertion to place themselves in a proper light before the people, to disarm prejudice, and to avert the danger which threatens liberty of conscience" (*The Great Controversy,* p. 616).

Learn the principles of health and how to help the sick. "As religious aggression subverts the liberties of our nation, those who would stand for freedom of conscience will be placed in unfavorable positions. For their own sake they should, while they have opportunity, become intelligent in regard to disease, its causes, prevention, and cure. And those who do this will find a field of labor anywhere. There will be suffering ones, plenty of them, who will need help, not only among those of our own faith, but largely among those who know not the truth" (*Medical Ministry,* p. 321).

Develop unity and fellowship with fellow believers. Hebrews 10:25 counsels us to get together more often and exhort one another as we see the day approaching. Over and over we are told to "press together." One of the characteristics of Christ's disciples after He returned to heaven was how they loved one another.

Learn to be self-sufficient. It was reported in the Washington *Post* recently that more than 95 percent of Americans subsist entirely on food from the store. Our counsel is to become more independent. "Privation may be the lot of every soul who now believes and obeys the truth. Christ has told us that we will have reproach. If persecution for the truth's sake is to come, it is important that every line of work become familiar to us, that we and our families may not suffer through lack of knowledge. We can and should have tact and knowledge in trades, in building, in planting, and in sowing. A knowledge of how to cultivate the land will make rough places much smoother. This knowledge will be counted a great blessing, even by our enemies" (*Manuscript Releases,* vol. 19, p. 26).

Get out of the cities. We have had this counsel for many years. It is no mystery to us now why this counsel was given. We can see the crime, overcrowding, violence, sickness, poverty, noise, and stress of city living. Read through the little booklet *Country Living* for more pertinent information on this topic.

GOD'S PROMISED PROTECTION

We can bank on the fact that God loves us, and that no matter what, He will be with us and see us through to the kingdom of glory. The stories of the Bible show us that God doesn't need a large army to win a battle. In fact He doesn't need an army at all. Remember that one angel destroyed Sennacherib's army and one angel scattered the soldiers guarding the grave of Jesus. Re-read the stories of Gideon, Jonathan, Elijah, and Elisha. God has given us the promises in His Word to be claimed. One such promise is Isaiah 41:10: "Fear thou not; for I am with thee: be not dismayed; for I am thy God: I will strengthen thee; yea, I will help thee; yea, I will uphold thee with the right hand of my righteousness."

We don't need to worry about the future, because God has promised to be with us. "The prospect of being brought into personal danger and distress, need not cause despondency, but should quicken the vigor and hopes of God's people; for the time of their peril is the season for God to grant them clearer manifestations of His power" (*Maranatha*, p. 194). "God's people are not to fear. Satan cannot go beyond his limit. The Lord will be the defense of His people" (*ibid.,* p. 191).

THE ABOMINATION OF DESOLATION

This unusual term is mentioned in Daniel 12 and Matthew 24. In her comments on these verses, Ellen White reports, "The time is not far distant, when, like the early disciples, we shall be forced to seek a refuge in desolate and solitary places. As the siege of Jerusalem by the Roman armies was the signal for flight to the Judean Christians, so the assumption of power on the part of our nation [the United States] in the decree enforcing the papal sabbath will be a warning to us. It will then be time to leave the large cities, preparatory to leaving the smaller ones for retired homes in secluded places among the mountains" (*ibid.,* p. 180).

God in His infinite wisdom will allow some to be laid to rest before the persecution comes so they won't have to bear it. "The Lord 'doth not afflict willingly nor grieve the children of men.' Lam. 3:33. 'Like as a father pitieth his children, so the Lord pitieth them that fear Him. For He knoweth our frame; He remembereth that we are dust.' Ps. 103:13, 14. He knows our heart, for He reads every secret of the soul. He knows whether or not those for whom petitions are offered would be able to endure the trial and test that would come upon them if they lived. He knows the end from the beginning. <u>Many will be laid away to sleep before the fiery ordeal of the time of trouble shall come upon our world.</u> This is another reason why we should say after our earnest petition: 'Nevertheless not my will, but Thine, be done.' Luke 22:42. Such a petition will never be registered in heaven as a faithless prayer" (*Counsels on Health,* p. 375).

"If God is for us, who can be against us?

"He who did not spare His own Son, but delivered Him up for us all, how shall He not with Him also freely give us all things?

"Who shall bring a charge against God's elect? It is God who justifies.

"Who is he who condemns? It is Christ who died, and furthermore is also risen, who is even at the right hand of God, who also makes intercession for us.

"Who shall separate us from the love of Christ? Shall tribulation, or distress, or persecution, or famine, or nakedness, or peril, or sword?

"As it is written: 'For Your sake we are killed all day long; we are accounted as sheep for the slaughter.'

"Yet in all these things we are more than conquerors through Him who loved us.

"For I am persuaded that neither death nor life, nor angels nor principalities nor powers, nor things present nor things to come, nor height nor depth, nor any other created thing, shall be able to separate us from the love of God which is in Christ Jesus our Lord" (Romans 8:31-39).

CHAPTER 14

The Great Detour

In just two lifetimes from the fall of man in the Garden of Eden (Adam was a contemporary of Methuselah, who died the year the flood came, for 243 years), men became so wicked that God had to destroy the world with a flood. The record states, "Then the Lord saw that the wickedness of man was great in the earth, and that every intent of the thoughts of his heart was only evil continually. . . . So the Lord said, 'I will destroy man whom I have created from the face of the earth, both man and beast, creeping thing and birds of the air, for I am sorry that I have made them. . . . The earth also was corrupt before God, and the earth was filled with violence" (Genesis 6:5-11). So God started all over with Noah and his family. The Bible describes Noah as "a just man, perfect in his generations. Noah walked with God" (Genesis 6:9).

Despite clear directions from God's Word, man keeps wanting to go his own way and do his own thing. Some time after the Flood the descendants of Noah decided to build a city with a tower so tall that it would reach to the heavens. Perhaps they were trying to be able to escape any future judgments of God. But God came down and halted construction by confusing their language, and the people scattered all over the earth. Many Bible scholars believe that this scattering of the family and language lines was the beginning of the various language and ethnic groups that we have today.

A LOST GENERATION

The descendants of Jacob—called "Israel" by God and "Israelites" by historians—left Egypt at the time of the Exodus. They passed through the Red Sea, probably at the northern end of the Gulf of Suez, and then went to Mount Sinai, where they received the Law from God and built the portable tabernacle. While Moses was in the mountain receiving the Ten Commandments from God the people came to Aaron and asked him to make them a god that they could see and worship.

Aaron made them a golden calf and set up an alter before it for worship. The context makes it clear that this image was not to represent a foreign god, but Yahweh, the God of the Hebrews (see Exodus 32:5). The children of Israel were consequently rebuked and punished, not for replacing their God with another, but for making an idol, thus placing their God side by side with the gods of other nations.

After almost a year near Mount Sinai, they were to move into the promised Canaan—and occupy it (see Numbers 10:11, 12; 13:1-3). Unfortunately, right on the borders of Canaan they rebelled against God after hearing the report of the 12 spies who had been sent ahead to check out the land. This uprising at Kadesh-barnea compelled God to change the program, so that the nation spent 38 more years in the desert (Deuteronomy 2:4) until the entire rebellious generation had died. Only the two faithful spies, Caleb and Joshua, survived the wilderness wandering.

SHOWDOWN ON MOUNT CARMEL

Fifty years after the heyday of Israel under kings David and Solomon God's people fell into a state of deep apostasy. King Ahab of the northern kingdom married a Phoenician girl named Jezebel. To put it mildly, she was a very bad influence on Ahab and the nation of Israel. The Bible reports, "Now Ahab the son of Omri did evil in the sight of the Lord, more than all who were before him" (1 Kings 16:30). It was a very low point in Israel's history. It was because of this condition that God called Elijah as His prophet to deal with this sad state of affairs. It was time for a showdown between God and Baal.

And so following directions from God, Elijah marched right into the presence of the king and announced, "As the Lord God of Israel lives, before whom I stand, there shall not be dew nor rain these years, except at my word" (1 Kings 17:1). And as abruptly as he had entered, Elijah turned on his heels and left. He was not seen or heard for three years; though Ahab's servants searched diligently for him.

The drought on the northern kingdom was severe. Conditions were terrible —crop failures, dust storms, lakes and rivers dried up. Things became so desperate that the king himself went out looking for some place to water the royal horses to keep them from dying. Then God came to Elijah and said, "Go, present yourself to Ahab, and I will send rain on the earth" (1 Kings 18:1). And so Elijah came out of hiding and came to see the king. The Bible records their meeting after three and a half years of drought. "Then it happened, when Ahab saw Elijah, that Ahab said to him, 'Is that you, O troubler of Israel?' And he answered, 'I have not troubled Israel, but you and your father's house have, in that you have forsaken the commandments of the Lord, and you have followed the Baals. Now therefore, send and gather all Israel to me on Mount Carmel, the four hundred and fifty prophets of Baal, and the four hundred prophets of Asherah, who eat at Jezebel's table'" (1 Kings 18:17-19).

Israel had fallen so low that they were worshiping false gods and bowing down to idols! As stated in the passage above, their ratio of false prophets to good was 850 to 1 on Mount Carmel. When the people, along with the king and the false prophets, assembled on the mountain Elijah challenged them, "'How long will you falter between two opinions? If the Lord is God, follow Him; but if Baal, then follow him.' But the people answered him not a word" (verse 21).

Elijah proposed that both he and the prophets of Baal, who were 450 strong, each prepare for a burnt offering, but that neither would put a fire under the wood. Then, he said, whichever god was the true God would send fire from heaven to burn the sacrifice. Immediately the people said, "It is well spoken,"—or as we would say—"That's a good idea." Since the people agreed, the prophets of Baal had no choice but to proceed.

You might remember the story of how the prophets of Baal jumped, danced, and shouted all day long around their altar—from morning, through noon, and on to the time of the evening sacrifice—and no fire came. The Bible says, "But there was no voice; no one answered, no one paid attention" (verse 29).

Then it was Elijah's turn. He called the people to come near. He repaired the broken-down altar of the Lord by using 12 large stones—one for each of the twelve sons of Jacob. He instructed the people to dig a trench around the altar and to lay the wood and the sacrifice on it. Then he said to the people, "Bring four barrels of water and pour it on the sacrifice and the wood." When they had done this, he said, "Do it a second time," and they did. Then he asked them to do it a third time, and they did. Twelve barrels of water were poured on the sacrifice and the wood. The water even filled the trench around the altar. Everything was soaked! Elijah wanted the people to know that the fire came from God.

Elijah knew a truth that we all need to know, and it is an awesome fact. God can light wet wood! We may feel that we have to have everything just right in order for God to work. But God doesn't need newspaper and dry kindling. God is not limited to the person who can speak the best, or say things in just the right way. God just tells us that He can ignite wet wood. And when we are ready, He will light the fire. Do circumstances seem formidable where you are? That's no problem with God. No situation is too difficult for Him!

Then, since it was the time for the evening sacrifice, Elijah knelt down and prayed a simple prayer. There was no jumping, shouting, or dancing. His prayer was only 63 well-chosen words. "Lord God of Abraham, Isaac, and Israel, let it be known this day that You are God in Israel, and that I am Your servant, and that I have done all these things at Your word. Hear me, O Lord, hear me, that this people may know that You are the Lord God, and that You have turned their hearts back to You again" (verses 36, 37). As soon as his prayer ended, "Then the fire of the Lord fell and consumed the burnt sacrifice, and the wood and the stones and the dust, and it licked up the water that was in the trench" (verse 38). When the people saw this they spontaneously fell on their faces and said, "The Lord, He is God! The Lord, He is God!"

Elijah instructed the people to take the prophets of Baal and execute them all. Then following Elijah's fervent prayer, there was a heavy rain. Later in his prophetic ministry Elijah was taken to heaven in a chariot of fire (see 2 Kings 2:11, 12). I have mentioned this story in some detail because the Bible indicates that Elijah would return before the coming of Christ. "Behold, I will send you Elijah the prophet before the coming of the great and dreadful day of the Lord. And he will turn the hearts of the fathers to the children, and the hearts of the children to their fathers, lest I come and strike the earth with a curse" (Malachi 4:5, 6).

Apparently, this prophecy has been partially fulfilled in the person of John the Baptist at the time of Christ's first advent and will be fulfilled in greater fullness "before the coming of the great and dreadful day of the Lord." As Christians we do not believe that the literal "Elijah" will return to the earth just before the Second Coming. But like John the Baptist, those who herald the soon coming of Christ will come in "the spirit and power of Elijah" with a message of repentance, revival, and reformation. When the angel Gabriel came to Zacharias and announced that he would have a son whose name should be called John, he also told him what John's work would be. "And he will turn many of the children of Israel to the Lord their God. He will also go before Him [Jesus] in the spirit and power of Elijah, 'to turn the hearts of the fathers to the children,' and the disobedient to the wisdom of the just, to make ready a people prepared for the Lord" (Luke 1:16, 17). John would not actually be Elijah (John 1:21) but he would come in the spirit and power of Elijah and do the work predicted in Malachi 4:5, 6. So, likewise, we should not expect a literal return of the prophet Elijah in connection with the Second Coming, but rather a message of repentance to make ready a people for the coming of the Lord. And just like on Mount Carmel, it will be a message to those who "have forsaken the commandments of the Lord" (1 Kings 18:18).

Those who are familiar with the history of God's chosen people in the Old Testament times well know that their spiritual relation with God was an up and down experience—being down more than up. Things got so bad that when Jesus came the first time the religious leaders of the day were instrumental in killing Him on the cross. But what about the church established by Christ? Have we fared any better in the Christian era? Again, history reveals a gradual drifting away from the teachings of Jesus and the inspired Word of God.

THE GREAT APOSTASY OF THE CHURCH

That there would be an apostasy in the Christian church should not be a surprise to anyone. John, Paul, and Jesus Himself predicted it. During His last major conversation with His disciples in a private meeting Jesus warned them of the coming deception. "'Take heed that no one deceives you,'" He said, "'for false christs and false prophets will arise and show great signs and wonders, so as to deceive, if possible, even the elect'" (Matthew 24:4, 24). His followers would experience a period of "great tribulation," but they would survive (Matthew 24:21, 22). Impressive signs would mark the end of this persecution and would reveal the nearness of Christ's return (Matthew 24:29, 32, 33).

Paul also warned: "'After my departure, savage wolves will come in among you, not sparing the flock. Also from among yourselves men will rise up, speaking perverse things, to draw away the disciples after themselves.'" (Acts 20:29, 30). These "wolves" would lead the church into apostasy or a "falling away."

Paul said that this apostasy would occur before Christ's return. It was such a certainty that the fact that it had not yet taken place was a sure sign that Christ's coming was not yet imminent. "Let no one deceive you," he wrote, "for that Day will not come unless the falling away comes first, and the man of sin [also called the lawless one] is revealed, the son of perdition, who opposes and exalts himself above all that is called God or that is worshiped, so that he sits as God in the temple [church] of God, showing himself that he is God" (2 Thessalonians 2:3, 4).

Actually, this apostasy had already begun in Paul's day. The methods of the "man of sin" were satanic, "with all power, signs, and lying wonders, and with all unrighteous deception" (2 Thessalonians 2:9, 10). And before the end of the first century John stated that "many false prophets have gone out into the world." Indeed, he said, "the spirit of the Antichrist" is "already in the world" (1 John 4:1, 3).

THE RISE OF THE MAN OF SIN

As the early church left its "first love" experience (Revelation 2:4), it compromised its purity of doctrine. Its high standards of personal conduct, and the invisible bond of unity provided by the Holy Spirit were also compromised. Worship became more formal, and leaders were chosen based on personality and popularity rather than orthodoxy of belief. Over time leaders were attempting to extend their authority over neighboring churches.

The Holy Spirit's guidance of the local church was replaced by authoritarianism at the hands of a single official, the bishop, to whom every church member was personally subject and through whom alone he had access to salvation. Church leaders became concerned with ruling the church rather than serving it. Gradually the concept of a priestly hierarchy developed that placed itself between the individual and his Lord.

As the importance of the individual and the local church declined, the bishop of Rome emerged as the supreme power in Christianity. With help from the civil government and the emperor, the bishop of Rome became known as the pope and was recognized as the visible head of the universal church. This gave him supreme power and authority over all church leaders throughout the world.

Under the leadership of the papacy—the little horn power of Daniel 7—the Christian church fell into even deeper apostasy. As the church became more popular it fell even further from its original simplicity and faith. Standards were lowered to the point that even the unconverted felt comfortable in the church. Many people who knew little about genuine Christianity joined the church in name only. They brought with them, reminiscent of the days of Jezebel, their pagan doctrines, idols, styles of worship, festivals, feasts, and various symbols.

Many Bible students believe that this compromise between Christianity and paganism led to the formation of what Paul called "the man of sin." The church became a mammoth system of false religion with a mixture of truth and error. And so the prediction of 2 Thessalonians 2 does not condemn individuals, but exposes the religious system that is responsible for the great apostasy. Many of the individual members within the system are part of God's universal church because they are living according to all the light they have.

Since the Roman bishop came to power with the aid of the civil government the ties between church and state continued to grow until they were united in an unholy alliance. For example, in 533 A.D. in a letter incorporated into the Code of Justinian, the emperor Justinian declared the bishop of Rome head over all the churches. Accordingly, when Justinian's general Belisarious liberated Rome in 538 A.D., the bishop of Rome was freed from the control of the Ostrogoths, whose Arianism had resulted in their restricting the developing Catholic Church. Now the bishop of Rome could exercise the powers that Justinian's earlier decree had granted him. He could increase the authority of the "Holy See." And so began the 1260 years of persecution by the church that the Bible had predicted (Daniel 7:25; Revelation 12:6, 14; 13:5-7).

Soon the church, with the assistance of the state, tried to force its decrees and teachings on all Christians. Many people surrendered their beliefs rather than suffer persecution, while those who were faithful to the Bible teachings were subjected to severe persecution. The Christian world became a great battlefield. Many were imprisoned or executed in the name of God! Historians now know that during the 1260-year persecution millions of faithful believers experienced great suffering, while many paid for their loyalty to Christ with their lives. Pope John Paul II acknowledged that the church was responsible for such persecution in the Middle Ages, and he appointed a committee to look into the matter so that apologies could be made "as we enter into the new millennium." I speak here of the atrocities of the Inquisition.

Every drop of innocent blood that was spilled in the name of Christianity put a stain on the name of God and Jesus Christ. Probably nothing has done more harm to the cause of Christianity than this ruthless persecution. This activity of the church grossly distorted how the character of God is viewed by Christians and non-Christians alike, and the false doctrines of purgatory and eternal torment led many to reject Christianity altogether.

Voices within the Catholic Church protested its merciless killing of opponents, its arrogant claims and demoralizing corruption. The church was unwilling to reform, and this led to the Protestant Reformation in the sixteenth century. The success of Protestantism was a great blow to the authority and prestige of the church of Rome. The church launched a counter reformation to crush the Reformation, but it gradually lost the battle against those who were striving for civil and religious freedom.

Then finally, just as the Bible predicted in Revelation 13:3, the Roman Catholic Church received a deadly blow. The French revolutionary government saw the Roman religion as an enemy of the Republic and directed Napoleon to take the pope prisoner. At Napoleon's orders General Berthier entered Rome and proclaimed the political rule of the papacy at an end. He took the pope captive and carried him off to France, where he died in exile. This event that occurred in 1798 marked the end of the 1260 years of papal domination that was predicted in Daniel 7:25 and Revelation 13:5.

A LEGACY OF ERRORS

Unfortunately, during this long period of spiritual decline a number of unscriptural teachings came into the church. Satan, using a most subtle technique, gradually brought in such things as prayers for the dead, the change of the Sabbath from the seventh to the first day of the week, the worship of Mary, the doctrine of purgatory, the institution of the papacy, and the worship of the cross and of images and relics. Other false practices and beliefs followed: the use of Holy water, canonization of dead saints, fasting on Fridays, the Mass, the establishment of the priesthood, the celibacy of the priests, the rosary, the sale of indulgences, the dogma of transubstantiation, confession of sins to the priest, the elevation of tradition to equal authority with the Bible, papal infallibility, the immaculate conception and bodily assumption of Mary, and much more.

But just as the Bible predicted a falling away from biblical truth as we have noted above, it also predicted a reformation—a return to the basics of Christianity. "Those from among you shall build the old waste places; you shall raise up the foundations of many generations; and you shall be called the Repairer of the Breach, the Restorer of Streets to Dwell In" (Isaiah 58:12). In the providence of God, many who find themselves on the long detour away from biblical orthodoxy are turning around and beginning the road back home. Thousands upon thousands of men, women, and young people are being led by the Spirit of God to study for themselves the Word of God and are taking steps to return to the God of Abraham, Isaac, and Jacob—the Christ of the early church.

CHAPTER 15

The Road Back

For centuries the teachings of the Christian church were a mixture of Scripture and tradition. But in God's providence the time came to give Scripture its rightful place and to make the Bible available to the people. The Protestant Reformation began the long road back to biblical fidelity. Many who were studying the Bible for the first time longed to learn the true biblical faith. Others stuck with tradition, too apathetic to change.

In the fourteenth century John Wycliffe called for a reformation of the church, not just in England but in the entire Christian world. At that time the Bible was not readily available to the common man. Wycliffe provided the first translation of the entire Bible into English. He is now called the morning star of the Reformation because his teachings of salvation through faith in Christ alone and that the Scriptures alone were to be the source of Christian faith and practice laid the foundation for the great Protestant Reformation. His teachings had a major influence on other Reformers such as Huss, Jerome, and Luther.

God used Martin Luther in Germany to further this change. As a young priest, Luther was disturbed by the sale of indulgences by the church. This was the payment of money to the church in exchange for forgiveness of personal sins as well as the sins of those who were suffering in the flames of purgatory. To Luther, this was bad theology. He wrote out 95 reasons he felt this was unbiblical, and nailed them to the church door in Wittenberg. This action put Luther in direct confrontation with papal authority and was the primary spark that ignited the Reformation. In spite of the almost overwhelming power of the papacy to frighten those in opposition to her teachings, Luther stood firm in his two great convictions—that salvation was by faith in Christ alone and that the Scriptures are the only standard for Christian faith and practice.

THE LONG ROAD BACK

Let me use a few illustrations to describe the problem encountered by the Reformation. First, the church didn't get in its fallen condition overnight. It was a gradual fall over literally centuries of time. It couldn't be changed overnight, either. This is much like a person who after years of inactivity and overeating decides to get on a fitness program. To tone up and lose weight can't be done overnight. The lifestyle must be changed and health reclaimed.

Because the apostasy transpired over many centuries it was almost imperceptible to any individual at any point in time. It's somewhat like the growing-up process of a child. The child may not notice much change. But when he or she makes a visit to Grandma's after a year's lapse, Grandma exclaims, "Oh, how much you have grown!" Similarly, a person may not notice much, if any, change in the church; that is because it is too gradual. But over time the church has gone so far from the path to the kingdom that very few even remember what that path looks like.

Another factor is the level of mental sharpness of the church. The Bible describes the church at the end as being asleep (Matthew 25:5). Quite often those who are asleep do not enjoy being awakened. But the Bible gives us many warnings to wake up. "And do this, knowing the time, that now it is high time to awake out of sleep; for now our salvation is nearer than when we first believed. The night is far spent, the day is at hand. Therefore let us cast off the works of darkness, and let us put on the armor of light. Let us walk properly, as in the day, not in revelry and drunkenness, not in lewdness and lust, not in strife and envy. But put on the Lord Jesus Christ, and make no provision for the flesh, to fulfill its lusts" (Romans 13:11-14).

During the early period of the Reformation many of the unbiblical teachings of the church, such as prayers for the dead, veneration of saints and relics, celebration of the Mass, worship of Mary, purgatory, penance, holy water, celibacy of the priesthood, the rosary, the Inquisition, transubstantiation, extreme unction, and dependence upon tradition, were repudiated and abandoned. In fact, the Protestant Reformers were nearly unanimous in identifying the papal system as the "man of sin," the "mystery of iniquity," and the "little horn" of Daniel 7. They saw it as the entity that was to persecute God's true people during the 1260 years of Revelation 12:6, 14 and 13:5, before the second coming of Jesus.

WHY SO MANY DENOMINATIONS?

The reformation of the Christian church should not have ended in the sixteenth century. The Reformers made much progress, but they did not rediscover all the light lost during the apostasy. They took Christianity out of deep darkness, but it still stood in the shadows. They broke the vice-like grip of the medieval church, gave the Bible to the people in their own languages, and restored the basic gospel. But there were many other Bible truths, such as baptism by immersion, immortality as a gift given by Christ at the time of the resurrection of the righteous, the seventh day as the Bible Sabbath, and other basic Bible truths waiting to be rediscovered.

The successors of the early Reformers failed to advance in Bible knowledge much beyond their predecessors. In fact, many called themselves by the names of the Reformers and did not study further to seek even more of the forgotten truths. This led to the many different denominations in the Protestant world. People who followed each Reformer camped around these great individuals but for some reason would not accept any further light than their leader had discovered. It was apparently God's idea, however, for each generation to stand on the foundation laid by former students of the Bible and build on that until the entire truth of God's Word would be restored.

THE DEVIL AND THE CHURCH

The twelfth chapter of the book of Revelation gives a brief but explicit history of the New Testament church and reveals the characteristics of the last or remnant of that church. A great red dragon is pictured as about to pounce on the woman clothed with the sun. Already it had brought about the downfall of one third of heaven's angels (Revelation 12:4, 7-10). Now if it could devour the Infant about to be born to the woman, it would win the war.

The woman standing before the dragon is clothed with the sun and has the moon under her feet; she wears a crown of 12 stars. The male Child, to whom she gives birth, is destined to "rule all nations with a rod of iron." The dragon attacks the Child, but its efforts to kill the Child are not successful. Instead, the Child is "caught up to God and His throne" (verse 5).

The angry dragon then turns his attention to the woman, the Child's mother, who is miraculously given wings and is taken into the wilderness to a place prepared for her by God. There God feeds and takes care of her for a time and times and half a time—three and a half prophetic years, or 1260 prophetic days (Revelation 12:13, 14). This is obviously the same prophetic time period during which the true church suffered persecution at the hands of the little-horn power of Daniel 7. Now, let's see if we can figure out all this symbolic language.

In Bible prophecy a pure woman represents God's faithful church. A woman described as a fornicator or adulterer represents God's people who have apostatized (Ezekiel 16; Isaiah 57:8; Jeremiah 31:4, 5; Hosea 1–3; Revelation 17:1-5). The dragon is the "serpent of old, called the Devil and Satan" (Revelation 12:9), who was waiting to devour the male Child—the long-expected Messiah, Jesus Christ. The dragon used as his instruments of death the Roman Empire and the apostatized people of God. But nothing, not even death on the cross, could distract Jesus from His mission as the Savior of mankind.

Christ defeated Satan by dying on the cross. Speaking of His crucifixion, Jesus said, "Now is the judgment of this world; now the ruler of this world will be cast out" (John 12:31). With this great event the heavenly choir sings the song of victory with a loud voice. "Now salvation, and strength, and the kingdom of our God, and the power of His Christ have come, for the accuser of our brethren, who accused them before our God day and night, has been cast down. . . . Therefore rejoice, O heavens, and you who dwell in them!" (Revelation 12:10-12).

But while heaven rejoices, earth must take warning: "Woe to the inhabitants of the earth and the sea! For the devil has come down to you, having great wrath, because he knows that he has a short time" (verse 12). Apparently, the devil's intensity at the end is fueled by the fact that he knows that time is short. God's people are almost home!

As we have noted, true to the prophecy the church was persecuted for 1260 prophetic days or 1260 literal years. But though the church suffered greatly, it still survived. Though God's faithful people were scattered all over the earth—"the wilderness"—God provided protection for them. At the end of this prophetic period, which ended in 1798, God's true people began to emerge and join together in response to the signs of Christ's soon return. John describes this faithful group as "the rest of her offspring, who keep the commandments of God and have the testimony of Jesus Christ" (verse 17). This same verse indicates that the devil hates this remnant group and makes war with it.

LOOKING FOR THE REMNANT

Naturally, those who are looking for biblical truth and are making preparation for meeting Jesus at His second coming will be interested in becoming a part of His last-day church. The church is important to Jesus. He organized it, gave His life for it, and gave gifts to it. But how does one find the true church today? The book of Revelation gives two almost identical descriptions of this group. The first is where we have just been studying—Revelation 12:17. This verse contains a description of the last remnant in God's chosen line of loyal believers—His loyal witnesses in the last days just before Christ's second coming. "And the dragon was enraged with the woman, and he went to make war with the rest of her offspring, who keep the commandments of God and have the testimony of Jesus Christ." Here, in this description of the devil's battle with the last-day church, John used the expression, "the rest of her offspring." That expression means the "remaining ones" or "remnant" (KJV).

The other description given by John of the last-day faithful ones is in Revelation 14:12. It states, "Here is the patience of the saints; here are those who keep the commandments of God and the faith of Jesus." So the remnant at the time of the end cannot easily be mistaken. The Bible describes them in specific terms. They keep the commandments of God and have the testimony of Jesus Christ. In addition, they have the responsibility of proclaiming, just before Jesus returns, God's final message of warning to the world. That message is recorded in Revelation 14:6-12. Let us consider more closely each of these characteristics.

The first characteristic is "the faith of Jesus." God's remnant people are characterized by a faith similar to that which Jesus had. They reflect Jesus' unshakable confidence in God and the authority of Scripture. They believe that Jesus Christ is the Messiah of prophecy, the Son of God, who came as the Savior of the world. Their faith encompasses all the truths of the Bible—those that Jesus and the apostles believed and taught.

Accordingly, God's remnant people will proclaim the everlasting gospel of salvation by faith in Christ. They will warn the world that the hour of God's judgment has arrived. Like Elijah and John the Baptist, the remnant will prepare the way of the Lord. They will proclaim the soon-coming Lord. They will be involved in a great worldwide mission to complete the divine witness to humanity (Revelation 14:6, 7; 10:11; Matthew 24:14).

The second characteristic of the remnant is that they "keep the commandments of God." In any generation those who return to the Lord will keep His commandments. Genuine faith in Jesus commits the remnant to follow His example. "He who says he abides in Him," John said, "ought himself also to walk just as He walked" (1 John 2:6). Jesus kept His Father's commandments, and they too will obey God's commandments (John 15:10).

Inasmuch as they are the remnant, God's last-day church will practice what the early church preached. And their actions must harmonize with their profession. Jesus said, "Not everyone who says to me, 'Lord, Lord,' shall enter the kingdom of heaven, but he who does the will of My Father in heaven" (Matthew 7:21). Through the strength Christ gives them, they obey God's requirements, including all 10 of the commandments, God's unchanging moral law (Exodus 20:1-17; Matthew 5:17-19; 19:17; Philippians 4:13). Obviously this will include the restoration of the keeping of the seventh-day Sabbath, the fourth commandment.

This was predicted of the remnant by the prophet Isaiah. "Those from among you shall build the old waste places; you shall raise up the foundations of many generations; and you shall be called the Repairer of the Breach, the Restorer of Streets to Dwell In. If you turn away your foot from the Sabbath, from doing your pleasure on My holy day, and call the Sabbath a delight, the holy day of the Lord honorable, and shall honor Him, not doing your own ways, nor finding your own pleasure, nor speaking your own words, then you shall delight yourself in the Lord; and I will cause you to ride on the high hills of the earth, and feed you with the heritage of Jacob your father. The mouth of the Lord has spoken" (Isaiah 58:12-14).

Right on time, just when the end-time prophecies began their fulfillment, Christians rediscovered the seventh-day Sabbath and began to keep it holy. Christian Sabbathkeepers now number in the millions, and thousands more are joining them every day. The Seventh-day Adventist Church has been at the forefront in this movement.

A third characteristic of God's remnant people at the end of time is that they possess "the testimony of Jesus." John defines "the testimony of Jesus" as "the spirit [or gift] of prophecy" (Revelation 19:10). The remnant will be guided by the testimony of Jesus conveyed through the gift of prophecy. This gift of the Spirit was to function continuously throughout the history of the church, until "all come to the unity of the faith and the knowledge of the Son of God, to a perfect man, to the measure of the stature of the fullness of Christ" (Ephesians 4:13). It is therefore one of the major characteristics of the remnant.

The Bible says that when Jesus returned to heaven after His first advent He "gave gifts to men" (verse 8). In five places, the New Testament names some of these divine gifts to the Christian church: Romans 12:6-8; 1 Corinthians 12:4-11; 1 Corinthians 13:1-3; 1 Corinthians 14; and Ephesians 4:11-16. It is significant to note that only one gift occurs in all five places. It is the gift of prophecy! Apparently our Lord Jesus recognized the need for continuing contact with His people, especially as the time of the end approached. It would not be like God, who has communicated with humans down through the ages, to abandon them at the very end, right before the most climactic event since the Creation. We know that "the Lord God does nothing, unless He reveals His secret to His servants the prophets" (Amos 3:7).

Such prophetic guidance makes the remnant a people of prophecy who proclaim a prophetic message. They will understand prophecy and teach it and have the gift of prophecy in their midst. The revelation of truth that comes to the remnant helps them accomplish their mission of preparing the world for Christ's return.

The timing of the work of the remnant is another characteristic of this group. The Bible indicates that the remnant appears on the world's stage after the time of the great persecution (Revelation 12:14-17). The earth-shaking events of the French Revolution, which led to the captivity of the pope at the end of the 1260-year period in 1798 and the fulfillment of the three great cosmic signs—in which the sun, moon, and stars testified of the nearness of Christ's return—led to a major revival of the study of prophecy. Many were convinced that the second coming of Christ was imminent. Throughout the world many Christians recognized that "the time of the end" had arrived (Daniel 12:4).

As Christians saw the fulfillment of many Bible prophecies during the second half of the eighteenth and the first half of the nineteenth century, a powerful interconfessional revival movement took place that centered on the Second Advent hope. This hope brought a deep spirit of unity among its adherents, and many joined together to proclaim to the world Christ's soon return. This movement was centered on the Word of God. People were convinced that God was calling a remnant to continue the reformation of the Christian church.

THE REMNANT PEOPLE GIVE
THE LAST WARNING TO THE WORLD

The book of Revelation clearly outlines the message and mission of the remnant people of God. Their message is so important that it is represented as angel messengers flying in mid-heaven and crying with loud voices. The Bible records the messages in Revelation 14:6-12. The timing is so precise that they could be only from heaven. These three messages comprise God's answers to the overwhelming satanic deception that sweeps the world just before Christ returns (Revelation 13:3, 8, 14-16). Then immediately after the giving of God's last appeal to the world, Christ returns to reap the harvest of the earth (Revelation 14:14-20). As we travel the road back toward the kingdom of God we must all respond to these messages and in turn share them with the world.

THE FIRST ANGEL'S MESSAGE

"Then I saw another angel flying in the midst of heaven, having the everlasting gospel to preach to those who dwell on the earth—to every nation, tribe, tongue, and people—saying with a loud voice, 'Fear God and give glory to Him, for the hour of His judgment has come; and worship Him who made heaven and earth, the sea and springs of water'" (Revelation 14:6, 7).

This first message given by the remnant contains the everlasting gospel. In view of the judgment they reaffirm the everlasting gospel that sinners can be justified by faith and receive Christ's righteousness. The message—virtually the same given by Elijah and John the Baptist —calls the world to repentance. It calls for everyone to "fear" or reverence God, and to give "glory" or honor to Him. This call to the world also announces "the hour of His judgment has come." This adds urgency to the message.

Next comes the call to worship the Creator. By commanding us "to worship Him who made heaven and earth, the sea and springs of water" this message calls attention back to the fourth commandment. This is easy to conclude when we compare this passage (Revelation 14:7) with the fourth commandment (Exodus 20:8-11). This first message leads people into true worship of the Creator, an experience that involves honoring His memorial of Creation—the seventh-day Sabbath of the Lord. God instituted the Sabbath at Creation (Genesis 2:1-3) and affirmed it in the Ten Commandments (Exodus 20:8-11). In addition to the Sabbath being a memorial of Creation, it is also a sign that God is the One who sanctifies the keeper. "Surely My Sabbaths you shall keep, for it is a sign between Me and you throughout your generations, that you may know that I am the Lord who sanctifies you" (Exodus 31:13; see also Ezekiel 20:12). Unfortunately this important sign of God's Creation and redemption is neglected by the vast majority of God's created beings.

THE SECOND ANGEL'S MESSAGE
"Babylon is fallen, is fallen, that great city, because she has made all nations drink of the wine of the wrath of her fornication" (Revelation 14:8).

From early history the city of Babylon symbolized defiance of God. Its tower was a monument to apostasy and a center of rebellion. Throughout the Bible the struggle between God's city, Jerusalem, and Satan's city, Babylon, illustrates the conflict between good and evil. Because of the apostasy and persecution, most Protestants of the Reformation and post-Reformation era have referred to the church of Rome as spiritual Babylon, the enemy of God's people. Revelation 17 gives a study of the false religious system just as Revelation 12 describes the true church.

The message of the second angel brings out the universal nature of the Babylonian apostasy and her coercive power, saying that "she has made all nations drink of the wine of the wrath of her fornication." The "wine" of Babylon represents her heretical teachings. Apparently, Babylon will pressure the powers of state to enforce universally her false religious teachings and decrees. The "fornication" that is mentioned here represents the illicit relationship between Babylon and the nations, that is, between the apostate church and civil powers. The church is supposed to be married to Christ and gets her support from Him. Accordingly, when she seeks the support of the state she commits spiritual fornication (see James 4:4).

Babylon is said to have fallen because she rejects the message of the first angel—the gospel of righteousness by faith in the Creator. Just as the church of Rome apostatized during the first few centuries of the Christian era, so many Protestants have departed from the great Bible truths of the Reformation or never went beyond their leaders in seeking truth. Sadly, this fall of Babylon involves much of the Christian world. And so the final angel depicted in Revelation 18 says, "Come out of her, my people, lest you share in her sins, and lest you receive of her plagues" (verse 4).

THE THIRD ANGEL'S MESSAGE

"If anyone worships the beast and his image, and receives his mark on his forehead or in his hand, he himself shall also drink of the wine of the wrath of God, which is poured out full strength into the cup of His indignation. He shall be tormented with fire and brimstone in the presence of the holy angels and in the presence of the Lamb. And the smoke of their torment ascends forever and ever; and they have no rest day or night, who worship the beast and his image, and whoever receives the mark of his name. Here is the patience of the saints; here are those who keep the commandments of God and the faith of Jesus" (Revelation 14:9-12).

The message of the third angel proclaims God's most solemn warning against worshiping the beast and his image. Everyone who rejects these messages from God will ultimately worship the beast. As we have discussed earlier, the beast described in Revelation 13:1-10 is the church-state union that dominated the Christian world during the 1260-year period. This apostate church was described by Paul as the "man of sin" (2 Thessalonians 2:3, 4) and by the prophet Daniel as the "little horn" (Daniel 7:8, 20-25; 8:9-12). Accordingly, the image of the beast represents that form of apostate religion that will be developed when churches that have lost the true spirit of the Reformation will unite with the state to enforce their teachings on others. This union of church and state will be a perfect image to the beast.

We are informed by this message that during the final conflict between good and evil two distinct classes will be found. One class will advocate a gospel of tradition and human devisings and will worship the beast and his image. They will bring upon themselves the most grievous judgments. The other class, by contrast, will live by the true gospel and "keep the commandments of God and the faith of Jesus" (Revelation 14:12). The bottom-line final issue will involve true and false worship—the true and the false gospel. When this issue is clearly brought before the world, those who reject God's memorial of His creatorship—the Bible Sabbath—choosing to worship and honor Sunday in the full knowledge that it is not God's appointed day of worship, will receive the "mark of the beast." This mark is a mark of rebellion. It involves choosing a day that humanity has established in place of the one that God established at Creation and memorialized in the Ten Commandments.

The choice to be involved in either of these two groups involves suffering. So the choice is not an easy one. Those who choose to obey God will experience the wrath of the dragon (Revelation 12:17) and eventually be threatened with death (Revelation 13:15), while those who choose to worship the beast and his image will incur the seven last plagues and finally "the lake of fire" (Revelation 15; 16; 20:14, 15).

But though both choices involve suffering, their results are very different. The worshipers of the Creator will escape the deadly wrath of the dragon and finally stand together with the Lamb on Mount Zion (Revelation 14:1). The worshipers of the beast and his image, on the other hand, receive the full wrath of God and die in the presence of the holy angels and the Lamb (verses 9, 10; Revelation 20:14). God has children in all churches and among the unchurched whom He is calling at this final time for decision. The two ways have never been more significant than now. God is calling people out of apostasy and preparing them for Christ's return.

A POWERFUL FOURTH ANGEL

God is so compassionate and eager to save those who are presently involved in a false or apostate religious system that He sends a final appeal to the world with such power that the entire world is lit up. John speaks of this final appeal in Revelation 18: "After these things I saw another angel coming down from heaven, having great authority, and the earth was illuminated with his glory. And he cried mightily with a loud voice, saying, 'Babylon the great is fallen, is fallen, and has become a dwelling place of demons, a prison for every foul spirit, and a cage for every unclean and hated bird! For all the nations have drunk of the wine of the wrath of her fornication, the kings of the earth have committed fornication with her, and the merchants of the earth have become rich through the abundance of her luxury.' And I heard another voice from heaven saying, 'Come out of her, my people, lest you share in her sins, and lest you receive of her plagues. For her sins have reached to heaven, and God has remembered her iniquities'" (verses 1-5).

That voice from heaven is calling to all of us today. It is time for us to take stock of our lives and the direction we are going. If we, for whatever reason, have taken the broad road that most of the rest of the world are traveling—that road that leads to destruction—it's time to take the road back to the Creator God and His commandments. Don't put off this important decision. Your eternal life is at stake. We are almost home!

Appendixes

The following chapters are given as a prophetic background to the contemporary developments of this book:

I. Prophecy Is Simple (The Four World Empires)
II. The Rise and Fall of the Little Horn Power
III. The United States—World Superpower
IV. Unmasking the Antichrist
V. The Seal of God
VI. The Mark of the Beast

For extra reading on the subject I recommend:

The Bible—first and foremost—get to know Christ and His prophetic guidance in the books of Daniel, Matthew, and Revelation.

Books by Ellen White:

The Great Controversy
Maranatha
Last Day Events
Early Writings
Selected Messages, vol. 3, pp. 380-431

Other books:

God Cares, vols. 1 and 2, by C. Mervyn Maxwell
Jesus Is My Judge—Meditations on the Book of Daniel,
    by Leslie Hardinge
Even at the Door, by G. Edward Reid

Personal Bible Study Guides:

Discover, The Voice of Prophecy, P.O. Box 55,
    Los Angeles, CA 90053
Unlocking Revelation, Light Bearers Ministry, P.O. Box 1888,
    Malo, WA 99150

For top-quality inspirational tapes from Adventist speakers:

Contact American Cassette Ministries, P.O. Box 922,
    Harrisburg, PA 17108 (Free Catalog)

Prophecy Is Simple

(The Four World Empires)

O nly two Bible books are primarily apocalyptic. Two very unique books pull back the veil and display the ultimate destiny of mankind. They portray a revelation of God in history and predict the future with precise accuracy. These two books are Daniel and Revelation. Both Daniel and John were in their later years when they penned their works. Both had since their youth developed a deep and abiding relationship with the God of heaven.

Understanding Daniel is a prerequisite for understanding Revelation. And understanding the first part of Daniel is essential to understanding the last part. Apocalyptic prophecy is progressive and presupposes an understanding of previous prophecy and of each previous step in the revelation. As indicated in the appendix title above, God never intended that prophecy would be complex. In fact, just the opposite is true. He wants prophecy to be a "revelation" of Himself and His activities on behalf of mankind. However, we are told that "None of the wicked shall understand, but the wise will understand" (Daniel 12:10). In other words, spiritual things are spiritually discerned. The Bible is its own best interpreter and by spending time in the Word we will gain understanding.

The Babylonian captivity of Israel was a real low point in the history of God's people. Warned of—predicted—for many years by Jeremiah and other prophets, this experience was devastating for the morale of Israel. Their thoughts were characterized by the words of the psalmist:

"By the rivers of Babylon,
"There we sat down, yea, we wept
"When we remembered Zion.
"We hung our harps

"Upon the willows in the midst of it.
"For there those who carried us away
      captive asked of us a song.
"And those who plundered us requested mirth,
"Saying, 'Sing us one of the songs of Zion!'
"[But] How shall we sing the Lord's song
      in a foreign land?" (Psalm 137:1-4).

And yet in spite of the captivity problems, which were the result of their own course of action, God was with them and prospered the faithful ones.

Since the first chapter of Daniel gives the setting for the book, it cannot be overlooked. It tells the story of four young men—only in their late teens—Jewish captives far from home. Offered the rich and unhealthful foods of the king the young men asked for simple food. They recognized their bodies as the temple of God. "Daniel purposed in his heart that he would not defile himself with the portion of the king's delicacies, nor with the wine which he drank . . . 'give us vegetables to eat and water to drink,'" he requested. (See Daniel 1:8, 12.) During their training period, "God gave them knowledge and skill in all literature and wisdom; and Daniel had understanding in all visions and dreams" (Daniel 1:17). At the end of their training period they were personally examined by the king. "And in all matters of wisdom and understanding about which the king examined them, he found them ten times better than all the magicians and astrologers who were in all his realm" (verse 20).

The second chapter of Daniel is fundamental to an understanding of the rest of that book and to the later book of Revelation. In the wisdom of God, chapter two is remarkably pleasant to read and easy to understand. And like the first chapter, its profound message is delivered to us as a story. It is simple enough to tell a child and yet in 45 short verses it lays out the entire course of history from Daniel's day to the second coming of Christ!

We read that the Babylonian king Nebuchadnezzar had a remarkable dream one night. It woke him up and he couldn't go back to sleep. The Bible says that "his spirit was so troubled that his sleep left him." He then called in all his "wise men" or counselors. The Bible calls

them "magicians, astrologers, sorcerers, and Chaldeans." He told them
that his dream was very significant but that he couldn't remember it,
and furthermore he wanted to know its meaning. The "wise men" were
used to giving their "interpretations" of dreams, but they were power-
less to come up with the dream as well. Nebuchadnezzar told them that
if they could tell him what he had dreamed they would be given gifts,
rewards, and great honor. If not, they would be cut in pieces and their
houses would be made an ash heap. One can only imagine the fear that
swept over the wise men.

The wise men made a final appeal. No king or ruler had ever asked
his wise men such a thing as that before, they said, and no one could
do what he was asking them to do "except the gods, whose dwelling is
not with flesh." The king became furious and gave a command to his
guards that all the wise men should be destroyed.

Apparently Daniel and his three faithful friends were not in the
group before the king. Perhaps their junior status had kept them away.
When the king's guard came to take Daniel and his companions to the
execution, the Bible says Daniel, with tact and wisdom, asked Arioch,
the captain of the king's guard, "Why is the decree from the king so
harsh?" Obviously, Daniel was well-liked by those who knew him because Arioch then told him the whole story.

Upon hearing the story, Daniel ventured into the king's presence
and begged time to petition his God to reveal the dream and its interpretation. The king granted the request. Immediately Daniel ran to his
house and contacted his three friends, Hananiah, Mishael, and Azariah
(their Hebrew names), asking them to join him in prayer "that they
might seek mercies from the God of heaven concerning this secret, so
that Daniel and his companions might not perish with the rest of the
wise men of Babylon" (verse 18).

These young men had confidence in God. He had been with them
before. They had turned to Him many times before for guidance and
protection. Now, with contrition of heart they submitted themselves
anew to the Judge of the earth, pleading that He would grant them deliverance in this their time of special need.

God revealed the secret dream of the king to Daniel in a night vision. No doubt when Daniel woke, he quickly wrote out some notes so
he wouldn't forget his dream. He offered a prayer by saying,

"I thank You and praise You, O God of my fathers;
"You have given me wisdom and might,
"And have now made known to me what
    we asked of You,
"For You have made known to us the king's
    demand" (verse 23).

Going to Arioch, Daniel told him, "Don't kill the wise men, take me to the king and I will give him the interpretation." The Bible says that "Then Arioch quickly brought Daniel before the king, and thus said to him [apparently taking a little credit to himself], 'I have found a man of the captives of Judah, who will make known to the king the interpretation'" (verse 25).

There stood Daniel, the Jewish captive, courteous, calm, and self-possessed. The king, perhaps remembering him as the outstanding student he had examined some time before, asked, "Are you able to make known to me the dream which I have seen and its interpretation?" Daniel could have just said, "Yes." But he didn't. Instead he gave a little preface to his answer. He said, "The secret which the king has demanded, the wise men . . . cannot declare to the king. But there is a God in heaven who reveals secrets, and He has made known [not to me but] to King Nebuchadnezzar what will be in the latter days" (verses 27, 28). Here is an indication that God wants us to know about future events and the last days!

Then Daniel began to tell the dream. You can be sure that everyone in the room, especially the king, was listening closely.

"You, O king, were watching; and behold, a great image! This great image, whose splendor was excellent, stood before you; and its form was awesome." The king moved to the edge of his throne and exclaimed, "That's it! You've got it! Go on!" Daniel continued,

"This image's head was of fine gold, its chest and
    arms of silver, its belly and thighs of bronze,
"Its legs of iron, its feet partly of iron and partly
    of clay.
"You watched while a stone was cut out without

> hands, which struck the image on its feet
> of iron and clay, and broke them in pieces.
> "Then the iron, the clay, the bronze, the silver, and
> the gold were crushed together, and became
> like chaff from the summer threshing floors;
> the wind carried them away so that no trace
> of them was found. And the stone that struck
> the image became a great mountain and filled
> the whole earth" (verses 32-35).

I can imagine the king, forgetting royal protocol, springing to his feet and hugging Daniel and saying, "You are exactly right, young man. Now, what does it mean?" Since he knew it was the very dream which had troubled him, he was receptive for its interpretation. Daniel responded, "Now we [apparently including his three friends as is later evident] will tell the interpretation of it before the king" (verse 36).

The interpretation, recorded in your Bible, is a model of clarity. The Bible interprets itself—it is indeed simple!

The Interpretation

The king sat back down and Daniel continued,

> "You, O king, are a king of kings. For the God of heaven has given you a kingdom, power, strength, and glory;

> "And wherever the children of men dwell [the known world], or the beasts of the field and the birds of the heaven, He has given them into your hand, and has made you ruler over them all—**you are this head of gold**" (verses 37, 38).

As you can see from what I have underlined above, the king of Babylon ruled the entire known world. But is the head of gold referring to the king himself or to his kingdom? The next verse gives the answer.

> "But after you shall arise another kingdom [not another "king"] inferior to yours; then another, a third **kingdom** of bronze, which shall rule over all the earth."

Please note that these successive kingdoms "rule over all the earth." They are world empires! But Daniel is not finished yet.

"And the <u>fourth kingdom</u> shall be as strong as iron, inasmuch as iron breaks in pieces and shatters everything; and like iron that crushes, that <u>kingdom</u> will break in pieces and crush all the others.

"Whereas you saw the feet and toes, partly of potter's clay and partly of iron, the <u>kingdom</u> shall be divided; yet the strength of the iron shall be in it, just as you saw the iron mixed with ceramic clay.

"And as the toes of the feet were partly of iron and partly of clay, so the kingdom shall be partly strong and partly fragile.

"As you saw iron mixed with ceramic clay, they will mingle with the seed of men; but they will not adhere to one another, just as iron does not mix with clay.

"And in the days of these kings [following the division of the fourth empire] the God of heaven will set up <u>a kingdom</u> which shall never be destroyed; and the kingdom shall not be left to other people; it shall break in pieces and consume all these kingdoms, <u>and it shall stand forever</u>" (verses 39-44).

The bottom line is simple. There would be four world empires starting with Babylon—only four. The fourth one would not be conquered as the first three were by a succeeding world empire; but the fourth would be "divided" or broken up among various "kings." Oh yes, many leaders would try to make another world empire, but their attempts would fail.

Daniel concluded the interpretation for King Nebuchadnezzar by saying, "Inasmuch as you saw that the stone was cut out of the mountain without hands, and that it broke in pieces the iron, the bronze, . . . the silver, and the gold—<u>the great God has made known to the king what **will** come to pass after this. **The dream is certain, and its interpretation is sure**</u>" (verse 45). Daniel was confident of the dream and its interpretation because he was confident in God!

Picture the scene in the king's royal quarters. The king prostrated himself before Daniel (verse 46) and commanded that they should present an offering and incense to him. The king told Daniel that his God is the God of gods, and truly the Lord is a revealer of secrets—"since you could reveal this secret."

The king gave Daniel many great gifts and made him ruler over the whole province of Babylon and the chief administrator of the wise men. Daniel, in his greatness and humility, petitioned the king on behalf of his three friends, and they were given positions of leadership as well.

Sometimes in a study of history it appears that events were shaped because of the strength or prowess of man, but this prophecy reveals the hand and wisdom of God. Before these world empires came upon the stage of action, God looked down the ages and predicted their rise and fall. When we now look back, by studying history, we can see the literal fulfillment of divine prophecy.

Daniel lived long enough to see the beginning of the second world empire. The elder statesman was summoned to come to Belshazzar's feast for another interpretation—the handwriting on the wall! Daniel's last words to the king were, "Your kingdom has been divided, and given to the Medes and Persians" (Daniel 5:28).

The prophet Ezra confirms this in the words of the Persian king: "Thus says Cyrus king of Persia: <u>All the kingdoms of the earth the Lord God of heaven has given me</u>" (Ezra 1:2).

Then later through a "heavenly messenger" God revealed to Daniel the identity of the third empire as well! The messenger asked, "Do you know why I have come to you? And now I must return to fight with the prince of Persia; and when I have gone forth, indeed the prince of <u>Greece</u> will come" (Daniel 10:20). Three out of four is not bad. Do you think the Bible also reveals the identity of the fourth empire? Yes, it does—In the New Testament! In Luke 2:1 we learn that Caesar Augustus issued a decree that "<u>all the world</u>" should be registered for tax purposes. He must, then, have had jurisdiction over all the world. Who was Caesar Augustus?—a Roman emperor. <u>So Rome was the fourth kingdom.</u> The legs of iron in Nebuchadnezzar's dream could represent no other kingdom, because Rome was the only universal kingdom that came to power after Grecia. So when Jesus appeared among men almost 2,000 years ago the course of history had already reached the legs of iron.

Dr. C. Mervyn Maxwell, in his excellent Daniel resource book summarizes the sequence this way: "After he [Nebuchadnezzar] died in 562 B.C. the Babylonian Empire ran rapidly downhill. Media and Persia, powers inferior to Babylon during Nebuchadnezzar's lifetime, were united together and linked to Lydia by Cyrus, king of Persia. They conquered Babylon in 539 B.C. The Medo-Persian Empire continued for a while to expand in wealth, power, and size (adding Egypt); but like Babylon it too went into decline. In 331 B.C. it was vanquished by Alexander the Great, founder of the Macedonian Greek Empire. At Alexander's death his dominion was divided into a number of Hellenistic Greek kingdoms. Meanwhile Rome was evolving in the west and, in due course, began to influence the Hellenistic kingdoms. By 168 B.C. Rome dominated the Mediterranean as the fourth empire of the statue prophecy.

"Babylonian, Medo-Persian, Greek, Roman—the list of empires is simple and can be memorized in a moment. Any good history book will confirm the sequence" (Maxwell, *God Cares,* vol. 1, pp. 34, 35).

How could this vision and history lesson ever be relevant to *Sunday's Coming!?* The answer: Daniel 2 is foundational. It is basic to understanding all prophecy that historically follows it. It provides the structure upon which one can add the additional details from other prophecies regarding these same and subsequent players in human history.

The Bible's own interpretation is sure. And a basic truth of Daniel 2 is that all of the major elements but the second coming of Christ are already written in the history books! We are indeed living in those "later times" spoken of by Daniel.

The Rise and Fall
of the Little Horn Power

The second chapter of Daniel gives us the basic structure of world history right down to the second coming of Christ. In fact, by the time of Christ's first advent, history had already reached the time of the fourth and final "world empire." So what about all the time between then and now? Do we have any indication from Bible prophecy what we should expect in those intervening years? Certainly: God wants us to know what is happening and what we may expect in the future. And in Daniel 7 we are informed in great detail of the activities of players in the drama of the ages. It is a wonderful validation of the truth that "Amidst the strife and tumult of nations, He that sitteth above the cherubim still guides the affairs of the earth.

"The history of nations that one after another have occupied their allotted time and place, unconsciously witnessing to the truth of which they themselves knew not the meaning, speaks to us. To every nation and to every individual of today God has assigned a place in His great plan. Today men and nations are being measured by the plummet in the hand of him who makes no mistake. All are by their own choice deciding their destiny, and God is overruling all for the accomplishment of His purposes.

"The history which the great I AM has marked out in His word, uniting link after link in the prophetic chain, from eternity in the past to eternity in the future, tells us where we are today in the procession of the ages, and what may be expected in the time to come. <u>All that prophecy has foretold as coming to pass, until the present time, has been traced on the pages of history, and we may be assured that all which is yet to come will be fulfilled in its order.</u>

"The final overthrow of all earthly dominions is plainly foretold in the word of truth. . . . That time is at hand. Today the signs of the times declare that we are standing on the threshold of great and solemn events. Everything in our world is in agitation. . . . The present is a time of overwhelming interest to all living. Rulers and statesmen, men who occupy positions of trust and authority, thinking men and women of all classes, have their attention fixed upon the events taking place about us. They are watching the strained, restless relations that exist among the nations. They observe the intensity that is taking possession of every earthly element, and they recognize that something great and decisive is about to take place—that the world is on the verge of a stupendous crisis.

"Angels are now restraining the winds of strife, that they may not blow until the world shall be warned of its coming doom; but a storm is gathering, ready to burst upon the earth; and when God shall bid His angels loose the winds, there will be such a scene of strife as no pen can picture.

"The Bible, and the Bible only, gives a correct view of these things" (*Education,* pp. 178-180). So let's get back to the Word for its exciting unveiling of more truth.

Daniel 7 begins by giving the date as "the first year of Belshazzar king of Babylon." This helps us to date the time of the vision. Historians tell us that Nebuchadnezzar was succeeded on the Babylonian throne by Nabonidus who "entrusted the kingship" to Belshazzar in 553 B.C.—the date of this vision. Nebuchadnezzar had been dead for nine years, and things weren't going very well for Babylon.

Daniel was no longer a young man. He was about 70, though apparently not fully retired. The fall of Babylon described in chapter 5 and his experience in the lions' den of chapter 6 were still in the future. The chapters of the book of Daniel—like that of Revelation—are not all arranged chronologically. Fifty years had passed since the vision of Daniel 2. No doubt that experience was still vivid in the mind of Daniel.

Then we read that "Daniel had a dream and visions of his head while on his bed" (verse 1). He wrote down the dream, making an outline of the main facts. What he saw was "the four winds of heaven were stirring up the Great Sea.

"And four great beasts came up from the sea, each different from the other.

"The first was like a lion, and had eagle's wings. I watched till its wings were plucked off; and it was lifted up from the earth and made to stand on two feet like a man, and a man's heart was given to it.

"And suddenly another beast, <u>a second, like a bear.</u> It was raised up on one side, and had three ribs in its mouth between its teeth. And they said to it: 'Arise, devour much flesh!'

"After this I looked, and there was <u>another, like a leopard,</u> which had on its back four wings of a bird. The beast also had four heads, and dominion was given to it.

"After this I saw in the night visions, and behold, <u>a fourth beast, dreadful and terrible, exceedingly strong.</u> It had huge iron teeth; it was devouring, breaking in pieces, and trampling the residue with its feet. It was different from all the beasts that were before it, and it had ten horns" (verses 2-7).

Then Daniel observed a very unique feature in the dream—a <u>little horn.</u> It is really the focus of this chapter because it—the little horn—describes something not mentioned in the empire progression of Daniel 2. Daniel puts it this way:

"I was considering the horns, and there was <u>another horn, a little one,</u> coming up among them, before whom three of the first horns were plucked out by the roots. And there, in this horn, were eyes like the eyes of a man, and a mouth speaking pompous words" (verse 8).

Daniel continued to watch the heavenly portrayal until he was shown the awesome view of a heavenly judgment where "the Ancient of Days was seated . . . the court was seated, and the books were opened." Then he was apparently distracted by the sounds of the little horn.

"I watched then <u>because of the sound of the pompous words which the horn was speaking;</u> I watched till the beast was slain, and its body destroyed and given to the burning flame.

"As for the rest of the beasts, they had their dominion taken away, yet their lives were prolonged for a season and a time" (verses 11, 12).

In his account Daniel says that he was next given a view of the second coming of the Son of Man and the setting up of His kingdom "which shall not pass away." But the vision troubled him and he wanted a better understanding of what it meant. He was particularly concerned about the fourth beast with its ten horns and curious about its "little horn." Daniel states that he came near to "one of those who stood by." We may assume that it was an angel—a heavenly messenger. He asked the angel, "the truth of all this."

The Interpretation

God clearly wants us to understand prophecy. He does not want us to be in darkness. Immediately, He provided an interpretation to Daniel through an angel. So "he told me and made known to me the interpretation." The angel first gave Daniel a short summary:

> "Those great beasts, which are four, are four kings which arise out of the earth. But the saints of the Most High shall receive the kingdom, and possess the kingdom forever, even forever and ever" (verses 17, 18).

Just two sentences. That's all he was given until he asked for more. But surely the angel wanted Daniel to see the similarity with the vision of chapter 2—the vision of the metal image. There would be four kingdoms and then God's everlasting kingdom. But Daniel wasn't satisfied with that simple explanation. He wanted to know more about the fourth beast and its horns and the strange "little horn." And so the Bible record continues:

> "Thus he [the angel] said:

> "The fourth beast shall be a fourth kingdom on earth,

> "Which shall be different from all other kingdoms, and shall devour the whole earth, trample it and break it in pieces" (verse 23).

Knowing that the fourth beast is the fourth kingdom, we recognize at once that we are seeing the same series of world powers that we discussed in the last chapter while reviewing Daniel 2: Babylonian, Medo-Persian, Greek, and Roman empires, followed in due time by the kingdom of God. But now more details are given.

The angel continued his interpretation:

"The ten horns are ten kings who shall arise from this kingdom.

"And another shall rise after them;

"He shall be different from the first ones,

"And shall subdue three kings.

"He shall speak pompous words against the Most High,

"Shall persecute the saints of the Most High,

"And shall intend to change times and law.

"Then the saints shall be given into his hand for a time and times and half a time" (verses 24, 25).

The angel's interpretation of the mysterious little horn clearly helps to identify it as papal Rome—later to be known as the Roman Catholic Church. Let's review the clues given by the angel for a positive identification.

1. **Location.** It arose out of the fourth beast. It came up among the ten horns (nations) of western Europe into which the civil or pagan Roman Empire was divided (verses 8, 24).

Did papal Rome originate out of the old Roman Empire? Yes.

2. **Time of rise.** It appeared after the ten other horns, that is, after the breakup of the Roman Empire—during the sixth century A.D. Further, it would rise after three of the horns (kings) had been uprooted (verses 8, 20, 24).

The "Christian church" founded by Christ and the apostles existed from the first century, but the papal domination did not begin until after the fall of the Roman Empire. Did papal Rome arise after the fifth century? Yes.

(Three of the barbarian kingdoms that arose out of the Roman Empire espoused the views of Arius, who denied the divinity of Christ. All the other barbarian kingdoms came to accept the Christian faith.)

From A.D. 476 on, the three Arian powers dominated portions of the territory of Rome, but each in turn met defeat as the rulers of the Eastern Roman Empire rallied to support the Roman Church in the West. In 533 Justinian, the emperor of the Eastern Empire, officially recognized the bishop (later to be called pope) of Rome as the head of all the Christian churches. But because of the Arian domination of Rome, the pope had no opportunity to actually exercise this officially recognized power. Five years later, in 538, Belisarius, one of Justinian's generals, routed the Ostrogoths, the last of the Arian powers, from the city of Rome. So by the military intervention of the Eastern Empire the pope was freed from the dominating influence of states that restrained his activities in the civil sphere. This date, A.D. 538, plays a significant part in another clue that helps to identify the little horn as the papacy.

3. **The nature of the little horn.** It was "different" or diverse from the other horns and though it was little at first it became "greater than his fellows" (verses 7, 8, 20, 24). The little horn was different— it would speak against the Most High and persecute the saints. The "difference" was that it would be both political and religious in nature.

Was papal Rome different than the other "kingdoms" that emerged from the Roman Empire? Yes, indeed.

4. **Rise to power.** It would "put down three kings" or "pluck them up by the roots" (verses 8, 24). As mentioned in two above, three of the ten kingdoms that emerged from the ashes of pagan Rome were "Arian" in religious thinking. These were the Heruls, the Vandals, and the Ostrogoths. They were, with the aid of the Eastern Empire, defeated by Rome to allow for its more dominant control. These three kingdoms have no modern counterparts.

Did papal Rome uproot three kingdoms as it "came to power"? Yes.

5. **Attitude toward God.** The little horn would speak great things against the Most High (verses 8, 20, 25). What does it mean to "speak great words against the Most High"? It is generally understood among Bible scholars that speaking against the Most High is equivalent to taking on the prerogatives of God and/or blaspheming His name. Much could be written on this topic. The following should be sufficient to make the point of identification.

"The pope's power—and his religious and political claims—increased for centuries. In 1076 Pope Gregory VII informed the subjects of Henry IV, emperor of Germany, that if Henry would not repent of his sins, they would not need to obey him. Henry was the most powerful monarch in Europe at the time, but he nonetheless made a pilgrimage to Canossa in the Alps, where the pope was residing, and waited three painful days, barefoot in the snow, until Pope Gregory forgave him.

"Taking his cue from Gregory VII, Pope Pius V in 1570, in the bull (or decree) *Regnans in excelsis* ('He who reigns in the heavens') declared that the Protestant queen of England, Elizabeth I (1558-1603), was an accursed heretic who hereafter should have no right to rule and whose citizens were all, by papal authority, forbidden to obey her. 'Professor McKenzie [Jesuit professor John L. McKenzie of Notre Dame University] acknowledges in his gracious manner that 'the teaching authority of the Roman Catholic Church is vested at any given moment in men, who are not all of equal virtue and competence.' He continues: '[Pope] Pius V was and is respected as a holy and learned man, but his deposition of Elizabeth I of England is recognized as one of the greatest blunders in the history of the papacy.'

"The admission that the 'teaching authority of the Roman Church' is vested in men of unequal virtue and competence contrasts with the claim made as recently as the 1890's by Pope Leo XIII. In an encyclical letter, 'On the Chief Duties of Christians as Citizens,' dated January 10, 1890, Leo XIII asserted that 'the supreme teacher in the Church is the Roman Pontiff. Union of minds, therefore, requires . . . complete submission and obedience of will to the Church and to the Roman Pontiff, <u>as to God Himself.</u>' On June 20, 1894, in 'The Reunion of Christendom,' Leo claimed further that 'we [that is, we popes] hold upon this earth the place of God Almighty'" (Maxwell, *God Cares,* vol. 1, p. 125).

Does papal Rome claim the prerogatives of God? Yes.

6. **Attitude toward God's people.** The little horn was to persecute or "wear out the saints of the Most High" (verses 21, 25). According to the angel's interpretation to Daniel this power would persecute God's people. Those whom papal Rome considered heretical faced civil punishment. History attests that <u>millions</u> were put to death under this religio-political system.* For a firsthand look, visit the archbishop's fortress in Salsburg, Austria, where during the "middle" or "dark ages" for a period

of over 400 years Salsburg was a "city state" and the archbishop was also the king. Take the guided tour of the fortress and see the torture chamber where enemies of the archbishop and "heretics" were tortured until they "confessed" and then they were executed.

Did papal Rome persecute the saints? Yes.

7. **Attitude toward God's law.** The little horn would attempt to or "think to" change times and law (verse 25). It would view God's law as needing changes and would attempt to make changes in that law by its own authority. Several examples will illustrate this. Many could be given. Significantly, the Roman Catholic Church does not adhere to the basic Protestant notion that the Bible and the Bible only should be the standard of faith and practice. There are three major "sources of truth" for the Roman Catholic: the Bible, the "magisterium" or the teaching authority of the church, and, of course, the ex-cathedra words of the pope.

Now here are some claims of the Roman Church regarding changes in God's law:

"Around the year 1400 Petrus de Ancharano made the claim that 'the pope can modify divine law, since his power is not of man, but of God, and he acts in the place of God on earth, with the fullest power of binding and loosening his sheep.'

"This astonishing assertion came to practical fruitage during the Reformation. Luther claimed that his conscience was captive only to Holy Scripture. *Sola Scriptura* was his slogan. 'The Bible and the Bible only.' No churchly tradition would be allowed to guide his life.

"But one day it occurred to Johann Eck and to other Catholic churchmen to taunt Luther on his observance of Sunday in place of the Bible Sabbath. Said Eck, 'Scripture teaches: "Remember to hallow the Sabbath; six days shall you labor and do all your work, but the seventh day is the Sabbath day of the Lord your God," etc. Yet,' insisted Eck, 'the *church* has changed the Sabbath into Sunday on its own authority, on which *you* [Luther] have no Scripture.'

"At the great Council of Trent (1545-1563), convened by the pope to staunch the onrush of Protestantism, Gaspare de Posso, the archbishop of Reggio, in an address of January 18, 1562, brought the issue up again. 'The authority of the church,' he said, 'is illustrated most clearly by the scriptures; for while on the one hand she [the church] recommends them, declares them to be divine, [and] offers them to us to be read, . . . on the other hand, the legal precepts in the Scriptures taught by the Lord have ceased by virtue of the same authority [the church]. The Sabbath, the most glorious day in the law, has been changed into the Lord's day . . . These and other similar matters have not ceased by virtue of Christ's teaching (for He says He has come to fulfill the law, not to destroy it), but they have been changed by the authority of the church'" (Maxwell, *God Cares,* vol. 1, p. 128).

Hundreds of years later the Roman Church still asserts she can change God's law. Recently I purchased two books from a Catholic organization, Our Lady's Book Service, operated by the "Servant and Jesus and Mary" in Constable, New York. Both books are proported to have the "Imprimatur" or blessing of the church. One book, by the renowned James Cardinal Gibbons, archbishop of Baltimore, states: "The scriptures alone do not contain all the truths which a Christian is obliged to practice. Not to mention other examples, is not every Christian obligated to sanctify Sunday and to abstain on that day from unnecessary servile work? Is not the observance of this law among the most prominent of our sacred duties? But you may read the Bible from Genesis to Revelation, and you will not find a single line authorizing the sanctification of Sunday. The Scriptures enforce the religious observance of Saturday, a day which we never sanctify" (Gibbons, *The Faith of Our Fathers,* pp. 72, 73, 1876, reprinted by TAN Books and Publishers, 1980).

The other book is Peter Geiermann's Catechism. His comments, in question-and-answer format, on the Sabbath commandment are as follows:

"Q. *What is the Third Commandment?* [note: Catholics place the Sabbath Command third]

"A. The Third Commandment is: Remember that thou keep holy the Sabbath day.

"Q. *Which is the Sabbath day?*

"A. Saturday is the Sabbath day.

"Q. *Why do we observe Sunday instead of Saturday?*

"A. We observe Sunday instead of Saturday because the Catholic Church transferred the solemnity from Saturday to Sunday" (Rev. Peter Geiermann, C.SS.R., *The Convert's Catechism of Catholic Doctrine,* p. 50).

In addition, in Catholic listings of the Ten Commandments the second commandment is dropped altogether. Many of the others have been abbreviated, robbing them of their full meaning. And the tenth is divided in order to make a total of ten. In the comments on the fourth commandment in the New Catechism (called the third by the RCC) paragraph number 2190 it states: "The sabbath, which represented the completion of the first creation, has been replaced by Sunday which recalls the new creation inaugurated by the Resurrection of Christ" (*The Catechism of the Catholic Church*, 1994 edition, p. 529).

Did papal Rome try to change God's law? Yes.

8. **Length of time permitted to rule.** It—the little horn—was to rule for "a time, and times and half a time" (v. 25). Again, this is not complicated. A time = one year or 360 days in prophecy. Times = two years or 720 days, and half a time = half a year or 180 days. Add them up and you get 1260 days. This harmonizes with Revelation 13:5 where this period is spoken of as 42 months (42 months x 30 days per month = 1260 days) and in Revelation 12:6 where the time is actually recorded as 1260 days.

Maxwell gives a good explanation of this. "We are dealing here with symbols. The Bible says that the four beasts are symbols of four kings or kingdoms, that the horns likewise symbolize kingdoms, and that the waters are symbolic of multitudes of people [Rev. 17:15]. The Bible also indicates that in symbolic prophecy days represent years.

"You may recall that when Daniel lived in Babylon, the prophet Ezekiel lived at Nippur, not very far away. In the symbolic prophecy of Ezekiel, chapters 4 to 6, God said expressly to Ezekiel, 'I assign you, a day for each year.' Ezekiel 4:6" (Maxwell, *God Cares*, vol. 1, p. 124).

Remember, as we noted in number 2 (Time of rise), the papal Roman Catholic Church came to power in 538 A.D. If we add to that the 1260 years of the time it was given to rule, that brings us to 1798. And so it happened in 1798, 1260 years after 538, that the French general Berthier, under the direction of the military government of France, arrested Pope Pius VI in the Sistine chapel and took him captive, where he ultimately died in exile.

Did papal Rome dominate Europe during the 1260-year period from 538 to 1798? Yes.

These eight identifying characteristics of the "little horn" clearly point to the papal Roman Church. What other power, different than other powers, arose after the fall of the Roman Empire from among the divided kingdoms, destroyed three of the kingdoms, spoke blasphemy against God, persecuted God's saints, tried to change God's law, and dominated Europe for 1260 years? None but the Roman Catholic Church. No other power or entity even comes close to meeting the conditions. The little horn power is quite obviously the Roman Catholic Church.

But this takes us only to 1798. Does God leave us there to wonder what will happen next? Not at all. Remember how prophecy is progressive and builds on what happens or is given before? In order to fill in the prophetic picture right up to the 1990s we go to the apocalyptic book of Revelation. God gave the apostle John the same view of the future that He gave Daniel. However, by the time of John the first three world empires were already history, and he was living during the fourth and final world empire. Summarizing what had been given before, God quickly brought John up to speed in an impressive vision.

"Then I stood on the sand of the sea. And I saw a beast rising up out of the sea, having seven heads and ten horns, and on his horns ten crowns, and on his heads a blasphemous name. Now the beast which I saw was like a leopard, and his feet were like the feet of a bear, and his mouth like the mouth of a lion. And the dragon gave him his power, his throne, and great authority" (Revelation 13:1, 2).

This beast rose up out of the sea, which represents a populated area (Revelation 17:15). Then John saw a unique symbol—a beast with the body of a leopard, the feet of a bear, and the mouth of a lion. These are the same symbolic animals of Daniel 7. In his vision Daniel saw a lion (symbolizing Babylon), a bear (Medo-Persia), a leopard (Greece), and finally a "dreadful and terrible" beast (Rome). According to his vision, the fourth empire, Rome, would come to be dominated in its final stage by a "little horn," a terrible power that would persecute God's people for "a time, times, and half a time."

John's vision and prophecy are so similar to the description of the little horn in Daniel 7, and it unquestionably points to the time when the apostate papal church system of the Middle Ages began to dominate the state. The apostle Paul referred to this power as the "man of sin," and the "mystery of iniquity" (see 2 Thessalonians 2:3, 4).

One aspect of Revelation 13 is most significant. After ruling for

1260 years during the Middle Ages until 1798, the papacy appeared to receive a deadly wound. But this chapter in Revelation reveals an additional fact. The deadly wound heals, and all the world wonders after the beast (Revelation 13:3). Evidently, the papacy will play a major role in end-time events.

In identifying the role of the papacy and Roman Catholicism, I want to emphasize that I have no bone to pick with Catholic people. Without question there are many wonderful, God-fearing individuals in the Roman Catholic Church. The Bible is quite clear on that (Revelation 14:7 and 18:4). God does not condemn these dear people. Rather, it is the system to which God objects—the mingling of church and state, or as Revelation 17:1 shows, the prostitution of the church to the state.

The bottom line here is very simple and straightforward. In the outline of prophecy as given through the books of Daniel and the Revelation, papal Rome as a system is a major player. One can draw no other logical conclusion.

---

* For considerable documented evidence see my book *Even at the Door,* chapter four and the appendix to chapter four.

APPENDIX III

The United States—
World Superpower

Many nations have played important bit parts in history. However, only a relatively small number actually play a major role in Bible prophecy and salvation history. They are Babylon, Medo-Persia, Greece, Rome, the papacy, and the United States of America. There are many explicit characteristics of the sixth power that help to identify it as the last great earthly power to play a role in salvation history.

Daniel was promised by an angel that his book, though it would be sealed for a period of time, would be opened and understood at the time of the end (see Daniel 12:4, 9, 10). Revelation, on the other hand, was to be just that—a revelation of Jesus Christ which would show His servants things which must shortly take place (see Revelation 1:1; 22:6, 7). It is when we use our own human speculation regarding prophetic interpretation instead of using the Bible itself to be its own interpreter that we come up with all kinds of weird interpretations. Remember, God wants us to know.

It has been the traditional interpretation of Seventh-day Adventists that the second beast, mentioned in Revelation 13 (verse 11), the land beast, the beast with horns like a lamb, is the United States of America. The reason it is important to identify this beast is that whatever nation it is eventually cooperates with the revived or "healed" papacy at the end of time. These two will be the final players in the great drama of the ages.

In the last chapter when discussing the little horn, we noted that apparently when God gave John his vision in Revelation 13, He took it for granted that His servant John would be familiar with the book of Daniel and its beasts in chapter 7. So basically, Revelation 13 does not go all the way back to Babylon and move systematically forward as Daniel

212

2 and 7 do. Instead, the vision of Revelation 13 makes a quick two-verse summary to bring John up to speed and then proceeds to give more details that help to make a positive ID of the little horn power.

But now another beast rises out of the earth. "He had two horns like a lamb and spoke as a dragon" (Revelation 13:11). Again the biblical clues give unmistakable evidence as to its identity. Here are some of the biblical identifying characteristics of this beast with horns like a lamb.

1. It arises about the time when the first beast, the papacy, is wounded (verses 3, 11).
2. It, unlike the first beast of Revelation 13 and the beasts of Daniel 7, comes up out of the earth (verse 11).
3. It has two horns like a lamb (verse 11).
4. It speaks like a dragon (verse 11).
5. It has a worldwide influence (verses 12, 14).
6. It has authority like the first beast (verse 12).
7. It supports the first beast (verses 14, 15).
8. It encourages worship of the first beast (verse 15).
9. It performs great signs (verses 13, 14).
10. It becomes a persecuting power (verses 15, 17).
11. It causes many to receive the mark of the beast (verse 16).

"Beasts" in apocalyptic language represent kings or kingdoms. Accordingly, we can begin by looking for a kingdom or nation that fits the clues given in Revelation 13. It is an almost inescapable conclusion that the clues point to the United States of America. The clues reveal:

1. **The time of its rise to power.** We should look for a country that is rising to power around 1798, the time when the papacy received its "deadly wound." The pilgrims landed in the "New World" in the early 1600s. The various settlements known as colonies slowly began to bond together during the "colonial period." In 1776 the colonies unified to the point that the Declaration of Independence was drawn up. In 1787 the Constitution was ratified, and in 1789 the Bill of Rights was formulated. In 1791 the Bill of Rights was adopted. As we noted in the last appendix it was a French general (Berthier) who took the pope captive in 1798, and it is no doubt significant that it was that very same year that the French government recognized the United States as a nation.

Ellen White makes this observation: "What nation of the New World was in 1798 rising into power, giving promise of strength and greatness, and attracting the attention of the world? The application of the symbol admits of no question. One nation, and only one, meets the specifications of this prophecy; <u>it points unmistakably to the United States of America</u>" (*The Great Controversy*, p. 440).

2. **The location of the new power.** The other beasts or kingdoms in the prophetic lineup all rose from the sea, which as we have seen from Revelation 17:15 represents "peoples, multitudes, nations, and tongues." All of the other nations came to power amidst the peoples of the earth by conquering them. Babylon conquered its surrounding nations including Israel; Medo-Persia conquered Babylon, etc., but this beast came up "out of the earth." So the nation we are looking for is one that "developed" or "grew up" by exploration, colonization, and development. Only one place on earth was "undeveloped" as far as the rest of the world was concerned—the North American continent. And it certainly was colonized by people moving here from other nations. Literally millions came to America from Ireland, Italy, Germany, and other countries of Europe initially and then from all parts of the world. Who hasn't heard of Ellis Island and the Statue of Liberty? In fact, fitted right into the pedestal or base of the Statue of Liberty is this famous poem:

The New Colossus
"Not like the brazen giant of Greek fame,
With conquering limbs astride from land to land;
Here at our sea-washed, sunset gates shall stand
A mighty woman with a torch, whose flame
Is the imprisoned lightning, and her name
Mother of Exiles. <u>From her beacon-hand</u>
<u>Glows world-wide welcome;</u> her mild eyes command
The air-bridged harbor that twin cities frame.

"'Keep ancient lands, your storied pomp!' cries she with silent lips.
<u>'Give me your tired, your poor,</u>
<u>Your huddled masses yearning to breath free,</u>
The wretched refuse of your teaming shore.
<u>Send these, the homeless, tempest-tost to me,</u>
<u>I lift my lamp beside the golden door!'"</u>
—Emma Lazarus

And so they came—by the millions! And still today they want to come! The new nation idea called by many the "American experiment," has been a part of the core of American history. But it was not without a struggle. There was a great civil war: Americans fighting Americans over differences in ideology.

Just a little over an hour's drive from my home is the little community of Gettysburg, Pennsylvania. The battle fought there on July 1 to 3 of 1863 marked a turning point in the war. The circumstances leading to this particular battle are very intriguing. General George G. Meade led a Northern army of about 90,000 men to victory against General Robert E. Lee's Southern army of about 75,000. The two forces met accidently in the little town of Gettysburg, Pennsylvania. The shooting began when a Confederate brigade ran into Union cavalrymen in Gettysburg on July 1.

The two armies spent the first day maneuvering for position. Northern troops settled south of town in a strong defensive position. Lee tried to crack the left side of the Union's defenses on the second day. The attack crushed a Northern corps, but failed to occupy the position. On July 3, Lee decided to aim directly at the Union center. In a famous charge, General George E. Pickett's troops advanced across an open field and up the slopes of Cemetery Ridge into murderous Northern fire. They reached the crest of the ridge, but could not hold the position. Lee withdrew his battered forces to Virginia. But the casualty list was long. More than 38,000 men lay dead on the battlefield.

Later that same year it was decided that a memorial should be established at Gettysburg. Part of that battlefield would be dedicated to be a cemetery for those who died there. On November 19, 1863, President Abraham Lincoln came up on the train "to say a few words" on the occasion of setting aside this special cemetery. He was not the featured speaker. The famous orator Edward Everett spoke for two hours before Lincoln gave his two-minute talk. Few have any knowledge of what Everett said in those two hours, but Lincoln's "few words" are known by all Americans as the Gettysburg Address. In those days everyone knew that America was unique, but wondered if the American experiment could work.

"Four score and seven years ago <u>our fathers brought forth</u> <u>on this continent, a new nation,</u> conceived in Liberty, and dedicated to the proposition that all men are created equal.

"Now we are engaged in a great civil war, testing whether that nation, or any nation so conceived and so dedicated, can long endure. We are met on a great battlefield of that war. We have come to dedicate a portion of that field, as a final resting place for those who here gave their lives that that nation might live. It is altogether fitting and proper that we should do this.

"But, in a larger sense, we can not dedicate—we can not consecrate—we can not hallow—this ground. The brave men, living and dead, who struggled here, have consecrated it, far above our power to add or detract. The world will little note, nor long remember what we say here, but it can never forget what they did here. It is for us the living, rather, to be dedicated here to the unfinished work which they who fought here have thus far so nobly advanced. It is rather for us to be here dedicated to the great task remaining before us—that from these honored dead we take increased devotion to that cause for which they gave the last full measure of devotion—that we here highly resolve that these dead shall not have died in vain—that this nation, under God, shall have a new birth of freedom—and that government of the people, by the people, for the people, shall not perish from the earth."

—Abraham Lincoln, Gettysburg, Pennsylvania, Nov. 19, 1863

The Emma Lazarus poem on the Statue of Liberty and Lincoln's Gettysburg Address show clearly that from a simply historical perspective the United States is truly a "new nation." There can be no question that the United States fits the second clue.

3. **It has two horns like a lamb**. Some interpreters have called this beast a lamblike beast. The Bible doesn't call the beast lamblike. It says that its horns are lamblike. Lamblike describes the horns not the beast. Ellen White makes 17 references to this in her writings and she always says the horns are lamblike—not the beast. There is a great difference in meaning. The beast grows to be big and powerful but it has "lamblike" horn. Maybe a buffalo—which some have pictured— would be more like the beast which John saw.

Why make such a big deal out of the lamblike description? It is quite simple. A misinterpretation can lead to a wrong conclusion! A former Adventist minister with nearly a million copies of his book in print, believes that the second beast of Revelation 13 is the antichrist. His reasoning is simple. He says if this beast is lamblike but not "the" lamb or Christ, then it must be the antichrist. This error could not have come up if one would just read the scripture carefully. The "horns" are "lamblike," not the beast. What do the two horns represent, then? I believe they could quite logically represent the "gentle" characteristics of Republicanism and Protestantism—a nation without a despotic king and a church without an authoritarian pope. The bottom line here is that the new nation would have civil and religious liberty.

"At the time when the Papacy, robbed of its strength, was forced to desist from persecution, John beheld a new power coming up to echo the dragon's voice, and carry forward the same cruel and blasphemous work. This power, the **last** that is to wage war against the church and the law of God, is represented by a beast with lamblike horns. The beasts preceding it had risen from the sea; but this came up out of the earth, representing the peaceful rise of the nation which it symbolized—the United States.

"The 'two horns like a lamb' well represent the character of our own government, as expressed in its two fundamental principles,— Republicanism and Protestantism. These principles are the secret of our power and prosperity as a nation. Those who first found an asylum on the shores of America, rejoiced that they had reached a country free from the arrogant claims of popery and the tyranny of kingly rule. They determined to establish a government upon the broad foundation of civil and religious liberty" (Ellen White, *The Signs of the Times,* Feb. 8, 1910).

4. **It becomes very powerful.** Revelation says, "speaks like a dragon." The United States is the only remaining world "superpower" today. No country on earth has the political or military muscle of the United States today. Yet this clue is fulfilled only partially at present. We may expect to see it further fulfilled in the near future.

"The dragon," of course, is Satan. But Satan also works through the other dragon-like beasts of prophecy. So apparently the United States will become more "Satan-like" near the end. Some might wonder how the United States could ever "speak as a dragon" and become a persecuting power. But the Bible says it will happen.

"The founders of the nation wisely sought to guard against the employment of secular power on the part of the church, with its inevitable result—intolerance and persecution. The Constitution provides that 'Congress shall make no law respecting an establishment of religion, or prohibiting the free exercise thereof' and that 'no religious test shall ever be required as a qualification to any office of public trust under the United States.' Only in flagrant violation of these safeguards to the nation's liberty, can any religious observance be enforced by civil authority. But the inconsistency of such action is no greater than is represented in the symbol. It is the beast with lamblike horns—in profession pure, gentle, and harmless—that speaks as a dragon" (*The Great Controversy*, p. 442).

5. **It has worldwide influence.** With the demise of the former Soviet Union the United States "leads" the world. For example, there would have been no "liberation" of Kuwait without the United States. The success of the "Desert Storm" war was possible only with the power and technology of the United States.

This worldwide influence was recognized by Malachi Martin in *The Keys of This Blood,* published in 1990. On the cover and in the introduction to his book Martin says that there was a three-way struggle going on for world dominion between the pope (Roman Catholicism), Gorbachev (the Soviet Union), and the Capitalist West (the United States and its allies). Martin expects the pope to be the victor in the struggle and that "those of us under seventy will at least see the basic structures of the new world government installed" (pp. 15, 16). He goes on to say, "It is not too much to say, in fact, that the chosen purpose of John Paul's pontificate—the engine that drives his papal grand policy and that determines his day-to-day, year-by-year strategies—is to be the victor in that competition, now well under way" (p. 17).

There can be no question that the United States does have worldwide influence today. But in the future, "As America, the land of religious liberty, shall unite with the papacy in forcing the conscience and compelling men to honor the false sabbath, the people of every country on the globe will be led to follow her example." Ellen White concludes, "Our people are not half awake to do all in their power, with the facilities within their reach, to extend the message of warning" (*Testimonies for the Church,* vol. 6, p. 18).

6. **It exercises all the authority of the first beast (the papacy).**
This will be fulfilled "When the Protestant churches shall unite with the secular power to sustain a false religion, for opposing which their ancestors endured the fiercest persecution; when the state shall use its power to enforce the decrees and sustain the institutions of the church—then will Protestant America have formed an image to the papacy [the beast], and there will be a national apostasy which will end only in national ruin" (Ellen G. White, *Signs of the Times,* March 22, 1910).

7. **It—the United States—supports the first beast—the papacy.** Many state Sunday laws were established around the turn of the century. But one essential ingredient was missing for them to constitute "the" national Sunday law. The missing ingredient was a cooperation between the United States and the papacy. In fact, as history bears out, there was a very strong anti-Catholic bias in the United States. How things have changed today! During Ronald Reagan's presidency we established "full diplomatic relations with the central government of the Roman Catholic Church," and additionally, in what has been called the "Holy Alliance," we cooperated with the papacy in bringing about the downfall of Communism.

8. **It encourages worship of the first beast.** One of the major factors in the identification of the first beast (of Revelation 13 and the little horn of Daniel 7) is that it is "different." This "worship" clue does include that the allegiance involves not only a civil but also a religious entity. In plain language the United States will eventually encourage support of the Roman Catholic Church. In fact, that is happening right now! Churchmen like Chuck Colson, Pat Robertson, Billy Graham, and others are encouraging support of Rome. And civil leaders like President Clinton, Vice President Gore, and most of the Republican establishment are giving political support for the aims of Rome.

9. **It would perform great signs.** The "signs" mentioned in Revelation 13 are things like "fire coming down from heaven." Significantly this type of sign is now being predicted by "The Blessed Virgin Mother, Mary" in apparitions around the world.

10. **It becomes a persecuting power.** This characteristic of the beast with lamblike horns has yet to be revealed. "Our land is in jeopardy. The time is drawing on when its legislators shall so abjure the principles of Protestantism as to give countenance to Romish apostasy.

The people for whom God has so marvelously wrought, strengthening them to throw off the galling yoke of popery, will, by a national act, give vigor to the corrupt faith of Rome, and thus arouse the tyranny which only waits for a touch to start again into cruelty and despotism. With rapid steps are we already approaching this period" (Ellen White, *Signs of the Times,* July 4, 1899).

11. **It causes many to receive the mark of the beast.** The United States, founded on the principles of civil and religious liberty, and so blessed of God, will be instrumental in bringing about the mark of the beast.

Taken together these clues are very clear. They point unmistakably to the United States as the second beast of Revelation 13—the beast with lamblike horns.

Unmasking the Antichrist

The antichrist is described as the great opponent and counterfeit of Christ, by whom he is finally to be conquered. The term antichrist may mean one who is opposed to Christ, or one who assumes the place of Christ, or one who combines both of these roles by assuming the prerogatives of Christ. The term antichrist occurs only in the New Testament and only in the writings of John (1 John 2:18, 22; 4:3; and 2 John 7).

It seems that John takes it for granted that his readers understand that the full manifestation of antichrist is in the last days. He speaks, however, of many antichrists in his day (1 John 2:18). He also uses the singular term "antichrist." Under the figure of the leopard beast of Revelation 13 he depicts a great power that would oppose Christ and His people.

Satan is "the ultimate" antichrist. He has opposed Christ through various human agencies. He has introduced many heresies through the centuries, all suited to deceive. In John's day Docetism and Gnosticism were doubtless considered anti-Christian. Through the centuries many Bible scholars, even some Roman Catholics, have identified the papacy as antichrist. I concur with this view and will share the evidence for this conclusion in this appendix.

At the very end of human history Satan will play a direct, personal role in world affairs (2 Thessalonians 2:9). In fact, Satan's personation of Christ will be followed quickly by the real second coming of Christ.

If the antichrist was already working in John's day and will be working intensely at the end of time, it could not be a specific man. It is rather the devil working through a "system" of evil.

In *Jesus Is My Judge—Meditations on the Book of Daniel,* Dr. Leslie Hardinge gives over 100 Bible clues for the identity of the antichrist. He makes the point, as do many other scholars, that the antichrist John speaks of is also the little horn of Daniel 7 and 8.

Chuck Colson, writing in *Evangelicals and Catholics Together,* observes, "About the only moral value postmodernists [our generation] seem to be able to advance is total, undiscriminating tolerance, but being able to tolerate anything is a formula for accepting the status quo. Those who accept people as they are have no interest in helping them change, even when their condition and behavior is ruining their lives . . . Mere tolerance is a weak and passive virtue compared to the active energy of Christian love" (p. 22).

The attitude that says I'm OK—you're OK, or just do your own thing, or if it makes you feel good—do it, is not appropriate for a Christian who is committed to fulfilling the gospel commission. Failure to warn of error and danger is unconscionable. Failure to state what the danger is in a clear and concise way is also just as bad.

While maintaining a spirit of love toward those deceived, Ellen White called Romanism a "mammoth system of deception" and wrote that "The people need to be aroused to resist the advances of this most dangerous foe to civil and religious liberty." She went on to say, "Papists place crosses upon their churches, upon their altars, and upon their garments. Everywhere is seen the insignia of the cross. Everywhere it is outwardly honored and exalted. But the teachings of Christ are buried beneath a mass of senseless traditions, false interpretations, and rigorous exactions. . . . Conscientious souls are kept in constant terror fearing the wrath of an offended God, while many of the dignitaries of the church are living in luxury and sensual pleasure" (*The Great Controversy*, pp. 570, 566, 568).

"The apostle Paul warned the church not to look for the coming of Christ in his day. 'That day shall not come,' he says, 'except there come a falling away first, and that man of sin be revealed.' 2 Thessalonians 2:3. Not until after the great apostasy, and the long period of the reign of the 'man of sin,' can we look for the advent of our Lord. The 'man of sin,' which is also styled 'the mystery of iniquity,' 'the son of perdition,' and 'that wicked,' **represents the papacy,** which, as foretold in prophecy, was to maintain its supremacy for 1260 years. This period ended in 1798. The coming of Christ could not come before that time" (*ibid.,* p. 356).

But how could the "Christian" church become so enmeshed with error as to be an antichrist power? The answer seems to be the "Christianizing" of paganism. It is quite clear to students of church history that Constantine's "conversion" to Christianity and his acceptance into the church was a matter of mutual convenience. Over the years much of paganism came into the belief and practice of the church. John Henry Newman, Rome's most famous English convert, gave the following list of church practices that came directly from paganism:

"The use of temples, and those dedicated to the particular saints, and ornamented on occasion with branches of trees, incense, lamps and candles; votive offerings on recovery from illness, holy water, asylums, holy days and seasons, use of calendars, processions, blessings on fields, sacerdotal vestments, the tonsure, the ring in marriage, turning to the East, images at a later date, perhaps the ecclesiastical chant, and Kyrie Eleison are all of pagan origin, and sanctified by adoption into the Church" (Cardinal J. H. Newman: *An Essay on the Development of Christian Doctrine,* p. 373).

There are many other pagan practices in Romanism today such as: "The sacrificing Priesthood, penances, absolution and the Confessional, Papal Infallibility, the titles 'Holy Father' and 'supreme pontiff,' the worship or veneration of Saints and relics (such as the Turin Shroud) and of idols, images, statues and symbols; stone altars; the rosary, the monstrance and wafer, prayers for the dead, extreme unction, purgatory and limbo, plenary indulgences, ritualism, monasticism and mysticism; add to these pilgrimages, crosses and crucifixes, celibacy, the Mother and Child worship; Mary's continuing virginity, the scapular, canonization of Saints, Cardinals, nuns, the mitre, fish on Friday, the (mystic) keys, Lent; the sign of the cross, the 'Sacred Heart,' Easter (from Astarte the goddess of spring, associated with the sun rising in the east), baptismal regeneration and justification by works; Peter 'the rock,' rather than Peter's faith in Christ; all these things and many besides, are at the heart of modern Roman Catholicism. Not all are widely practiced in Western Protestant countries, but they are nevertheless deeply embedded in Church tradition. All are unsupported by Scripture and many are expressly forbidden in the Bible" (Michael de Semlyen, *All Roads Lead to Rome,* pp. 61, 62).

The discerning student will quickly note that the two major doctrinal errors in the end-time scenario, Sunday sacredness and the immortality of the soul, both come directly from paganism—from the devil—and not the Holy Scriptures.

The Authority of Scripture

Some say that it is unfair to judge the modern church by the church of the past. The church has changed, they say. Yes, many public practices have changed such as using English in the services here in America, the priest facing the congregation, etc. But what doctrine or pagan practice has changed? Can you name even one? I can't. Sadly, the Roman Catholic Church holds that the Bible alone is not a sufficient guide for faith and practice. I will quote three Catholic authors for evidence of that "antichrist" position.

"The Scriptures alone do not contain all the truths which a Christian is bound to believe, nor do they explicitly enjoin all the duties which he is obliged to practice. Not to mention other examples, is not every Christian obliged to sanctify Sunday and to abstain on that day from unnecessary servile work: Is not the observance of this law among the most prominent of our sacred duties? But you may read the Bible from Genesis to Revelation, and you will not find a single line authorizing the sanctification of Sunday. The Scriptures enforce the religious observance of Saturday, a day which we never sanctify.

"The Catholic Church correctly teaches that our Lord and His Apostles inculcated certain important duties of religion which are not recorded by the inspired writers. For instance, most Christians pray to the Holy Ghost, a practice which is nowhere found in the Bible.

"We must therefore, conclude that the Scriptures alone cannot be a sufficient guide and rule of faith because they cannot, at any time, be within the reach of every inquirer; because they are not of themselves clear and intelligible even in matters of the highest importance, and **because they do not contain all the truths necessary for salvation**" (James Cardinal Gibbons, *The Faith of Our Fathers,* pp. 72, 73).

In 1994 the Roman Catholic Church produced the new *Catechism of the Catholic Church.* The full edition of the Catechism had not been revised since the sixteenth century (1566). It was also the first full edition of the Catechism to be printed in English. It sold over 10,000,000 copies in the first six month of circulation. Significantly, it has the Imprimatur of the Vatican in the form of the signature of Cardinal Joseph Ratzinger, the director of the Congregation for the Doctrine of the Faith which is "the Roman Inquisition's latest incarnation" (*Time,* December 6, 1993, p. 58). *Time* goes on to report that "The Cardinal

[Ratzinger] likes to explain his faith through the story of one of his theology professors, a man who questioned the thinking behind the church's 1950 declaration that the Assumption of the Virgin Mary into Heaven was an infallible tenet. He said, 'No this is not possible—we don't have a foundation in Scripture. It is not possible to give this as dogma.' This led the professor's Protestant friends to hope they had a potential convert. But the professor immediately reaffirmed his abiding Catholicism. 'No, at this moment I will be convinced that the church is wiser than I.' Ratzinger asserts, 'It was always my idea to be a Catholic, to follow the Catholic faith and not my own opinions.' Theologians may wrangle all they want, he says, but faith in the end is something ineffable, springing from the heart. And once it is felt there, he says, 'then the mind will accept it too'" (*Time,* Dec. 6, 1993, p. 60). This great enforcer of the Catholic faith states in essence that it doesn't matter if your belief is biblical or not—if the church teaches it, you will accept it.

Ellen White gave this very perceptive insight into this topic. "The Roman Church reserves to the clergy the right to interpret the Scriptures. On the ground that ecclesiastics alone are competent to explain God's word, it is withheld from the common people. Though the Reformation gave the Scriptures to all, yet the selfsame principle which was maintained by Rome prevents multitudes in Protestant churches from searching the Bible for themselves. They are taught to accept its teachings *as interpreted by the church;* and there are thousands who dare receive nothing, however plainly revealed in Scripture, that is contrary to their creed or the established teaching of their church" (*The Great Controversy,* p. 596).

But here again hasn't the church changed? Now the Catholic Church encourages the study of the Bible. There are even Bible study groups. Yes, one can study all he wants to, but to remain a Catholic you must accept the interpretation of the church above the plain meaning of Scripture.

Perhaps the best example of this is the stated belief of Roman Catholic attorney and author, Keith Fournier. He is a college graduate, a law school graduate, a college administrator, and now works full-time for the Christian Coalition as the director of the American Center for Law and Justice. He states that he is a born-again Christian, a tongues-speaking, Holy Spirit-filled, Evangelical Catholic. He is a "professional Christian," who has been involved in the Charismatic movement and the ecumenical movement and has written several books on religious topics—and yet in spite of all this he will not make a biblical decision apart from the teaching of the church. He says, "I am thoroughly convinced that the church of Christ must be both hierarchial and charismatic, institutional and dynamic, and that she is indeed the universal sign (sacrament) of salvation still revealing Christ's presence in the world. Therefore I have submitted myself to the teaching office of the Catholic Church and its leadership. I do this willingly and by conscious choice."

Fournier goes on to say, "I have often heard friends refer to themselves as 'Bible-toting believers.' Well, I am too, but as a Catholic, I believe that there is a magisterium, a teaching office, that provides ongoing guidance in the application of that Book to my life. **Hence I am a magisterium-toting Catholic.** I appreciate the moral clarity the magisterium provides" (Keith Fournier, *A House United,* p. 32).

ANTI-CATHOLIC BIGOTRY?

Many "politically correct" Christians say that to point out the errors of the Catholic Church is prejudiced and bigoted. We need to keep in mind that "It is true that there are real Christians in the Roman Catholic communion. Thousands in that church are serving God according to the best light they have . . . But Romanism as a system is no more in harmony with the gospel of Christ now than in any former period of her history. The Protestant churches are in great darkness, or they would discern the signs of the times. The Roman Church is far-reaching in her plans and modes of operation. She is employing every device to extend her influence and increase her power in preparation for a fierce and determined conflict to regain control of the world, to re-establish persecution, and to undo all that Protestantism has done. Catholicism is gaining ground on every side . . . Protestants have tampered with and patronized popery; they have made compromises and concessions which papists themselves are surprised to see and fail to understand" (*The Great Controversy,* pp. 565, 566).

Is it prejudice to expose error? Is it bigotry to stand for the truth of God's Word and encourage others to join you? If you think it is, then what kind of message will you give during the latter rain and the loud cry? The message of Revelation 18 is twofold: "Babylon is fallen" and "Come out of her My people." Think about it! The bottom line is that the truth must be spoken in love—but it must be spoken.

"As the time comes for it [the third angel's message] to be given with greatest power, the Lord will work through humble instruments . . . <u>The sins of Babylon will be laid open.</u> The fearful results of enforcing the observances of the church by civil authority, the inroads of spiritualism, the stealthy but rapid progress of the papal power—<u>all will be unmasked. Thousands upon thousands will listen who have never heard words like these. In amazement they hear the testimony that Babylon is the Church, fallen because of her errors and sins,</u> because of her rejection of the truth sent to her from heaven" (*ibid.,* pp. 606, 607).

CATHOLICS DISCUSS THE PAPACY

Over the years many Catholic leaders have deplored the gross immorality in the Catholic Church. In fact, Martin Luther, "as an Augustinian monk in the University of Wittenberg, came reluctantly to believe 'the papacy is in truth . . . very Antichrist.' " And "Through the centuries, various Roman Catholic spokesmen have felt that the pope—either the current one or a future one, or the papacy as a whole (the entire line of popes)—was the Antichrist. For example, during a time of deep spiritual laxness in Rome, Arnoff, the bishop of Orleans, deplored the Roman popes as 'monsters of guilt' and declared in the council called by the king of France in 991 that the pontiff, clad in purple and gold, was 'Antichrist, sitting in the temple of God, and showing himself as God.'

"When the Western church was divided for about 40 years between two rival popes, one in Rome and the other in Avignon, France, each pope called the other pope antichrist—and John Wycliffe is reputed to have regarded them both as being right: 'two halves of Antichrist, making up the perfect Man of Sin between them'" (Maxwell, *God Cares,* vol. 1, p. 117).

In the thirteenth century a terrible feud developed between Frederick II, ruler of the Holy Roman Empire, and Pope Gregory IX. During this controversy Eberhard II, archbishop of Salzburg, who was a supporter of Frederick, reported in public the results of his biblical studies—that the pope was the antichrist and the little horn of Daniel 7. "His boldest statement was made at a synod of Bavarian bishops held in Regensburg, or Ratisbon, in 1240 or 1241; where he gave utterance at the same time to a new interpretation of some lines of prophecy. Here, during this council, Eberhard, in a brilliant oration preserved by Aventinus, or Turmair, in his noted Bavarian Annals, clearly sets forth this identification of the prophecy of the Little Horn. In this striking presentation Eberhard not only openly calls the pope a wolf in shepherd's garb, the Son of Perdition, and Antichrist, but also gives his revolutionary exposition of the pope as the Little Horn of Daniel 7" (Leroy Edwin Froom, *The Prophetic Faith of Our Fathers*, vol. 1, pp. 797, 798).

Eberhard's declaration came at the height of the papal power, which was the midnight of Bible truth and religious freedom. Ellen White describes those days in this manner: "The Holy Scriptures were almost unknown, not only to the people, but to the priests. Like the Pharisees of old, the papal leaders hated the light which would reveal their sins. God's law, the standard of righteousness, having been removed, they exercised their power without limit, and practiced vice without restraint. Fraud, avarice, and profligacy prevailed. Men shrank from no crime by which they could gain wealth or position. The palaces of popes and prelates were scenes of vilest debauchery. Some of the reigning pontiffs were guilty of crimes so revolting that secular rulers endeavored to depose these dignitaries of the church as monsters too vile to be tolerated. For centuries Europe had made no progress in learning, arts, or civilization. A moral and intellectual paralysis had fallen upon Christendom" (*The Great Controversy*, p. 60).

Sadly, the papacy, Roman Catholicism, does indeed fit the prophetic definitions of the system through which the great antichrist, Satan, is working. "The papacy is just what the prophecy declared that she would be, the apostasy of the latter times" (*ibid.*, p. 571).

The Seal of God

I n the Bible the seal of God is good and its counterpart, the mark of the beast, is bad. No one gets both. Everyone who lives to see Jesus come will get one or the other. It is important to clearly identify the seal of God. We need to prepare for it. Actually, the sealing process is a trigger point in the book of Revelation. John says, "After these things I saw four angels standing at the four corners of the earth, holding the four winds of the earth, that the wind should not blow on the earth, on the sea, or on any tree.

"Then I saw another angel ascending from the east, having the seal of the living God. And he cried with a loud voice to the four angels to whom it was granted to harm the earth and the sea.

"Saying, 'Do not harm the earth, the sea, or the trees till we have sealed the servants of our God on their foreheads.'

"And I heard the number of those who were sealed. One hundred and forty-four thousand of all the tribes of the children of Israel were sealed" (Revelation 7:1-4).

Evidently, God's wrath is not poured out until His seal is placed on His servants. The seal, placed on their foreheads, identifies them and provides protection.

The King James Bible has 25 references to the word "seal." The general usage denotes something official: something with a permanent mark. The book of Esther records the word of the Persian king to Esther following the hanging of Haman. Wanting to protect Esther and all of the Jews in his realm, he told them, "You yourselves write a decree for the Jews, as you please, in the king's name, and seal it with the king's signet ring; for a letter which is written in the king's name and sealed with the king's signet ring no one can revoke" (Esther 8:8).

God loves each one of us dearly. A study of His seal reveals some amazing concepts. We are His by virtue of creation and redemption. He paid for us. And He is coming back soon to get us! Note the following exciting passage: "Now He who establishes us with you in Christ and has anointed us is God, who also has sealed us and given us the Spirit in our hearts as a deposit" (2 Corinthians 1:21, 22, NKJV). Here God seals us with His Spirit as a deposit. The KJV says, "He has given the earnest [as in earnest money] of the Spirit in our hearts." The NIV says, "He has put his Spirit in our hearts as a deposit, guaranteeing what is to come." And who is given the Holy Spirit? Acts 5:32 states, "And we are His witnesses to these things, and so also is the Holy Spirit whom <u>God has given to those who obey Him.</u>" This is one of the clues we are looking for. Obedience involves God's law. God's seal is given to those who obey His law.

Isaiah 8:16 commands, "Bind up the testimony, seal the <u>law</u> among my disciples." Here again the seal involves God's law. When we go to God's great moral law, the Ten Commandments as recorded in Exodus 20, it is easy for one to observe that the fourth commandment in particular identifies its author and on what basis He should be worshiped. A seal typically gives the name, title, and territory of a ruler. The fourth commandment contains these elements in regard to God. The name—"The Lord Thy God"; title—"Creator"; territory—"Heaven and Earth." With the fourth commandment, the Creator plainly indicates that it is the Sabbath which is to stand as His eternal seal. God plainly said this to Moses. "Speak also to the children of Israel, saying: '<u>Surely My Sabbaths you shall keep, for it is a sign between Me and you throughout your generations,</u> that you may know that I am the Lord who sanctifies you' " (Exodus 31:13). There is more evidence from Scripture: God says, "Moreover <u>I also gave them My Sabbaths, to be a sign between them and Me, that they might know that I am the Lord who sanctifies them.</u> 'I am the Lord your God: Walk in My statutes, keep My judgments, and do them; <u>hallow My Sabbaths, and they will be a sign between Me and you, that you may know that I am the Lord your God'</u> " (Ezekiel 20:12, 19, 20).

"<u>The Sabbath</u> is not introduced [at Mt. Sinai] as a new institution but as having been founded at creation [see Genesis 2:1-3]. It is to be remembered and observed as the memorial of the Creator's work. Pointing to God as the Maker of the heavens and the earth, it <u>distinguishes the true God from all false gods.</u> All who keep the seventh day signify by this act that they are worshipers of Jehovah. Thus the

Sabbath is the sign of man's allegiance to God as long as there are any upon the earth to serve Him. The fourth commandment is the only one of all the ten in which are found both the name and the title of the Lawgiver. It is the only one that shows by whose authority the law is given. Thus it contains the seal of God, affixed to His law as evidence of its authenticity and binding force" (*Patriarchs and Prophets,* p. 307).

In changing the Sabbath the papal power violated the seal of God on the law. God's followers are called upon to restore the Sabbath of the fourth commandment to its rightful position as the Creator's memorial, the sign of His authority and His covenant with His people.

THE SIGNIFICANCE OF THE SEAL

"Not all who profess to keep the Sabbath will be sealed" (*Testimonies for the Church,* vol. 5, p. 213). A survey of the chapter from which this statement is taken indicates that knowledge of the Sabbath and a merely legalistic observance of it falls far short of evidencing a saving relationship with God. Then what, in addition to Sabbathkeeping, is necessary to receive the seal of God? "The seal of God will never be placed upon the forehead of an impure man or woman. It will never be placed upon the head of an ambitious, world-loving man or woman. It will never be placed upon the forehead of men or women of false tongues or deceitful hearts. All who receive the seal must be without spot before God—candidates for heaven" (*ibid.,* p. 216). In other words, those who receive the seal of God will not only be Sabbathkeepers, they will also be converted, committed, loving, and honest Christians.

Ellen White explains that those who are sealed have settled "into the truth, both intellectually and spiritually, so that they cannot be moved" (*Manuscript Releases,* vol. 10, p. 252). They believe the truth and they practice the truth. They believe in the perpetuity of God's law and they trust Him to sanctify them. "No other institution which was committed to the Jews tended so fully to distinguish them from surrounding nations as did the Sabbath. God designed that its observance should designate them as His worshipers. It was to be a token of their separation from idolatry, and their connection with the true God. But in order to keep the Sabbath holy, men must themselves be holy. Through faith they must become partakers of the righteousness of Christ" (*The Desire of Ages,* p. 283).

Earlier we noted that 2 Corinthians 1:22 states we are sealed by God's Spirit as an earnest pledge, deposit, or guarantee. Let's now consider what that truly means. "The sealing is a pledge from God of perfect security to His chosen ones (Ex. 31:13-17). Sealing indicates you are God's chosen. He has appropriated you to Himself. As the sealed of God we are Christ's purchased possession, and no one shall pluck us out of His hands. The seal given in the forehead is God, New Jerusalem. 'I will write upon him the name of My God, and the name of the city of My God' (Rev. 3:12)" (*Manuscript Releases,* vol. 15, p. 225).

Neither the seal of God nor the mark of the beast are visible marks to the human eye. It is also important to note that though the mark of the beast can be received either in the hand or on the forehead, the seal of God can be received only on the forehead. Most Bible students believe that with regard to the Sunday law and the mark of the beast one can choose to believe and support it—mark on the forehead, or choose to not make any waves and just go along with it—mark in the hand. Obviously, no one will "just go along" with the seal of God. It is something one must be willing to die for.

So, then, what is this seal that is placed on the foreheads of the saved? "It is a mark which angels, not human eyes, can read; for the destroying angel must see the mark of redemption. The intelligent mind has seen the sign of the cross of Calvary in the Lord's adopted sons and daughters. The sin of the transgression of the law of God is taken away. They have on the wedding garment, and are obedient and faithful to all God's commands" (*The Gospel Herald,* June 11, 1902). The living righteous will receive the seal of God prior to the close of probation and it will be their passport through the gates of the Holy City. (See *Maranatha,* p. 211 and *The SDA Bible Commentary,* vol. 7, p. 970.)

Certainly the Sabbath is central to obeying God and receiving His seal. It is central to recognizing the great end-time apostasy. It is not an obscure interpretation by one or two Bible scholars. It is woven into the very fabric of God's Word to us. Early Adventists held the Sabbath aloft and treasured it. The following "facts" on the Sabbath come from an old tract published by the Review and Herald Publishing Association about the year 1885. Read through these significant—and still very true—facts to understand the continuing significance of the Sabbath.

ONE HUNDRED BIBLE FACTS UPON THE SABBATH QUESTION

Why keep the Sabbath day? What is the object of the Sabbath? Who made it? When was it made, and for whom? Which day is the true Sabbath? Many keep the first day of the week, or Sunday. What Bible authority have they for this? Some keep the seventh day, or Saturday. What scripture have they for that? Here are the facts about both days, as plainly stated in the Word of God:

SIXTY BIBLE FACTS CONCERNING THE SEVENTH DAY

1. After working the first six days of the week in creating this earth, the great God rested on the seventh day. Genesis 2:1-3.

2. This stamped that day as God's rest day, or Sabbath day, as Sabbath day means rest day. To illustrate: When a person is born on a certain day, that day thus becomes his *birthday*. So when God rested upon the seventh day, that day became His rest, or Sabbath day.

3. Therefore the seventh day must always be God's Sabbath day. Can you change your birthday from the day on which you were born? No. Neither can you change God's rest day to a day on which He did not rest. Hence the seventh day is still God's Sabbath day.

4. The Creator blessed the seventh day. Genesis 2:3.

5. He sanctified the seventh day. Exodus 20:11.

6. He made it the Sabbath day in the garden of Eden. Genesis 2:1-3.

7. It was made before the fall; hence it is not a type; for types were not introduced till after the fall.

8. Jesus said it was made for *man* (Mark 2:27); that is, for the race, as the word man here is unlimited; hence, for the Gentile as well as for the Jews.

9. It is a memorial of creation. Exodus 20:11; 31:17. Every time we rest upon the seventh day, as God did at creation, we commemorate that great event.

10. It was given to Adam, the head of the human race. Mark 2:27; Genesis 2:1-3.

11. Hence through him, as our representative, to all nations. Acts 17:26.

12. It is not a Jewish institution; for it was made 2,300 years before there ever was a Jew.

13. The Bible never calls it the Jewish Sabbath; but always, "the Sabbath of the Lord thy God." Men should be cautious how they

stigmatize God's holy rest day.

14. Evident reference is made to the Sabbath all through the patriarchal age. Genesis 2:1-3; 8:10, 12; 29:27, 28, etc.

15. It was a part of God's law before Sinai. Exodus 16:4, 27-29.

16. Then God placed it in the heart of His moral law. Exodus 20:1-17. Why did He place it there if it was not like the other nine precepts, which all admit to be immutable?

17. The seventh-day Sabbath was commanded by the voice of the living God. Deuteronomy 4:12, 13.

18. Then He wrote the commandment with His own finger. Exodus 31:18.

19. He engraved it in the enduring stone, indicating its imperishable nature. Deuteronomy 5:22.

20. It was sacredly preserved in the ark in the holy of holies. Deuteronomy 10:1-5.

21. God forbade work upon the Sabbath, even in the most hurrying times. Exodus 34:21.

22. God destroyed the Israelites in the wilderness because they profaned the Sabbath. Ezekiel 20:12, 13.

23. It is the sign of the true God, by which we are to know Him from false gods. Ezekiel 20:20.

24. God promised that Jerusalem should stand forever if the Jews would keep the Sabbath. Jeremiah 17:24, 25.

25. He sent them into the Babylonian captivity for breaking it. Nehemiah 13:18.

26. He destroyed Jerusalem for its violation. Jeremiah 17:27.

27. God has pronounced a special blessing on all the Gentiles who will keep it. Isaiah 56:6, 7.

28. This is in the prophecy which refers wholly to the Christian dispensation. See Isaiah 56.

29. God has promised to bless any man who will keep the Sabbath. Isaiah 56:2.

30. The Lord requires us to call it *"honorable."* Isaiah 58:13. Beware, ye who take delight in calling it the "old Jewish Sabbath," "a yoke of bondage," etc.

31. After the holy Sabbath has been trodden down "many generations," it is to be restored in the last days. Isaiah 58:12, 13.

32. All the holy prophets kept the seventh day.

33. When the Son of God came, He kept the seventh day all His life. Luke 4:16; John 15:10. Thus He followed His Father's example at creation. Shall we not be safe in following the example of

both the Father and the Son?

34. The seventh day is the Lord's day. See Revelation 1:10; Mark 2:28; Isaiah 58:13; Exodus 20:10.

35. Jesus was the Lord of the Sabbath (Mark 2:28); that is, to love and protect it, as the husband is the lord of the wife, to love and cherish her. 1 Peter 3:6.

36. He vindicated the Sabbath as a merciful institution designed for man's good. Mark 2:23-28.

37. Instead of abolishing the Sabbath, He carefully taught how it should be observed. Matthew 12:1-13.

38. He taught His disciples that they should do nothing upon the Sabbath day but what was *"lawful."* Matthew 12:12.

39. He instructed His apostles that the Sabbath should be prayerfully regarded 40 years after His resurrection. Matthew 24:20.

40. The pious women who had been with Jesus carefully kept the Sabbath after His death. Luke 23:56.

41. Thirty years after Christ's resurrection, the Holy Spirit expressly calls it *"the Sabbath day."* Acts 13:14.

42. Paul, the apostle to the Gentiles, called it "the Sabbath day" in A.D. 45. Acts 13:27. Did

not Paul know? Or shall we believe modern teachers, who affirm that it ceased to be the Sabbath at the resurrection of Christ?

43. Luke, the inspired Christian historian, writing as late as A.D. 62, calls it "the Sabbath day." Acts 13:44.

44. The Gentile converts called it the Sabbath. Acts 13:42.

45. In the great Christian council, A.D. 52, in the presence of the apostles and thousands of disciples, James calls it "the Sabbath day." Acts 15:21.

46. It was customary to hold prayer meeting upon that day. Acts 16:13.

47. Paul read the Scriptures in public meetings on that day. Acts 17:2, 3.

48. It was his custom to preach upon that day. Acts 17:2.

49. The book of Acts alone gives record of his holding 84 meetings upon that day. See Acts 13:14, 44; 16:13; 17:2; 18:4, 11.

50. There was never any dispute between the Christians and the Jews about the Sabbath day. This is proof that the Christians still observed the same day that the Jews did.

51. In all their accusations against Paul, they never charged him with disregarding the

Sabbath day. Why did they not, if he did not keep it?

52. But Paul himself expressly declared that he had kept the law. "Neither against the law of the Jews, neither against Caesar, have I offended any thing at all." Acts 25:8. How could this be true if he had not kept the Sabbath?

53. The Sabbath is mentioned in the New Testament 59 times, and always with respect, bearing the same title it had in the Old Testament, *"the Sabbath day."*

54. Not a word is said anywhere in the New Testament about the Sabbath being abolished, done away with, changed, or anything of the kind.

55. God has never given permission to any man to work upon it. Reader, by what authority do you use the seventh day for common labor?

56. No Christian of the New Testament, either before or after the resurrection, ever did ordinary work upon the seventh day. Find one case, and we will yield the question. Why should modern Christians do differently from Bible Christians?

57. There is no record that God has ever removed His blessing or sanctification from the seventh day.

58. As the Sabbath was kept in Eden before the fall, so it will be observed eternally in the new earth after the restitution. Isaiah 66:22, 23.

59. The seventh-day Sabbath was an important part of the law of God, as it came from His own mouth, and was written by His own finger upon stone at Mount Sinai. See Exodus 20. When Jesus began His work, He expressly declared that He had not come to destroy the law. "Think not that I am come to destroy the law, or the prophets." Matthew 5:17.

60. Jesus severely condemned the Pharisees as hypocrites for pretending to love God, while at the same time they made void one of the Ten Commandments by their tradition. The keeping of Sunday is only a tradition of men.

We have now presented 60 plain Bible facts concerning the seventh day. What will you do with them?

FORTY BIBLE FACTS CONCERNING THE FIRST DAY OF THE WEEK

1. The very first thing recorded in the Bible is work done on Sunday, the first day of the week. Genesis 1:1-5. This was done by the Creator Himself. If God made the earth on Sunday, can it be wicked for us to work on Sunday?

2. God commands men to work upon the first day of the week. Exodus 20:8-11. Is it wrong to obey God?

3. None of the patriarchs ever kept it.

4. None of the holy prophets ever kept it.

5. By the express command of God, His holy people used the first day of the week as a common working day for 4,000 years, at least.

6. God Himself calls it a *"working"* day. Ezekiel 46:1.

7. God did not rest upon it.

8. He never blessed it.

9. Christ did not rest upon it.

10. Jesus was a carpenter (Mark 6:3), and worked at His trade until He was 30 years old. He kept the Sabbath and worked six days in the week, as all admit. Hence He did many a hard day's work on Sunday.

11. The apostles worked upon it during the same time.

12. The apostles never rested upon it.

13. Christ never blessed it.

14. It has never been blessed by any divine authority.

15. It has never been sanctified.

16. No law was ever given to enforce the keeping of it, hence it is no transgression to work upon it. "For where no law is, there is no transgression." Romans 4:15; (1 John 3:4).

17. The New Testament nowhere forbids work to be done on it.

18. No penalty is provided for its violation.

19. No blessing is promised for its observance.

20. No regulation is given as to how it ought to be observed. Would this be so if the Lord wished us to keep it?

21. It is never called the Christian Sabbath.

22. It is never called the Sabbath at all.

23. It is never called the Lord's day.

24. It is never even called a rest day.

25. No sacred title whatever is applied to it. Then why should we call it holy?

26. It is simply called "the first day of the week."

27. Jesus never mentioned it in any way, never took its name upon His lips, so far as the record shows.

28. The word Sunday never appears in the Bible at all.

29. Neither God, Christ, nor inspired men, ever said one word in favor of Sunday as a holy day.

30. The first day of the week is mentioned only eight times in all the New Testament. Matthew 28:1; Mark 16:2, 9; Luke 24:1; John 20:1, 19; Acts 20:7; 1 Corinthians 16:2.

31. Six of these texts refer to the same first day of the week.

32. Paul directed the saints to look over secular affairs on that day. 1 Corinthians 16:2.

33. In all the New Testament we have a record of only one religious meeting held upon that day, and it was even a night meeting. Acts 20:5-12.

34. There is not an intimation that they ever held a meeting upon it before or after that.

35. It was not their custom to meet on that day.

36. There was no requirement to break bread on that day.

37. We have an account of only one instance in which it was done. Acts 20:7.

38. That was done in the night—after midnight. Verses 7-11. Jesus celebrated it on Thursday evening, (Luke 22), and the disciples sometimes did it every day. Acts 2:42-46.

39. The Bible nowhere says that the first day of the week commemorates the resurrection of Christ. This is a tradition of men, which makes void the law of God. Matthew 15:1-9. Baptism commemorates the burial and resurrection of Jesus. Romans 6:3-5.

40. Finally, the New Testament is totally silent with regard to any change of the Sabbath day or any sacredness for the first day.

Here are 100 plain Bible facts upon this question, showing conclusively that the seventh day is the Sabbath of the Lord in both the Old and New Testaments.

Reprinted from a tract published by the Review and Herald Publishing Association about the year 1885.

APPENDIX VI

The Mark of the Beast

In Christian circles having the "mark of the beast" is synonymous with being "lost." And well it should. In every case those who receive the mark of the beast are contrasted with God's people and in most references they are consigned to hellfire.

The term "mark of the beast" is found only in the book of Revelation. "And that no one may buy or sell except one who has the mark or the name of the beast, or the number of his name" (Revelation 13:17). At first blush it would seem that receiving the mark of the beast is desirable because without it you can't buy or sell. Upon reading the context, however, one soon discovers that those who follow the leopard-like beast and the two-horned beast do not have their names written in the Book of Life (Revelation 13:8). And also the beast giving this mark receives his power, throne, and authority from the dragon—who is Satan!

The next two references to the mark of the beast are found in Revelation 14:9-12, right in the heart of the third angel's message. "And a third angel followed them, saying with a loud voice, 'If anyone worships the beast and his image, and receives his mark on his forehead or on his hand, he himself shall also drink of the wrath of God, which is poured out full strength into the cup of His indignation. And he shall be tormented with fire and brimstone in the presence of the holy angels and in the presence of the Lamb.

"And the smoke of their torment ascends forever and ever; and they have no rest day or night, who worship the beast and his image, and whoever receives the mark of his name.

"Here is the patience of the saints; here are those who keep the commandments of God and the faith of Jesus."

Those with the mark suffer the wrath of God [the seven last plagues] unmixed with mercy [His "strange"act] and are burned up. Those without the mark are those who keep the commandments of God and have faith in Jesus. The description of the saints in contrast with those who re-

239

ceive the mark of the beast is a significant point. The saints uphold God's commandments and have faith in Him. Could it be that those who receive the mark do <u>not</u> keep the commandments and have faith in Jesus? One thing we know for sure from this passage is that those who receive God's wrath are those who follow the beast and receive his mark.

The next mention of the mark of the beast is in Revelation 15:2, 3. John, seeing a vision of the future, says, "And I saw something like a sea of glass mingled with fire, and those who have the victory over <u>the beast,</u> over his image <u>and</u> over <u>his mark</u> and over the number of his name, standing on the sea of glass, having harps of God. They sing the song of Moses, the servant of God, and the song of the Lamb."

What an awesome, glad scene. It's one I plan to participate in one day soon. Those who refuse the mark of the beast—that is, gain the victory over the beast—eventually stand on the sea of glass in heaven and with one of God's harps <u>sing</u> the victory song—the song of Moses and the Lamb!

Again we read of the mark of the beast in Revelation 16:2. This entire chapter is taken up with the seven angels with the seven last plagues—the wrath of God. "So the first [angel] went and poured out his bowl [plague] upon the earth, and a foul and loathsome sore came upon the men who had the <u>mark of the beast</u> and those who worshiped his image."

Students of prophecy understand that the seven last plagues are poured out <u>without mercy</u> on those with the mark of the beast. This happens after the close of probation—when there is no longer mercy available for sinners. The wrath of God falls on those who have rejected Him and persecuted His faithful people. Thank God, His people are protected against these plagues by the seal of God!

The sixth mention of the mark of the beast is where we read of the fate of those who are deceived by the beast and the false prophet. "Then the beast was captured, and with him the false prophet who worked signs in his presence, by which he deceived those who received the mark of the beast and those who worshiped his image. These two were cast alive into the lake of fire burning with brimstone" (Revelation 19:20).

What a sad picture. <u>Those who receive the mark of the beast are deceived!</u> But because they rejected opportunities to hear the truth they receive the wrath of God and miss out on eternal life with God.

The seventh and final mention of the mark of the beast is in connection with the great judgment in heaven. Those who would not worship the beast or receive his mark live and reign with Christ 1,000 years! "And I saw thrones, and they sat on them, and judgment was committed to them. And I saw the souls of those who had been beheaded for their witness to Jesus and for the word of God, and who had not worshiped the beast or his image, and had not received his mark on their foreheads or on their hands. And they lived and reigned with Christ for a thousand years" (Revelation 20:4).

The conclusion, from a review of these passages, is basic and sobering: Those who receive the mark of the beast are lost—those who don't are saved.

EARTH'S FINAL WARNING

I believe the Seventh-day Adventist Church is the "remnant" church of Bible prophecy. I believe God has called us to proclaim the worldwide message of the three angels of Revelation 14:6-12.

Prophecy indicates another angel/message will come just before the second coming of Christ. This is a final warning to the world to escape from the wrath of God. This message, which lightens the whole world with its glory, has two parts: "Babylon is fallen"—a repeat of the second angel's message, and "Come out of her My people"—which is a repeat of the third angel's message (Revelation 18:1-4).

To give this message one must know who Babylon is, what the beast is, what its mark is, and be convicted of the need to warn others of their danger. This is a very sensitive subject, but we overlook it at the peril of our lives, our eternal lives, and those of many others.

WHO IS THE BEAST WITH THE MARK?

The context of Revelation 13 indicates that "the beast" is the leopard beast—the first beast introduced in this chapter. A study of prophecy shows clearly that the little horn power of Daniel 7 and the leopard beast of Revelation 13 are one and the same.

Both derive their power and authority from the dragon—Satan.
They both rise out of pagan Rome.
They both blaspheme God.
They both rule for 1260 years.
They both make war on the saints.

They both have worldwide influence.

And in Revelation 13 this power receives a wound that appears deadly, but it heals, and all the world wonders after it.

Revelation 13 tells of the blasphemous beast power cooperating with a new beast with two lamb-like horns. This new beast can be identified as the United States of America. These are the two last great powers involved in the great controversy against God. The evidence is almost overwhelming—the leopard beast and the little horn power describe papal Rome, the Roman Catholic Church.

BUT WHO IS BABYLON?

In the book of Revelation, John presupposes or assumes that his readers have a knowledge of the book of Daniel and the other Old Testament writers. The book contains literally hundreds of quotes from the Old Testament. As one reads through Revelation, witnessing the working of God in history, there is suddenly the announcement "Babylon is fallen, is fallen, that great city" (Revelation 14:8). There is no definition given as to the identity of Babylon—just, Babylon is fallen.

Remember, in the previous chapter John has been shown a "composite" beast made up of the beasts of Daniel 7. He certainly knows what Babylon represents and he believes his readers will too.

Ancient Babylon—the first world empire—came to its end, rejecting God. God's "handwriting on the wall," announced that "You have been weighed in the balances, and found wanting" (Daniel 5:27). That very night king Belshazzar was killed as the Medes and Persians attacked the city of Babylon and overthrew its kingdom.

In John's day the actual city of Babylon lay in ruins. But because of Babylon's oppression of His people in the days of Daniel, God used it as a symbol of how near the close of history Satan would try to destroy His people through a corrupt church. As ancient Babylon rejected God, so much of the professed Christian world is rejecting Him today, if not in actual words, certainly by their actions. Those who reject the judgment hour message of the first angel of Revelation 14 can only fall farther and farther away from God. According to the second angel, when the churches of Christendom unite themselves fully with the principles of the world, then the fall of Babylon will be complete.

God's people will then repeat the second angel's message with such power that in Revelation 18:1-4 it is described as illuminating the whole earth! Those who reject this message clearly fail to recognize Babylon's fall and will see in the union of church and state something good. Only those who keep the commandments and have the faith of Jesus will realize the nature of sin in the light of the cross, and will speak with power against the corruption of Babylon.

In particular they will expose Babylon's erroneous teachings, the "wine" that she induces all nations to drink. Among other things, this wine includes the teaching that Sunday is sacred and that man has an immortal soul by nature. The first error forms a bond between Roman Catholicism and Protestantism, and the second connects both with spiritualism.

In Revelation, Babylon is described as the one who receives the plagues. And to Babylon goes the call to "Come out of her." Since "the mark of the beast power" is the composite, leopard-looking beast, it is apparent that it and Babylon are one and the same. And we can see that the antichrist power is a system through which Satan works to war against the cause of God. Accordingly, all who act this part are part of the "system."

THE BEAST DESCRIBES HIS MARK

The beast, as we have noted several times before, represents papal Rome or the Roman Catholic system. One could surmise that the mark of the beast has to do with Sunday worship since the seal of God is found in the Sabbath and since the saints are described as those who keep the commandments. But beyond these clear biblical proofs we can make a positive identification of the mark by listening to Roman Catholic spokesmen.

In the thirteenth century Thomas Aquinas, whose authority as a Catholic theologian is unequaled, declared specifically, "In the New law the keeping of the Sunday supplants that of the Sabbath, not in virtue of the precept of the law, but through determination by the church and the custom of the Christian people" (Thomas Aquinas, *Summa theologiae,* 2a2ae, 122.4 ad 4, cited in *Daniel & Revelation Committee Series,* vol. 7, p. 95). Aquinas, the single most respected teacher of Roman Catholicism, taught that the change from Sabbath to Sunday was indeed brought about by the Roman Catholic Church.

This was also acknowledged at the great Council of Trent in an address by Gaspare [Ricciulli] de Fosso (Archbishop of Reggio), in an address in the 17th session of the Council, Jan. 18, 1562. He stated, "The Sabbath, the most glorious day in the law, has been changed into the Lord's day . . . These and other similar matters have not ceased by virtue of Christ's teaching (for He says He has come to fulfill the law, not to destroy it), but they have been changed by the authority of the church." (Original source cited in the *SDA Bible Student's Source Book,* p. 887.)

Many Catholic Catechisms make the claim that the "Church" changed the day of worship from the Sabbath to Sunday because of her power and authority. Here is one of many such examples:

"Q. *Have you any other way of proving that the Church has power to institute festivals of precept?*

"A. Had she not such power, she could not have done that in which all modern religionists agree with her; she could not have substituted the observance of Sunday the first day of the week for the observance of Saturday the seventh day, a change for which there is no Scriptural authority" (Stephen Keenan, *A Doctrinal Catechism,* p. 174).

Cardinal Gibbons of Baltimore stated, "The Divine institution of a day of rest from ordinary occupations and of religious worship, transferred by the authority of the Church from the Sabbath, the last day, to Sunday, the first day of the week, has always been revered in this country, has entered into our legislation and customs, and is one of the most patent signs that we are a Christian people.

"The neglect and abandonment of this observance would be sure evidence of a departure from the Christian spirit in which our past national life has been moulded. In our times, as in all times past, the enemies of religion are the opponents, secret or avowed, of the Christian Sabbath. A close observer cannot fail to note the dangerous inroads that have been made on the Lord's Day in this country within the last quarter of a century. He renders a service to his country who tries to check this dangerous tendency to desecration.

"It would not be difficult to show that the observance of Sunday is fraught with the greatest social blessing; as proof, look at the social ills that have befallen those Christian nations that have lost respect for it. Solicitous to avert from the United States those disastrous consequences, the Catholic Church has been a strenuous upholder of the sacred character of the Lord's Day" (James Cardinal Gibbons, *The Claims of the*

Catholic Church in the Making of the Republic, in John Gilmary Shea and others, *The Cross and the Flag, Our Church and Country,* pp. 24, 25; cited in full in *SDA Bible Students' Source Book,* p. 987).

Reading those three short paragraphs from Cardinal Gibbons lets one know of the significance of Sunday and the desire of the Catholic Church to see it observed in the United States as a "sign" that we are Christian people.

WHAT IS THE MARK OF THE BEAST?

Synthesizing what we have covered in the last four chapters, it can be seen that, **"The mark of the beast is willful, knowledgeable, end-time approval of coercive Sunday observance in *opposition* to the clear light on the Sabbath question and in *harmony* with classic Roman Catholicism. As such, the mark of the beast is evidence of personal *character* matured in opposition to God"** (Daniel & Revelation Committee Series, vol. 7, *Symposium on Revelation—Book II,* p. 118; bold and italics in original). Remember in the last chapter we discovered that the seal of God was evidence of an intellectual and spiritual settling into the truth? The mark of the beast is evidence of a character "matured" in opposition to God.

"When the test comes, it will be clearly shown what the mark of the beast is. It is the keeping of Sunday. Those who, after having heard the truth, continue to regard this day as holy bear the signature of the man of sin, who thought to change times and laws" (Ellen G. White, Letter 12, 1900, quoted in *The SDA Bible Commentary,* vol. 7, p. 980).

WHEN WILL THE MARK OF THE BEAST BE GIVEN?

From our study to this point, we understand that the seal of God and the mark of the beast are given just before the close of probation and just before the seven last plagues begin to fall. Just before the end the gospel will go to all the world with great power. The Bible says, "Therefore, to him who knows to do good and does it not, to him it is sin" (James 4:17). Thousands have died keeping Sunday, thinking it was the Bible Sabbath. But men will not be judged for light they never had. "Many have gone to their graves in full faith that Sunday was the Sabbath. . . . If we are rational beings, and the light has come to us, we shall be accountable for it. But those who have not had the light which is now shining upon the people of God concerning the Sabbath ques-

246 • SUNDAY'S COMING!

tion, will not be accountable for the light; for it has never been brought before them, and they have died without condemnation" (Ellen G. White, *Review and Herald,* April 25, 1893).

The real "when" of the mark of the beast is answered in this statement: "When Sunday observance shall be enforced by law, and the world shall be enlightened concerning the obligation of the true Sabbath, then whoever shall transgress the command of God, to obey a precept which has no higher authority than that of Rome, will thereby honor popery above God. He is paying homage to Rome, to the power which enforces the institution ordained by Rome. As men then reject the institution which God has declared to be the sign of His authority, and honor in its stead that which Rome has chosen as the token of her supremacy, they will thereby accept the sign of allegiance to Rome,— 'the mark of the beast.' And it is not until the issue is thus plainly set before the people, and they are brought to choose between the commandments of God and the commandments of men, that those who continue in transgression will receive 'the mark of the beast'" (*The Great Controversy,* [1888 edition], p. 449).

ONLY TWO SIDES AT THE END OF TIME

C. Mervyn Maxwell expresses graphically the situation in our world at the moment of crisis.

"Scripture indicates clearly that at the end of time personal choices will cause everyone to be on one side or the other. No one will be left in the middle.

"One side will worship the Creator (Rev. 14:7). The other side will worship the beast and his image (13:12; 14:9; 16:2; 19:20).

"One side will be trustworthy and true, without any lies in their mouths (14:5). The other side will have accepted the lies of the false prophet (19:20).

"One side will be pure and spotless (14:4, 5). The other side will be cowardly, faithless, polluted, murderers, fornicators, sorcerers, idolaters, liars (21:8).

"One side will have their names in the book of life (Dan. 12:1). The other will have had their names blotted out of the book of life (Rev. 17:8).

"One side will be unable to buy or sell but will escape the plagues (13:17; 18:4). The other side will be able to buy and sell (for a time) but will then suffer the plagues (13:17; 14:9-11; 16:2).

"One side is composed of guests invited to the Lamb's joyous wedding supper (19:9). The other side is fed to birds of prey at the terrible supper of God (19:17-21).

"One side praises God and sings joyfully in the presence of the Lamb (15:2-4; 14:3). The other side curses God and suffers torment in the presence of the Lamb (16:9-11, 21; 14:9-11).

"One side enters the eternal kingdom (Dan. 7:27; Rev. 22:14). The other suffers permanent punishment (Rev. 14:9-11).

"One side has the seal of God (7:1-3). The other side has the mark of the beast (13:16; 14:11).

"The easiest thing to do when the image of the beast is set up will be to go with the crowd. People who have believed the serpent's lies, that God's laws either should not, ought not, or cannot be obeyed, will find compliance easy. They will be influenced by Satan's signs and wonders (2 Thess. 2:9-12). They will "bow" to the image—and receive the mark of the beast, indicating their submission and obedience to human authority.

"But those who cherish Jesus and the 'faith of Jesus' and have learned to 'conquer' as Christ conquered (Rev. 3:21), will choose at the risk of their lives to honor God and worship Him in the way He has directed. They will consider loyalty to their Creator and Redeemer the most important consideration possible. These courageous ones will soon find themselves singing on the sea of glass (15:1-5)" (C. Mervyn Maxwell, *Roman Catholicism and the United States, Daniel & Revelation Committee Series*, vol. 7, Symposium on Revelation—Book II, pp. 119, 120).

Bible prophecy has indeed indicated the entire course of human history. All the world powers have taken their places and passed from the scene of action—just as God predicted. And, then, as predicted, the little horn power arose from among the kingdoms of the divided Roman empire. That power, we have identified as papal Rome, the Roman Catholic Church. It virtually ruled the world for 1260 years before receiving a deadly wound in 1798. Many thought that the papacy was "done for," but as the Bible predicted, the wound has been healed. Now—all the world is wondering after the beast. The United States has indeed arisen as a "new nation," maturing into the most powerful nation on the earth—the world's only superpower.

These two powers, the papacy and the United States, are to be the leading characters in the last act in the drama of the ages.